The Campus in the Modern World

The Campus in the Modern World

Twenty-five Essays

JOHN D. MARGOLIS

Department of English
Northwestern University

The Macmillan Company

Library of Congress catalog card number: 69–18252

THE MACMILLAN COMPANY
COLLIER-MACMILLAN CANADA, LTD., TORONTO, CANADA

PRINTED IN THE UNITED STATES OF AMERICA

Acknowledgments

1. "The Educated Person" by Mark Van Doren. Reprinted by permission of Miss Nannine Joseph, the author's agent, originally appeared in *Liberal Education* by Mark Van Doren. New York: Holt, Rinehart & Winston, Inc., 1943, Copyrighted, 1959, by Beacon Press, pp. 13–27.

2. "The Aims of Education" by Robert Maynard Hutchins. Reprinted by permission of the publisher, originally appeared in *Education for Freedom* by Robert M. Hutchins. Baton Rouge, Louisiana: Louisiana State University Press, 1943, pp. 19–38.

3. "General and Special Education" Report of the Harvard Committee. Reprinted by permission of the publishers from *General Education in a Free Society: Report of the Harvard Committee*. Cambridge, Massachusetts: Harvard University Press, copyright, 1945, by the President and Fellows of Harvard College, Chap. II of Part II, pp. 51–58.

4. "Liberal Education: A Common Adventure" by Stringfellow Barr. Originally appeared in the *Antioch Review*, Volume XV, Number 3, 1955, pp. 300–312. Reprinted by permission of Stringfellow Barr and the publisher.

5. "Modern Education and the Classics" by T. S. Eliot. From *Selected Essays* by T. S. Eliot (new edition, 1950), copyright, 1932, 1936, by Harcourt, Brace & World, Inc.; Copyright 1960, 1964, by T. S. Eliot, pp. 452–460. Reprinted by permission of the publishers. Reprinted by permission of Faber and Faber, Ltd.

6. "The Meaning of a University" by Howard Mumford Jones. Reprinted from *Atlantic Monthly* magazine, Vol. 216, Number 5, November 1965, pp. 157–160. Reprinted by permission of the author.

7. "Liberal Education and the Democratic Ideal" by A. Whitney Griswold. Reprinted by permission of the publisher from *Liberal Education and the Democratic Ideal* by A. Whitney Griswold. New Haven: Yale University Press, Copyright © 1959, pp. 1–7.

8. "The Autonomy of the University" by John S. Brubacher. Reprinted from the *Journal of Higher Education*, XXXVIII (May, 1967), pp. 237–249.

Copyright © 1967 by the Ohio State University Press and reprinted with its permission.

9. "Higher Education in the 21st Century" by Alvin C. Eurich. Reprinted from *Atlantic Monthly* magazine, Vol. 211, June 1963, pp. 51–55. Reprinted by permission of the author.

10. "Universities and Their Function" by Alfred North Whitehead. Reprinted with permission of the publisher, from *The Aims of Education* by Alfred North Whitehead. New York: The Macmillan Company, 1959, pp. 136–152.

11. "The College of *Liberal* Arts and Sciences" by Arthur Bestor. Reprinted by permission of the publisher, from *The Restoration of Learning* by Arthur Bestor. New York: Random House, Inc., 1956, pp. 393–408.

12. "College to University—And After" by Jacques Barzun. Reprinted from *The American Scholar*, Volume 33, Number 2, Spring 1964, Copyright © 1964 by the United Chapters of Phi Beta Kappa, pp. 212–219. By permission of the publishers.

13. "The Frantic Race to Remain Contemporary" by Clark Kerr. Reprinted by permission of the publisher, from *Daedalus*, Journal of the American Academy of Arts and Sciences, Boston, Volume 93, Number 4, Fall 1964, pp. 1051–1070.

14. "The Search for Internal Coherence" by James A. Perkins. Reprinted from *The University in Transition* by James A. Perkins. Princeton, N.J.: Princeton University Press, 1966, pp. 31–59. Reprinted by permission of Princeton University Press.

15. "The Squeeze on the Liberal University" by J. Douglas Brown. Reprinted from *Atlantic Monthly* magazine, Volume 213, Number 5, May 1964, pp. 85–87. Reprinted by permission of the author.

16. "The University: Mask for Privilege" by Richard Lichtman. Reprinted by permission of the Center for the Study of Democratic Institutions, from *The Center Magazine*, Volume 1, Number 2, January 1968, pp. 2–10.

17. "Intelligence, the University and Society" by Kenneth B. Clark. Reprinted from *The American Scholar*, Volume 36, Number 1, Winter 1966–67, Copyright © 1966 by the United Chapters of Phi Beta Kappa, pp. 23–32. By permission of the publishers.

18. "The Complacencies of the Academy: 1967" by Theodore Roszak. Reprinted from the *New American Review*, Number 1, September 1967, pp. 82–107. Reprinted by permission of Random House, Incorporated.

19. "The College as Rat Race" by Robert Paul Wolff. Reprinted from *The Radical Papers*, Irving Howe, ed. New York: Doubleday & Company, Inc., 1966, pp. 286–296. Reprinted by permission of *Dissent*, a Quarterly of Socialist Opinion.

20. "The University" by Jacques Maritain. Reprinted from *Education at the Cross-*

roads by Jacques Maritain. New Haven: Yale University Press, Copyright 1943, pp. 75–87. Reprinted by permission of the publisher.

21. "Toward the More Perfect University" by Clark Kerr. Reprinted from "The University in America" (occasional paper), Santa Barbara, California: Center for the Study of Democratic Institutions, 1967, pp. 9–16. Reprinted by permission of the publisher.

22. "A Simple Proposal" by Paul Goodman. Reprinted from *The Community of Scholars* by Paul Goodman. New York: Random House, Inc., 1962, pp. 159–175. Reprinted by permission of the publisher.

23. "College and the Alternatives" by John W. Gardner. Reprinted from *Excellence: Can We Be Equal and Excellent Too?* by John W. Gardner, New York: Harper & Row, Publishers, Inc., Copyright © 1961 by John W. Gardner, pp. 76–91. Reprinted by permission of Harper & Row, Publishers.

24. "Some Reasonable Alternatives" by John Keats. Reprinted from *The Sheepskin Psychosis* by John Keats. Copyright © 1963, 1965 by John Keats. Published by J. B. Lippincott Company. By permission of the publisher. Pages 174–190.

25. "A Case for Humane Intelligence" by Michael O'Neil. Reprinted from *To Make a Difference*, Otto Butz, ed. New York: Harper & Row, Publishers, Inc., Copyright © 1967 by Otto Butz, pp. 137–154. Reprinted by permission of Harper & Row, Publishers.

26. "America in the Twenty-third Century" by John W. Gardner. Reprinted by permission of John W. Gardner and *The New York Times.* © 1968 by The New York Times Company.

Foreword

America's colleges and universities today are passing through a period of crisis from which they cannot emerge unaffected. In a sense, the university is but sharing many of the problems of the nation as a whole: the population continues to grow dramatically, and the young constitute an increasingly large proportion of our society. Millions of poor and oppressed people are now demanding opportunities and rights that have long been denied them. The growth of large urban centers and the ever greater role of technology have led to a sense of depersonalization of life. And many people are forced to make vital and difficult decisions, when called upon to render loyalty and service to a government whose moral right to rule they have come to question.

No age, of course, has been entirely free of problems. Ours, however, seems to be encountering them with unusual intensity. And the crises of the sixties have been felt acutely in our institutions of higher learning.

Until recently, the ivy walls and iron gates of such institutions have offered insulation from such contemporary realities; the term "ivory tower" applied to colleges and universities was often apt. According to the noted diplomat and historian George F. Kennan, the process of learning traditionally has been associated with ". . . a certain remoteness from the contemporary scene—a certain detachment and seclusion, a certain voluntary withdrawal and renunciation of participation in contemporary life in the interests of the achievement of a better perspective on that life when the period of withdrawal is over."

Today, however, the college enjoys no such aloof withdrawal from contemporary affairs. The greatly expanded role of state and Federal governments in higher education, the impact of current events, and the increasingly active concern of many students with national and international problems have combined to bring the academic community down from its towerlike isolation to confront social and political issues it had previously ignored.

Largely as a result of these developments, students, teachers, administrators, and the public generally are being challenged to re-examine their basic principles regarding the aims of education, the privileges and responsibilities of the university, and the character of high education appropriate to the mid-twentieth century.

The dissension that has accompanied this re-examination could damage the university irreparably. But one can hope that from the difficult days of redefinition and readjustment will issue a healthier, more unified institution, more principled in its aspirations for higher education and more understanding of the practical realities in terms of which colleges and universities must operate.

This book does not concern itself, except in passing, with the contemporary issues that have occasioned this crisis in the American college; they are documented daily in the press and on television. Nor does it consider extensively the student activism that has dramatized this crisis for the world. Our interest, rather, is in exploring the fundamental questions of higher education in general, and American colleges and universities in particular—questions that are basic to the topical issues receiving such wide attention today.

No one whose life is close to that of any of our nation's colleges and universities can reasonably be unconcerned about the matters treated in these essays.

Although the distinction between the two has become increasingly obscure, traditionally there have been important differences between the undergraduate college, especially the independent four-year, liberal arts college, and the multipurpose university. Many of the specific problems treated in this book are felt more keenly in universities than in most colleges. None the less, most of the pressures bearing on the university are also felt in their wholly undergraduate counterparts. The university's problems are often those of the college, writ large. In this book the term "college" often is used generically to refer to both types of institutions.

We begin by considering two questions that must be prior to any discussion of particular issues in higher education: What *is* education? What are its goals? The essays in Part I offer a number of traditional—

and, today, rarely heard—statements regarding the aims of education and the nature of the educated man. It is hoped that in these statements some will find a persuasive argument for much in the liberal arts tradition that is being dismissed by many students as inapplicable to contemporary life. But even if the reader finds such ideas dated and anachronistic, he should be challenged to articulate for himself a definition of educational goals that are meaningful and relevant to him.

The second group of readings, Part II, provides some historical context for an understanding of perhaps the most vexing issue confronting the university: What should properly be the extent and nature of the ties between such an institution and society? The essays suggest that in the past the university has been and for an indefinite future will be engaged in a continuous struggle to achieve an appropriate reconciliation of society's demands and its own desire for autonomy and independence.

Some of the pressures being exerted on colleges and universities and the institutional responses they have been forced to make are explored in Part III. Although the desirability of those responses may be questionable, there can be no doubt, after reading these essays, that institutions of higher learning are engaged in adjustments of great magnitude. One consequence of such adjustment has been the growing dissatisfaction of both students and faculty with the new shape of higher education. The contributors to Part IV articulate some of these criticisms. Their remarks call into question some beliefs and practices long fundamental to the American college.

Part V, the final group of essays, suggests some alternatives to the present organization of higher education in America. While some of the proposals are already being implemented in institutions around the country, others present the radical view that for some students higher education might be most effective in forms totally unlike those offered by contemporary academic institutions. It seems appropriate to, close this group with the essay of a perceptive and articulate undergraduate, Michael O'Neil, whose views on the university and the contemporary world bring together many of the themes running through this collection.

All but two of the twenty-four contributors to this book have been associated with American higher education as lecturers, professors, or administrators. Their various experiences and philosophies provide a broad spectrum of thought regarding the crises facing the American college. The differing approaches these writers take to the same issues and the frequent reference made by one to the ideas of another create a provocative dialogue within the book.

It is hoped that the same type of dialogue will occur in classrooms, dormitory rooms, or wherever the essays in this collection are read and discussed. Among the possible formal situations in which this book can be of use, three stand out. The thematic unity that underlies the essays and the considerable variety in point of view among them combine to provide exciting and timely material as a basis for discussion, critical analysis, and expository writing in freshman composition classes, and as a source book for research papers. Closely related is the value the readings can have in orientation and summer reading programs for students who are entering college and making firsthand acquaintance with these issues. Not least of all, courses in education should find here a significant gathering of some of the more important recent statements on American higher education.

Regardless of the specific use made of this book, it will serve its function if it plays some part in creating an intelligent awareness of the problems facing American colleges and universities, of the historical and philosophical implications of those problems, and of the possibility of their solution.

J. D. M.

Contents

PART I   The Goals of Higher Education: Some Traditional Views

INTRODUCTION   2

Mark Van Doren *The Educated Person*   5

Robert Maynard Hutchins *The Aims of Education*   18

Report of the Harvard Committee *General and Special Education*   31

Stringfellow Barr *Liberal Education: A Common Adventure*   39

T. S. Eliot *Modern Education and the Classics*   54

PART II   The Contemporary Situation in Perspective

INTRODUCTION   64

Howard Mumford Jones *The Meaning of a University*   68

A. Whitney Griswold *Liberal Education and the Democratic Ideal*   78

John S. Brubacher *The Autonomy of the University: How Independent Is the Republic of Scholars?*   84

Alvin C. Eurich *Higher Education in the 21st Century*   101

PART III   Colleges and Universities

INTRODUCTION   *114*

Alfred North Whitehead *Universities and Their Function*   118

Arthur Bestor *The College of* Liberal *Arts and Sciences*   130

Jacques Barzun *College to University—and After*   148

Clark Kerr *The Frantic Race to Remain Contemporary*   156

James A. Perkins *The Search for Internal Coherence*   179

J. Douglas Brown *The Squeeze on the Liberal University*   197

PART IV   Some Criticisms

INTRODUCTION   *208*

Richard Lichtman *The University: Mask for Privilege?*   212

Kenneth B. Clark *Intelligence, the University and Society*   234

Theodore Roszak *The Complacencies of the Academy: 1967*   245

Robert Paul Wolff *The College as Rat Race*   271

PART V   Some Alternatives

INTRODUCTION   *284*

Jacques Maritain *The University* 288

Clark Kerr *Toward the More Perfect University* 298

Paul Goodman *A Simple Proposal* 313

John W. Gardner *College and the Alternatives* 328

John Keats *Some Reasonable Alternatives* 341

Michael O'Neil *A Case for Humane Intelligence* 355

EPILOGUE

John W. Gardner *America in the Twenty-third Century* 377

The Goals of Higher Education: Some Traditional Views

Many recent campaigns to discourage potential dropouts have stressed the financial disadvantage under which one labors if he has not completed high school or college. In popular discussion, at least, the value of education seems to be measured primarily in dollars and cents. Many, however, would insist that there are, as well, less tangible but no less important values in education. It is appropriate at the outset to remind ourselves of some of them.

Just as few would question that the teaching of such necessary practical skills as reading, spelling, and mathematics is properly the central focus of elementary education, few today would deny that *among* the aims of a college education should be the preparation of the student for his productive functioning in the world. Often this preparation is accomplished through academic "majors" which prepare one for graduate or professional school, or through more specifically vocational programs, such as journalism or business or engineering, designed to enable the student to step into a career immediately upon graduation.

Increasingly, however, such preprofessional and vocational training is usurping the place of liberal studies and coming to dominate undergraduate education. Many of the same people who would maintain that the value of an education cannot be measured solely in dollars and cents hold that mere preparation for a career should not be the exclusive aim of a collegiate program. The essays in Part I reaffirm some of the goals of education which the movement towards courses of an immediately practical emphasis tends to overlook.

The nature of contemporary American society makes it especially necessary that students be prepared for something more than a trade. Specific job skills are often obsolescent at the very time they are being taught, and within a generation entire careers are created and others displaced. More important, then, than the ability to perform a particular occupational function is the ability to feel, to think, to reason, and to adapt to new ideas and circumstances unforeseen, perhaps, when a student was in school. It is such a development of the total mind and character that these writers propose. As well as being workers, journalists or businessmen or engineers, we are also human beings. In terms of the Harvard report (part of which appears in this section) we must be generalists as well as specialists; to be complete, education must address itself to our total selves. The Harvard report also points out that the development of mind and character by all people is especially important in a democratic society in which all are important not only as functionaries in the fulfillment of the nation's goals but also in which, if the democracy is a healthy one, the people themselves create and sanction those goals. Education must prepare us each to be the governor that by virtue of the franchise he is.

Behind several of the following essays lies the traditional ideal of "liberal" education. At a time when "liberal" and "conservative" have acquired narrowly political connotations, it is well to note their quite different meaning here. Rather than doctrinaire, liberal education is open-minded and tolerant; instead of centering around immediate social issues, it is concerned with understanding man's present predicament in the light of the collective human experience of the past. Paradoxically, among educators the heirs of the liberal ideal are generally more conservative in their endeavor to preserve in our increasingly technological society some of the values which distinguish the humane man from the mere human being, and the human being from the machine.

Nowhere else in this book is such frequent reference made to writers of previous ages. In "The Educated Person," Mark Van Doren draws on the words and ideas of no fewer than a dozen other thinkers. The explanation is not that Van Doren lacks originality. Rather, he is exemplifying in his own allusions to literature and history the conviction of liberal educators that men must be put in vital contact with their roots in the past. Like a plant, which must constantly be nourished through its roots in the ground, so the human spirit, if it is to flourish, must draw nourishment from the lives and thoughts of those who have gone before.

Such is the "great conversation" of which Stringfellow Barr writes in "Liberal Education: A Common Adventure"; any man can converse with the fathers of Western thought through reading and discussing the expressions of their minds, preserved for us in books. To initiate such a conversation with the past is one of the primary goals of liberal education. An exercise of the imagination and spirit, such an educational experience is designed to result in better mental fitness, just as calisthenics, when properly conducted, should lead to better physical fitness.

In its concern to develop not so much vocational skills as a quality of character, the humanistic education proposed in Part I seeks to temper the materialism of the present world with a concern for the immaterial, which is not the irrelevant, but the spiritual. Unfortunately, for many today the term "spiritual" carries with it the negative connotation of the pious and the churchly. But in another sense perhaps the use of that term in relation to education is appropriate. As church and home have lost much of their power to persuade the young in matters of values and principles, school and college have the opportunity—some would say the obligation—to provide the moral and ethical inspiration that many students are seeking. T. S. Eliot's "Modern Education and the Classics" offers a forceful and provocative statement of such a position.

It may thus be that the goal of liberal education is, as the adjective suggests, to liberate our minds and spirits from the parochial pressures of our hectic and narrow worlds in order to refresh ourselves with the vision of a richer and fuller humanity. Yet before one can speak adequately of liberal education he must have some understanding of what it might mean to be a human being in a world, like ours, increasingly inhumane. In "The Aims of Education" Robert Hutchins points out that any theory of education requires a metaphysics. Any philosophy of the goals of liberal education demands some consideration of what man is being liberated for. Each student, too, as he reflects on his own education should ask what he is being educated for.

A *man of broad humanistic interests, Mark Van Doren (1894–   ) is the author of numerous volumes of poetry, drama, fiction, and literary criticism; in 1940 he received the Pulitzer Prize for poetry. A revered teacher as well, he retired in 1959 after nearly four decades of service at Columbia University. In his* Autobiography *(1958) he reflects on his own lifelong education as a writer and teacher.*

1

The Educated Person

MARK VAN DOREN

The "Educated Man" about whom so much talk is made remains an abstraction of small interest if he is nothing but teacher's pet, a typical creature of the educator's dream. Nevertheless, he is necessary to any discussion, for he is education's clearest end. That is why he should be treated with respect, in terms of his own nature. He is less a certain kind of man than he is any man who has become free to use the intellect he was born with: the intellect, and whatever else is important. And something is gained, as the sequel may suggest, by calling him not a man but a person.

He has been brilliantly defined, over and over again, in

sentences whose brevity must be admired. He is one, for instance, "who knows what he is doing." This may claim too much for any mortal, but it aims in the right direction, as does the sister sentence which says he knows what he is saying. Alice never learned about that in the Wonderland which for us, if not for her, continues to be the best allegory of education. She never improved in the art of watching the words she used lest they be taken as referring to something different from the conventions she assumed; she never caught on to the fact that she might be as strange to others as others were to her; she got nowhere in the realm of possibility. "Why not?" was a rejoinder she failed to fathom.

The educated person, says Pascal, is one who has substituted learned ignorance for natural ignorance. That is valuable because it keeps ignorance in the picture, which otherwise would be false. "At home in the world"—the familiar phrase is a little too cozy for truth, though again it states the right desire; and it illuminates the image of aged persons blessed with the gift of occupation. For the last sign of education one can reveal is serenity in decrepitude, a sense that there is still something to be if not to do. Such persons in their prime had doubtless showed another sign: they could respect failure, or even idleness, if integrity came with it. And they were not too sure that they were judges of integrity, better and worse having been for them, as they surely are, big problems. "Those of us," remarked Rousseau, "who can best endure the good and evil of life are the best educated."

The list of insights is long. "An educated man is committed to reason—really committed." His habits are "the spirit of analysis and the perception of rule." He has, says William James, "a general sense of what, under various disguises, superiority has always signified and may still signify." He has learned, in other words from the same source, how to know a good man when he sees him. For Aristotle the educated man was one who had learned how to judge the competence of any teacher in any science. For Alexander Meiklejohn he is one "who tries to understand the whole of knowledge as well as one man can"; who is not discouraged by the legend that there is too much to know because he has kept faith with the principles of organization and analogy. More simply, he is one who knows how to read, write, speak, and listen—four major arts in which few are evenly proficient.

The educated person is free to disagree; and to agree. The first is now the more familiar act, so that many must believe it the sole proof of independence. Either can be proof, and both must be present before we acclaim the man. For only then are we convinced that he has taken truth for master.

"A cultivated intellect, because it is a good in itself, brings with it a power and a grace to every work and occupation which it undertakes." Thus Cardinal Newman, whom theology makes more lyric than the rest. He can invoke, with an ideality that is never absurd, a "clear, calm, accurate vision and comprehension of things, as far as the finite mind can embrace them, each in its place, and with its own characteristics upon it. It is almost prophetic from its knowledge of history; it is almost heart-searching from its knowledge of human nature; it has almost supernatural charity from its freedom from littleness and prejudice; it has almost the repose of faith, because nothing can startle it."

The path to this point, however, is thorny, and one has not arrived who was unwilling to be punished. "No one," says T. S. Eliot, "can become really educated without having pursued some study in which he took no interest—for it is a part of education to learn to interest ourselves in subjects for which we have no aptitude." The search for attractive studies—attractive, that is, before their true reward is comprehended—ends in the middle of a desert where distinction has been lost. The path has something puritan about it, something which the natural man resists in proportion to the very need he has for the happiness at its farther end.

That happiness consists in the possession of his own powers, and in the sense that he has done all he could to avoid the bewilderment of one who suspects he has missed the main thing. There is no happiness like this. Trust no philosopher who does not relish his existence and his thoughts.

His relish most recommends itself when it is hearty, and even when it is rude or alarming. It is not as if he had been led into a tomb.

The educator's tone is sometimes that of one who asks the student to smile for the last time before he offers himself as a sacrifice to society. The voices of culture are too often dull, blank, and soundless; or else there is a sniffle and a whine suggesting that education is good for something else, not for its own sure self. At least one classic educator, Rabelais, was a roarer. And nobody can doubt the culture of John Jay Chapman in our time, even though he could write like this: "Is the education of the young the whole of life? I hate the young— I'm worn out with them. They absorb you and suck you dry and are vampires and selfish brutes at best. Give me some good old rain-soaked clubmen—who *can't* be improved and make no moral claims—and let me play checkers with them and look out of the club window and think about what I'll have for dinner."

The man who commands his mind may be as reckless as that: as apparently arrogant, as exultant over some secret glory which is in fact the source of his fascination. For the arrogance is only apparent, as becomes clear when we see how he refuses to boast about his education; he lets it recommend itself. It does this when we note that he is not weakly sensitive to the doubting word, to the slur at what is privately most precious to him. He can survive disagreement, just as he can weather unanimity.

Nor does he count on the whole world's becoming good day after tomorrow. This does not keep him from being glad that there are those today who would eradicate demonstrable ills. He even assists, for if he accepts evil he does not love it, and he is under no illusion that campaigns against inequality will mean the disappearance of injury between men. Reform for him does not cure evil so much as contain it in its native country, chance. He is perhaps the only man who can fight it without the illusion that it will stay away.

All this is high praise, and may seem to call for more than one man could be. But that is what education at the top does call for—each man becoming more than he is. A paradox emerges here. Pindar said that our chief duty consists in "becoming who we are." Were we not that already? What of the change that is supposed to take place in the educated person?

In an important sense he is not changed. He does not become, that is, a tiger or a crocodile. He becomes, we hope, only more human than he was. But he was already human. Then there are degrees of humanity, the last one yielding not the least but the most recognizable man, the person most clearly and completely a specimen of his kind. The more one changes in this way, the more one remains the same. The more, in other words, one becomes what one could be.

William Whewell avoided such tangles by saying blandly that the purpose of education is "to connect a man's mind with the general mind of the human race." And Comenius remarked with his wonderful simplicity: "Schools are the workshops of humanity." But the subject of man, always inseparable from the subject of education, remains difficult and obscure, with paradox at its heart because those who deal with it are themselves men. It was never more worth exploring than it is now, when so much that happens dehumanizes, and when there must be a corresponding hunger for knowledge of what after all the human is.

Our studies have not been taking this direction. As a philosopher has remarked, we think we know primitive man, Western man, the man of the Renaissance, the workingman, but we do not even pretend to know man, or what we mean when we say the word. Scott Buchanan once listed seven metaphors currently implicit in the term:

> Man is a system of electrons.
> Man is a machine.
> Man is an animal.
> Man is a bundle of habits.
> Man is a soul.
> Man is an angel.
> Man is divine.

There are those for whom all of these would be metaphors save one; there are others, perhaps, whose discourse builds itself upon two or more of them without consciousness of inconsistency. When we are metaphorical about something and do not know that we are, we prove that we have never examined it strictly. We confess, indeed, that we do not think it worthy of examination. But sooner or later, if the thing is man, our indifference counts against us.

Man's study of man is always threatened with frustration because it is the case of a species being measured by itself, which of course is not scientific. But man as philosopher, asking himself the further question, "What am I?", runs into as many difficulties. It is the oldest human question, and in our wisdom we have not answered it. Perhaps our wisdom, such as it is, appears in the fact that we have never been satisfied with an answer—or perhaps it should be said, never rested in a metaphor. We have continued to treat the problem as real: as one to which we do not know a simple solution. For all our present shallowness of thought about the matter, we do still recognize that man's distinguishing feature is his inability to know himself. He is a creature doomed to desire more knowledge, at least on this one point, than he will ever have. As a result he is both more than he need be and less than he would be. If he could slay his desire he might be content to exist rather than live. But he wants to live; and yet he never lives enough; that is, he never knows enough, for in proportion as he knows he lives. His predicament in the universe is probably peculiar. It is even noble. But it is a predicament, and this is no news to the educated person who has met it in every great writer he has read.

No wonder Gregory Nazianzen decided that "to educate man is the art of arts, for he is the most complex and mysterious of all creatures." Pascal called man "an incomprehensible monster . . . so necessarily mad that not to be mad would amount to another form of madness." Such language may sound extreme in an age which lets its metaphors go undetected because it supposes it has hold of the fact, because it rests in psychology and sociology. But it is not a dead language. Why man is both mind and body, and how they unite—these are questions we cannot afford to be too sure we have waved away. They have astonished and terrified great men.

To become more human than one was, therefore, is not in so far to find peace. It may be only then that the war begins, the war of understanding. William James never forgot that man is an animal with a tendency toward superfluity or excess; his wants are "fantastic and unnecessary." "Prune down his extravagance, sober him, and you undo him." He is a nervous animal, straining to comprehend what he contains, straining even to contain it. For it is bigger than he is. It is not an animal. "We must love a being who is in us," said Pascal, "and is not ourselves." This being in man goes by many names, serves under many metaphors. Whatever it is, its authority is huge, and one who has heard it speak will never be complacent again. It is something we inherit, and something into which we are educated. No one denies this, yet many seem to be unaware that the process is more like a revolution than it is like going to buy a new suit of clothes.

The educated person knows his own species as well as he can. But today he is at a disadvantage because he lacks a scale whereon to set the object of his examination. Too few other beings are available for comparison. There are the animals, whom we have with us whether or no; and we do use them for the purpose, frequently admiring the mirror more than our reflection in it. The comparison of men with animals, however, is at best a meager exercise. A richer field existed when there were gods and heroes, as with the Greeks, or God and the angels, as with the Christians. Without the idea of angels we have a poorer knowledge of that creature who once was lower than they, though he was higher than worm or ox. And since angels were still lower than God, and different from Him, the cloud of distinction thickened into something solid which intellectually we have lost.

Seeing man in a middle position between animals and angels lights up his dimensions as nothing else does. Animals are unconscious of their ignorance; angels know without difficulty. The middle creature, conscious of his ignorance, knows with difficulty. This makes him a more various creature than either of his neighbors, particularly since he is unstable enough in the category where he is suspended to yearn constantly for another. He tries to be brute or angel. Our language still permits us to denounce one who would be animal; "beast" is an epithet universally understood, along with the specifications of dog, hog, snake, lizard, cow, elephant, and cat. It is rarely, however, that a man these days is pitied for acting as if he thought he was an angel—

a form of conduct, incidentally, which may make him more brute than before. Both mistakes are human. Man is the only being that can misconceive his nature. Animals do not conceive at all; angels conceive without effort or error.

Such a scale is one of man's most brilliant inventions; but our progress has been away from it. The thinner metaphors of animal and machine seem now to be all that we have, and even those are seldom recognized as functions of our speech. Perhaps there is no better explanation for the absence of irony in our art, or for the poor uses we make of poetry and history. Poetry is pretending, and history is something by which we prove that we could not have become other than what we are.

Man has a strange difficulty: he does not know what to be. No horse finds it hard to be a horse, or to know when he is one. He knows nothing else. And so, we assume, with angels—who know, however, what other things are, including man, though excluding God. What is it to be more of a man than one already is? It is not to grow taller, to have longer hair, to lose the body, to own the stars. Perhaps it is merely to know that such questions are important, and beset with perpetual difficulty. "We judge," said Pascal, "that animals do well what they do. Is there no rule whereby to judge men?" He thought there was. "To deny, to believe, and to doubt well are to a man what the race is to a horse."

To believe and doubt well. That is at least a program for the person whose perfection we have had in mind as the aim of education. Perfection, yet within the limits of his knowing nature. Those limits are harsh and final. There is nothing like them, however, in all the creature world. And let one distinction be clear. The individual is only a creature. The person has greater dignity. For he contains more than he is, and to the extent that he does so he appears to perform the miracle of being a part which possesses the whole.

The person in an individual is the man in him, the thing that politics respects when it is wise and good. It is what the doctrine of equality refers to. It is the medium through which individuals understand one another; it is the source of language and the explanation of love. And it solves many mysteries of the thing called personality. Individuality is less powerful; it is uniqueness, it is eccentricity, it is something we lack tongue to praise. He who is most a person is, strangely, the least personal of men; he is least hide-bound by a notion he has of his own integrity. He is surprised when he hears of that, having all the while been occupied with the world's variety. There are many things he prefers to himself and tries to be. What he tries most steadily to be is a man. And when we praise him we praise his humanity. We compliment individuals; we praise persons for the virtues in them which they share with other men. An old way of saying this is that good men—that is, men—tend to be alike. Virtue is single and general; courage is not what one is but has.

Yet another mystery appears. For the possession of human virtues in high degree marks men, after all, so that they cannot be mistaken for their fellows. Personality is unique as individuality can never be. To say as much is to recognize for the last time that men are not angels. Their natures are rich with accident, and their animal base is profound. At the top, however, they touch a power which they hesitate to call their own.

The educated person is, then, a human being. As such he must cope with a special question which history never tires of asking. Does being human always mean the same thing? What of change? How long will the present last? For it is in the present that we know what we know. The completely educated person is one, we must suppose, who has settled some sort of relation in his mind between past, future, and present.

It is said to be more difficult now than ever before to be wise about these three. But it was always difficult, and we should not be in too much of a hurry to believe those who see change as something peculiar to our time. Such visionaries live in a perpetual panic. I have a friend who says he lives always at 11:59, waiting for the moment of midnight to strike the bell of utter change. And indeed the vast transformations now gathering in the world, the concentrations of public and private power, the appalling shrinkage of space, the increased impersonality of business and state, the multiplying artifices of life are not to be dismissed with a stare. The oil age is really new, and cities that now reach to the sky may soon be rotting in their riches. If history is the story of revolutions, another chapter may be nearing its last paragraph. Yet the student cannot leave it at that. And if he is a good student he will continue, under no matter what difficulties, his search for a center from which he can view both new and old. Such a center is the only place where the intellect can feel at home.

The priests of change are melancholy fellows who have little hope for the intellect. For them the human person is a butterfly that new shapes may crush just as it learns to lift its wings; education has other things to do than prepare a home for humanity; wherever it is built will be the wrong place; the tide of change sets always elsewhere; for education to perfect the powers of the person is only to make ready a sacrifice. So they mix their figures as they sweat to say the one thing they have in mind, namely, that the coming alterations are bound to come—so bound, indeed, as to make it doubtful that even an education in them is necessary, since soon we shall know all things without the trouble of thought. To such prophets it would be ridiculous to suggest that men need not be so ineffectual; that wisdom in at least a few persons might modify the future, which is among other things man's future.

The absolutists of the new are unaware that the present as they see it is "but an ambiguous sentence," says Jacques Barzun, "out of its context." The problem is one of reading—an art which they despise. The past, which they mistakenly identify as the sole concern of liberal education, puts them on the defensive. They think of it, in John Dewey's words, as "a rival of the present," and accuse the intellectual of wishing to make the present "an imitation of the past." The problem is immensely more complicated than that. The educated person recognizes no dry stretch between now and then. They are one river, and the more he knows about its length the better. He is a citizen of his age; but if he is a good citizen he studies the oldest laws as well as yesterday's statutes. He wants to know where things came from that neither he nor any contemporary invented. They may rejuvenate invention itself; an understanding of them may increase the rate of change fantastically beyond the dream of a provincial in time. The changes he wants are radical; they are improvements in persons. But to even the superficial ones he is not hostile. He assumes them with the flowing of the river, which he does not suppose will stop, as some reformers do, when one shift is made. If it could stop now it would have stopped before, and the shift would never have been possible. He is ready for shifts; but he does not forget that in proportion as the speed of alteration grows the need for memory deepens. No man can be wise enough. No man will be wise at all if he refuses to make the attempt.

The problem is the primeval one of permanence and change. Nobody but a fool teaches either that change does not occur or that there is nothing but change. An unassisted eye corrects the first error, and only a little tutoring is needed to see through the second. But no amount of education can remove the darkness from the theme, or can make it easy to know what in any particular case one should understand. The life of the mind would be simple if there were no change or if every change were total, for in neither instance would there be a problem; or it would have been solved millenniums ago, granting that without differences there would ever have been names, and that without names there would have been ideas.

The most familiar form of the problem has to do with the nature of man, concerning which the educated person will know what he knows about any nature, namely, that in so far as it is a nature it does not change. For then we should have another nature; meaning that in the case of man he would have another name. The reason we can keep on talking about man is that he changes but his nature does not; when he was ape he was not man, and as long as he is man he will not be angel. As long as man is, he does not alter beyond the recognition he first earned by being daily and yearly different. One who insists that human life changes has nevertheless spoken the words "human life" as if he knew what they meant. They meant for him the thing he could see changing. When, if ever, it becomes some other sort of life, he will cease to say it is human life that changes.

The educated person is neither scared by novelty nor bored without it. What can bore him is the bulletin which states that tomorrow nothing is going to be recognizable. Such bulletins are posted by people who know nothing of the past; or of the future, for if they considered what they were saying they would be silent, since it could not matter tomorrow what they had mouthed today. The worst nuisance, probably, is he who tolls the bell for good and evil and by some legerdemain of logic calls their passing good. The human spirit, however, is very tough; it can survive such fools, as it has survived the horrors, real or supposed, of its countless institutions.

Past, future, and present—they are three gods in one, and worship of them should be wisely distributed. The educated person knows one thing at least: the past is a burden which crushes only those who ignore it, and so do not study how to balance it on their shoulders. It is there in spite of everything; known and used for what it is, it can lighten the entire load. Dismissed from the mind by "practical" men, it can bring them to deserve Robert Maynard Hutchins's definition of them as "those who practice the errors of their forefathers."

"We never live," said Pascal, "but we hope to live; and, as we are always preparing to be happy, it is inevitable we should never be so." The poor student is lectured too much about another life for which this one of books and classes is preparing him; as if this one in itself were nothing, or could not be good. It is in fact one of the best lives available to men, some of whom childishly spend all their later years reliving it, as if none other followed. The educated person knows what it means to say that eternity is most like the present. It is now or never. It is the present in all its vastness that makes us serious, that makes us moral and religious. "The present," says Alfred North Whitehead, "contains all that there is. It is holy ground." And by some miracle it is ours alone—an amazing fact, to which history and prophecy are but footnotes. The educated person is no stranger to that mood in which Pascal once meditated:

When I consider the short duration of my life, swallowed up in the eternity before and after, the little space which I fill, and even can see, engulfed in the infinite immensity of spaces of which I am ignorant, and which know me not, I am frightened, and am astonished at being here rather than there; for there is no reason why here rather than there, why now rather than then.

At sixteen, a freshman in Ober-lin College; at twenty-nine, dean of Yale Law School; at thirty, president of the University of Chicago, Robert May-nard Hutchins (1899–   ) has been one of the most distin-guished figures in American higher education. A caustic critic of current educational practices, he became the focus of much controversy as he intro-duced boldly innovative pro-grams at Chicago. He resigned as chancellor in 1951 to head the Fund for the Republic and, at present, the Center for the Study of Democratic Institu-tions. Here he begins by reflect-ing on a lecture series he delivered at Yale, published as The Higher Learning in America *(1936).*

The Aims of Education

ROBERT MAYNARD
HUTCHINS

Six years ago I had the honor of addressing my fellow Yale men on the Higher Learning in America. I was surprised to find that these lectures did not have the ef-fect they were intended to produce. Instead, all the move-ments they were designed to arrest, all the attitudes they were calculated to change, went rushing onward, in the case of the movements, or be-came more firmly entrenched, in the case of the attitudes.

I attacked triviality, and forty-two students enrolled in the Oklahoma University short course for drum majors.

I attacked vocationalism, and the University of California announced a course in cosmetology, saying, "The profession of beautician is the fastest growing in this state."

I deplored a curriculum of obsolescent information, and one of America's most distinguished sociologists announced that our information was increasing so rapidly that in order to get time to pour it all into our students we should have to prolong adolescence at least until age forty-five.

I asserted that higher education was primarily intellectual, and the President of the New York State College for Teachers said, "Education is not even primarily intellectual, certainly not chiefly intellectual. It is the process by which the emotions are socialized."

I lamented the confusion that besets American education, and the president of a highly confused and very large college announced that chaos was a good thing. Though I should prefer chaos to an order imposed by force, I had never supposed that chaos was an ideal toward which all right-thinking men should strive. Chaos had always seemed to me something you tried to get out of. I had always thought that what we wanted, both in politics and education, was a rational order, rationally arrived at.

One professor accidentally agreed with me. He made the following outrageous remarks in a book of his own: "There will always remain," he said, "certain permanent values which education must cultivate, such as intellectual honesty, love of truth, ability to think clearly, moral qualities." The fact that he was from Teachers College, Columbia, and could be assumed to be only teasing, did not save him. He was sharply rebuked by a professor from Ohio State University who said that here he must "part company with the author of this indisputably significant volume, for the suspicion grows that the author is still something of an absolutist." The author actually wanted education to cultivate intellectual honesty, the love of truth, the ability to think clearly, and moral qualities.

Now I will not deny that one or two people did pay some attention to my book. They had to. And they got it free in the course of their trade as book reviewers. One of these, who in his spare time is a professor at Yale, summed up the whole thing by saying that the trouble with me was my intense moral idealism. Such a quality would naturally distort anybody's view of education. A university president guilty of moral idealism? What is the world coming to? By some process of association of ideas I am reminded of the remarks of one of our alumni who in a recent discussion at the University of Chicago said that everything I had said about football was logical, perfectly logical, very logical indeed. "But," he said, "if the University abolishes football, my son, now fifteen years old, will not want to go there." In other words, "logical" is a term of reproach, and the University of Chicago should be illogical because one of its alumni has an illogical child. I have even heard the word "educational" in the same slurring connotation, as when a Princeton graduate wrote to Woodrow Wilson saying, "I will have nothing more to do with Princeton. You are turning my dear old college into an educational institution." A university president who is suspected of an interest in morals, in intellect, or even in education deserves the severest condemnation from those who have the true interests of our country at heart.

But all these things are as nothing compared with the menace of metaphysics. I had mildly suggested that metaphysics might unify the modern university. I knew it was a long word, but I thought my audience of learned reviewers would know what it meant. I was somewhat surprised to find that to them metaphysics was a series of balloons, floating far above the surface of the earth, which could be pulled down by vicious or weak-minded people when they wanted to win an argument. The explosion of one of these balloons or the release of the gases it contained might silence, but never convince, a wise man. The wise man would go away muttering, "Words, words, words," or "Antiscientific," "Reactionary," or even "Fascist." Knowing that there is nothing true unless experimental science makes it so, the wise man knows that metaphysics is simply a technical name for superstition.

Now I might as well make a clean breast of it all. I am interested in education, in morals, in intellect, and in metaphysics. I even go so far as to hold that there is a necessary relation among all these things. I am willing to assert that without one we cannot have the others and that without the others we cannot have the one with which I am primarily concerned, namely education.

I insist, moreover, that everything that is happening in the world today confirms the immediate and pressing necessity of pulling ourselves together and getting ourselves straight on these matters. The world is probably closer to disintegration now than at any time since the fall of the Roman Empire. If there are any forces of clarification and unification left, however slight and ineffectual they may appear, they had better be mobilized instantly, or all that we have known as Western Civilization may vanish.

Even assuming that normal conditions will soon be restored, we must grant that our country has long been afflicted with problems which, though apparently insoluble, must be solved if this nation is to be preserved or to be worth preserving. These problems are not material problems. We may have faith that the vast resources of our land and the technological genius of our people will produce a supply of material goods adequate for the maintenance of that interesting fiction, the American Standard of Living. No, our problems are moral, intellectual, and spiritual. The paradox of starvation in the midst of plenty illustrates the nature of our difficulties. This paradox will not be resolved by technical skill or scientific data. It will be resolved, if it is resolved at all, by wisdom and goodness.

Now wisdom and goodness are the aim of higher education. How can it be otherwise? Wisdom and goodness are the end of human life. If you dispute this, you are at once entering upon a metaphysical controversy; for you are disputing about the nature of being and the nature of man. This is as it should be. How can we consider man's destiny unless we ask what he is? How can we talk about preparing men for life unless we ask what the end of life may be? At the base of education, as at the base of every human activity, lies metaphysics.

So it is with science. As Dr. H. S. Burr of the Yale Medical School has put it: "One of the primitive assumptions of science is that we live in a universe of order; order determined by, and controlled through, the operation of fundamental principles capable of elucidation and reasonably exact definition. This assumption states that there is a metaphysics, a body of universal laws which can be grasped by the human intellect and utilized effectively in the solution of human problems."

So it is with ethics and politics. We want to lead the good life. We want the good state as a means to that life. Once more, to find the good life and the good state, we must inquire into the nature of man and the ends of life. The minute we do that we are metaphysicians in spite of ourselves. Moreover, if ethics is the science of human freedom, we must know at the beginning whether and in what sense man is free. Here we are metaphysicians once again. And the soundness of our moral conclusions depends on whether we are good metaphysicians or bad ones. So the more preposterous positions of Mill's *Essay on Liberty* originate in his mistaken or inadequate analysis of the doctrine of free will; and Aristotle's defense of natural slavery results from his failure to remember that according to Aristotelian metaphysics there can be no such thing as a natural slave.

So it is with education. Here the great criminal was Mr. Eliot, who as President of Harvard applied his genius, skill, and longevity to the task of robbing American youth of their cultural heritage. Since he held that there were no such things as good or bad subjects of study, his laudable effort to open the curriculum to good ones naturally led him to open it to bad ones and finally to destroy it altogether. Today, though it is possible to get an education in an American university, a man would have to be so bright and know so much to get it that he wouldn't really need it. Our institutions give full support to the proposition of Gibbon that "instruction is seldom of much efficacy except in those happy dispositions in which it is almost superfluous." Today the young American comprehends only by accident the intellectual tradition of which he is a part and in which he must live: for its scattered and disjointed fragments are strewn from one end of the campus to the other. Our university graduates have far more information and far less understanding than in the colonial period. And our universities present themselves to our people in this crisis either as rather ineffectual trade schools or as places where nice boys and girls have a nice time under the supervision of nice men and women in a nice environment.

The crucial error is that of holding that nothing is any more important than anything else, that there can be no order of goods and no order in the intellectual realm. There is nothing central and nothing peripheral, nothing primary and nothing secondary, nothing basic and nothing superficial. The course of study goes to pieces because there is nothing to hold it together. Triviality, mediocrity, and vocationalism take it over because we have no standard by which to judge them. We have little to offer as a substitute for a sound curriculum except talk of personality, "character," and great teachers, the slogans of educational futilitarianism.

We see, then, that metaphysics plays a double part in higher education. By way of their metaphysics educators determine what education they shall offer. By way of metaphysics their students must lay the foundations of their moral, intellectual, and spiritual life. By way of metaphysics I arrive at the conclusion that the aim of education is wisdom and goodness and that studies which do not bring us closer to this goal have no place in a university. If you have a different opinion, you must show that you have a better metaphysics. By way of metaphysics, students, on their part, may recover a rational view of the universe and of their role in it. If you deny this proposition you take the responsibility of asserting that a rational view of the universe and one's role in it is no better than an irrational one or none at all.

Let us, in the light of these principles, look at the relation of education to the improvement of society. We all want to improve society, and we want college graduates because of their education to want to improve society and to know how to do it. Differences appear when we come to the method by which these educational objects may be attained. Since the issue before us is education, I shall not attempt to deal with the problem of how a university may through its scientific investigations best prevent or cure soil erosion, juvenile delinquency, or war. I shall discuss only the method by which an institution may develop in its students a social consciousness and a social conscience.

At first glance it would seem that we should all agree that in order to talk about society or its improvement we should have to inquire into the nature of society, into the common and abiding characteristics of society, and of those unusual animals who compose it, namely men. We should want to consider the history of societies, their rise, development, and decay. We should wish to examine their object, the various ways of achieving it, and the degree to which each succeeded or failed. In order to talk about success or failure we should have to have some notions about what a good society was. Without such notions we could not appraise the societies that came under our eye or the one in which we lived. We should need to have some conception of a good society in order to decide what improvement was; for we all know that we have welcomed many measures as beneficent which when adopted have seemed to leave us in as unsatisfactory condition as we were in before. In short, if we approached the great task of improving society without prejudice, we should think at once of trying to understand the nature, the purpose, and the history of the institutions which man has created. The quest for social improvement is a perpetual quest. Ever since societies existed men have been trying to make them better. The ideas and the experience of mankind should, one would think, be placed in the hands of the rising generation as it goes forward on the perpetual quest.

This would mean that if we wanted a student to have a sense of social responsibility and the desire to live up to his obligations we should have to give him, to achieve this aim, whatever we gave him for other purposes—an education in history and philosophy, together with the disciplines needed to understand those fields. For the purpose of making him an improver of society we should hope to make him, in a modest way, master of the political wisdom of the race. Without some inkling of it he could not understand a social problem. He could not criticize a social institution. He would be without the weapons needed to attack or to defend one. He could not tell a good one from a bad one. He could not think intelligently about one.

It is hardly necessary for me to add that nobody can think about a practical problem like the problem of improving society unless he knows the facts. He cannot comment usefully on the situation in Germany unless he knows what the situation is. Neither can he do so unless he has some standard of criticism and of action. This standard cannot, of course, be a mathematical formula or some miraculous automatic intellectual gadget which when applied to the facts will immediately and infallibly produce the right answer. The practical world is a world of contingent singular things and not a mathematical system. No one has emphasized this point more forcefully than Aristotle. But this did not restrain him from attempting in the *Ethics* and *Politics* to work out the general principles of the good life and the good state, or from trying to show the utility of such principles in his society and, as I think, in any other.

If, then, we are to have standards of social criticism and social action, and if they are to be anything but emotional standards, they must result from philosophical and historical study and from the habit of straight thinking therein. It would be a wonderful thing if we were all so conditioned that our reflexes worked unanimously in the right direction when confronted by political and economic injustice, if we could be trained in infancy to recognize and fight it. But even if we could arrive at adolescence in this happy state I am afraid that our excellent habits might fall away under pressure. Something is needed to preserve them, and this is understanding. This is another way of saying that the intellect commands the will. Our parents should make every effort in our childhood to moderate our passions and to habituate us to justice and prudence. But the role of higher education in this connection must be to supply the firm and enduring groundwork to sustain these habits when the tumult of adult life beats upon them.

It seems obvious to me, therefore, that the kind of education I have been urging is the kind that helps to develop a social consciousness and a social conscience. Why isn't it obvious to everybody else? The first reason, I think, is the popularity of the cult of skepticism. I have been saying that I want to give the student knowledge about society. But we have got ourselves into such a state of mind that if anybody outside of natural science says he knows anything, he is a dogmatist and an authoritarian. Anybody who says, "I don't know because nobody can"; or, "Everything is a matter of opinion"; or, "I will take no position because I am tolerant and open-minded" is a liberal, progressive, democratic fellow to whom the fate of the world may safely be entrusted.

I regret that I am forced to remind you that the two most eminent skeptics of modern times were among its most stalwart reactionaries. Hume was a Tory of the deepest dye, and Montaigne was, too. This was a perfectly natural consequence of their philosophical position. Montaigne held, in effect, that "there was nothing more dangerous than to touch a political order once it had been established. For who knows whether the next will be better? The world is living by custom and tradition; we should not disturb it on the strength of private opinions which express little more than our own moods and humors, or, at the utmost the local prejudices of our own country." The decision to which the skepticism of Hume and Montaigne led them was the decision to let the world alone. There is another decision to which they could have come and at which others of their faith have actually arrived. If we can know nothing about society, if we can have only opinion about it, and if one man's opinion is as good as another's, then we may decide to get what we irrationally want by the use of irrational means, namely force. The appeal to reason is vain in a skeptical world. That appeal can only be successful if those appealed to have some rational views of the society of which they are a part.

A second reason why some people doubt the social utility of the education I favor is that they belong to the cult of immediacy, or of what may be called presentism. In this view the way to comprehend the world is to grapple with the reality you find about you. You tour the stockyards and the steel plants and understand the industrial system. There is no past. Any reference to antiquity or the Middle Ages shows that you are not interested in social progress. Philosophy is merely a function of its time and place. We live in a different time and usually a different place. Hence philosophers who lived yesterday have nothing to say to us today.

But we cannot understand the environment by looking at it. It presents itself to us as a mass of incomprehensible items. Simply collecting these items does not enlighten us. It may lead only to that worship of information which, according to John Dewey, still curses the social studies, and understanding escapes us still. We attack old problems not knowing they are old and make the same mistakes because we do not know they were made. So Stuart Chase and Thurman Arnold some years ago renewed the mediaeval controversy between the nominalists and the realists without showing that they realized that the subject had ever been discussed before or that they had the knowledge or training to conduct the discussion to any intelligible end.

The method of disposing of philosophy by placing it in a certain time and then saying that time is gone has been adequately dealt with by a contemporary historian. He says, "It ascribes the birth of Aristotelianism to the fact that Aristotle was a Greek and a pagan, living in a society based on slavery, four centuries before Christ; it also explains the revival of Aristotelianism in the thirteenth century by the fact that St. Thomas Aquinas was an Italian, a Christian, and even a monk, living in a feudal society, whose political and economic structure was widely different from that of the fourth-century Greece; and it accounts equally well for the Aristotelianism of J. Maritain, who is French, a layman, and living in the 'bourgeois' society of a nineteenth-century republic. Conversely, since they were living in the same times and the same places, just as Aristotle should have held the same philosophy as Plato, so Abelard and St. Bernard, St. Bonaventure and St. Thomas Aquinas, Descartes and Gassendi, all these men, who flatly contradicted one another, should have said more or less the same things."

You will see at once that skepticism and presentism are related to a third ism that distorts our view of the method of education for social improvement. This is the cult of scientism, a cult to which, curiously enough, very few natural scientists belong. It is a cult composed of those who misconceive the nature or the role of science. They say that science is modern; science is tentative; science is progressive. Everything which is not science is antiquated, or at best irrelevant. A writer in so respectable and learned a publication as the *International*

Journal of Ethics has called upon us to follow science in our quest for the good life, and the fact that he is a philosopher suggests that the cult of scientism has found members in the most unlikely places. For it must be clear that though we can and should use science to achieve social improvement, we cannot follow it to this destination. The reason is that science does not tell us where to go. Men may employ it for good or evil purposes; but it is the men that have the purposes, and they do not learn them from their scientific studies.

Scientism is a disservice to science. The rise of science is the most important fact of modern life. No student should be permitted to complete his education without understanding it. Universities should and must support and encourage scientific research. From a scientific education we may expect an understanding of science. From scientific investigation we may expect scientific knowledge. We are confusing the issue and demanding what we have no right to ask if we seek to learn from science the goals of human life and of organized society.

Finally, we have the cult of anti-intellectualism, which has some oddly assorted members. They range from Hitler, who thinks with his red corpuscles, through the members of the three other cults, to men of good will, who, since they are men of good will, are at the opposite pole to Hitler, but can give no rational justification for being there. They hold that philosophy of the heart which Auguste Comte first celebrated. Comte belonged to the cult of scientism. Therefore he could know nothing but what science told him. But he wanted social improvement. Hence he tried to make a philosophy and finally a religion out of science, and succeeded only in producing something which was no one of the three and which was, in fact, little more than sentimentalism.

Sentimentalism is an irrational desire to be helpful to one's fellow men. It sometimes appears as an ingratiating and even a redeeming quality in those who cannot or will not think. But the sentimentalist is really a dangerous character. He distrusts the intellect, because it might show him he is wrong. He believes in the primacy of the will, and this is what makes him dangerous. You don't know what you ought to want; you don't know why you want what you want. But you do know that you want it. This easily develops into the notion that since you want it, you ought to have it. You are a man of good will, and your opponents by definition are not. Since you ought to have what you want, you should get it if you have the power; and here the journey from the man of good will to Hitler is complete.

This is indeed the position in which the members of all four cults—skepticism, presentism, scientism, and anti-intellectualism—find themselves on questions of social improvement. Since they cannot know, they must feel. We can only hope that they will feel good. But we cannot be very hopeful. Where does the good will come from? Long ago the campaign before the Austrian plebiscite gave us the news for the first time that Hitler was guided by a special revelation. Most other men of good will do not claim such intimate contact with the Deity. But they are uniformly mysterious about the source of their inspiration. If it is not knowledge, and hence in this case philosophy, it must be habit—habit of the most irrational kind. A university can have nothing to do with irrational habits, except to try to moderate the bad ones and support the good ones. But if by hypothesis we cannot do this by rational means, we are forced to the conclusion that a university must be a large nursery school tenderly preserving good habits from shock, in the hope that if they can be nursed long enough they will last through life, though without any rational foundation. In this view the boarding school in the country would be the only proper training ground for American youth, and the University of Chicago could take no part in social improvement. In fact, it would be a subversive institution.

It hardly helps us here to say, as many anti-intellectuals do, that education must educate "the whole man." Of all the meaningless phrases in educational discussion this is the prize. Does it mean that education must do the whole job of translating the whole infant into a whole adult? Must it do what the church, the family, the state, the Y.M.C.A., and the Boy Scouts allege they are trying to do? If so, what is the place of these important or interesting organizations, and what becomes of that intellectual training which educational institutions might be able to give if they could get around to it? Are we compelled to assume that our students can learn nothing from life or that they have led no life before coming to us and lead none after they come? Moreover, what we are seeking is a guide to the emphasis that higher education must receive. Talk of the whole man seems to imply that there should be no emphasis at all. All "parts" of the man are of equal importance: his dress, his food, his health, his family, his business. Is education to emphasize them all? That would be like saying, if we were going to study the war, that in studying it we should emphasize the war. A flat equality among subjects, interests, and powers will hardly lead to the satisfactory development of any. Is it too much to say that if we can teach our students to lead the life of reason we shall do all that can be expected of us and do at the same time the best thing that can be done for the whole man? The task of education is to make rational animals more perfectly rational.

We see, then, that the quest for social improvement is a perpetual one. Men have always wanted not a different society, but a better one. What a better society is and how to get it has been one of the persistent problems of philosophy and one of the fundamental issues in the tradition of the Western World. Only those who recognize the important place that philosophy and the wisdom of the race must hold in education for citizenship can hope to educate men and women who can contribute to the improvement of society and who will want to do so. The cults of skepticism, presentism, scientism, and anti-intellectualism will lead us to despair, not merely of education, but also of society.

At a time when education at high school and college levels was becoming increasingly specialized, and when commercial, vocational, and technical courses were assuming a dominant role in curriculums, President James B. Conant of Harvard established a committee of twelve professors to explore "The Objectives of a General Education in a Free Society." The professors, many of them Harvard's most distinguished teachers and scholars, devoted nearly three years of intensive consideration to their study; their 267-page report was published in 1945. Since then it has gone through eighteen printings. In this excerpt "general education" is compared with its opposite and complement, "special education."

General and Special Education

REPORT OF THE HARVARD COMMITTEE

In the previous section we have attempted to outline the unifying elements of our culture and therefore of American education as well. In the present section we shall take the next step of indicating in what ways these cultural strands may be woven into the fabric of education. Education is broadly divided into general and special education; our topic now is the difference and the relationship between the two. The term, general education, is somewhat vague and color-less; it does not mean some airy education in knowledge in general (if there be such knowledge), nor does it mean education for all in the sense of universal education. It is used to indicate that part of a student's whole education which looks first of all to his life as a re-sponsible human being and citizen; while the term, special education, indicates that part which looks to the student's competence in some occupation. These two sides of life are not entirely separable, and it would be false to imagine education for the one as quite distinct from education for the other—more will be said on this point presently. Clearly, general education has somewhat the meaning of liberal edu-cation, except that, by applying to high school as well as to college, it envisages immensely greater numbers of students and thus escapes the invidium which, rightly or wrongly, attaches to liberal education in the minds of some people. But if one cling to the root meaning of liberal as that which befits or helps to make free men, then gen-eral and liberal education have identical goals. The one may be thought of as an earlier stage of the other, similar in nature but less advanced in degree.

The opposition to liberal education—both to the phrase and to the fact—stems largely from historical causes. The concept of liberal edu-cation first appeared in a slave-owning society, like that of Athens, in which the community was divided into freemen and slaves, rulers and subjects. While the slaves carried on the specialized occupations of menial work, the freemen were primarily concerned with the rights and duties of citizenship. The training of the former was purely vo-cational; but as the freemen were not only a ruling but also a leisure class, their education was exclusively in the liberal arts, without any utilitarian tinge. The freemen were trained in the reflective pursuit of the good life; their education was unspecialized as well as unvoca-tional; its aim was to produce a rounded person with a full under-standing of himself and of his place in society and in the cosmos.

Modern democratic society clearly does not regard labor as odious or disgraceful; on the contrary, in this country at least, it regards leisure with suspicion and expects its "gentlemen" to engage in work.

Thus we attach no odium to vocational instruction. Moreover, in so far as we surely reject the idea of freemen who are free in so far as they have slaves or subjects, we are apt strongly to deprecate the liberal education which went with the structure of the aristocratic ideal. Herein our society runs the risk of committing a serious fallacy. Democracy is the view that not only the few but that all are free, in that everyone governs his own life and shares in the responsibility for the management of the community. This being the case, it follows that all human beings stand in need of an ampler and rounded education. The task of modern democracy is to preserve the ancient ideal of liberal education and to extend it as far as possible to all the members of the community. In short, we have been apt to confuse accidental with fundamental factors, in our suspicion of the classical ideal. To believe in the equality of human beings is to believe that the good life, and the education which trains the citizen for the good life, are equally the privilege of all. And these are the touchstones of the liberated man: first, is he free; that is to say, is he able to judge and plan for himself, so that he can truly govern himself? In order to do this, his must be a mind capable of self-criticism; he must lead that self-examined life which according to Socrates is alone worthy of a free man. Thus he will possess inner freedom, as well as social freedom. Second, is he universal in his motives and sympathies? For the civilized man is a citizen of the entire universe; he has overcome provincialism, he is objective, and is a "spectator of all time and all existence." Surely these two are the very aims of democracy itself.

But the opposition to general education does not stem from causes located in the past alone. We are living in an age of specialism, in which the avenue to success for the student often lies in his choice of a specialized career, whether as a chemist, or an engineer, or a doctor, or a specialist in some form of business or of manual or technical work. Each of these specialties makes an increasing demand on the time and on the interest of the student. Specialism is the means for advancement in our mobile social structure; yet we must envisage the fact that a society controlled wholly by specialists is not a wisely ordered society. We cannot, however, turn away from specialism. The problem is how to save general education and its values within a system where specialism is necessary.

The very prevalence and power of the demand for special training makes doubly clear the need for a concurrent, balancing force in general education. Specialism enhances the centrifugal forces in society. The business of providing for the needs of society breeds a great diversity of special occupations; and a given specialist does not speak the language of the other specialists. In order to discharge his duties as a citizen adequately, a person must somehow be able to grasp the complexities of life as a whole. Even from the point of view of economic success, specialism has its peculiar limitations. Specializing in a vocation makes for inflexibility in a world of fluid possibilities. Business demands minds capable of adjusting themselves to varying situations and of managing complex human institutions. Given the pace of economic progress, techniques alter speedily; and even the work in which the student has been trained may no longer be useful when he is ready to earn a living or soon after. Our conclusion, then, is that the aim of education should be to prepare an individual to become an expert both in some particular vocation or art and in the general art of the free man and the citizen. Thus the two kinds of education once given separately to different social classes must be given together to all alike.

In this epoch in which almost all of us must be experts in some field in order to make a living, general education therefore assumes a peculiar importance. Since no one can become an expert in all fields, everyone is compelled to trust the judgment of other people pretty thoroughly in most areas of activity. I must trust the advice of my doctor, my plumber, my lawyer, my radio repairman, and so on. Therefore I am in peculiar need of a kind of sagacity by which to distinguish the expert from the quack, and the better from the worse expert. From this point of view, the aim of general education may be defined as that of providing the broad critical sense by which to recognize competence in any field. William James said that an educated person knows a good man when he sees one. There are standards and a style for every type of activity—manual, athletic, intellectual, or artistic; and the educated man should be one who can tell sound from shoddy work in a field outside his own. General education is especially required in a democracy where the public elects its leaders and officials; the ordinary citizen must be discerning enough so that he will not be deceived by appearances and will elect the candidate who is wise in his field.

Both kinds of education—special as well as general—contribute to the task of implementing the pervasive forces of our culture. Here we revert to what was said at the start of this chapter on the aims of education in our society. It was argued there that two complementary forces are at the root of our culture: on the one hand, an ideal of man and society distilled from the past but at the same time transcending the past as a standard of judgment valid in itself, and, on the other hand, the belief that no existent expressions of this ideal are final but that all alike call for perpetual scrutiny and change in the light of new knowledge. Specialism is usually the vehicle of this second force. It fosters the open-mindedness and love of investigation which are the wellspring of change, and it devotes itself to the means by which change is brought about. The fact may not always be obvious. There is a sterile specialism which hugs accepted knowledge and ends in the bleakest conservatism. Modern life also calls for many skills which, though specialized, are repetitive and certainly do not conduce to inquiry. These minister to change but unconsciously. Nevertheless, the previous statement is true in the sense that specialism is concerned primarily with knowledge in action, as it advances into new fields and into further applications.

Special education comprises a wider field than vocationalism; and correspondingly, general education extends beyond the limits of merely literary preoccupation. An example will make our point clearer. A scholar—let us say a scientist (whether student or teacher)—will, in the laudable aim of saving himself from narrowness, take a course in English literature, or perhaps read poetry and novels, or perhaps listen to good music and generally occupy himself with the fine arts. All this, while eminently fine and good, reveals a misapprehension. In his altogether unjustified humility, the scientist wrongly interprets the distinction between liberal and illiberal in terms of the distinction between the humanities and the sciences. Plato and Cicero would have been very much surprised to hear that geometry, astronomy, and the sciences of nature in general, are excluded from the humanities. There is also implied a more serious contempt for the liberal arts, harking back to the fallacy which identifies liberal education with the aristocratic ideal. The implication is that liberal education is something only genteel. A similar error is evident in the student's attitude toward his required courses outside his major field as something to "get over with," so that he may engage in the business of serious education, identified in his mind with the field of concentration.

Now, a general education is distinguished from special education, not by subject matter, but in terms of method and outlook, no matter what the field. Literature, when studied in a technical fashion, gives rise to the special science of philology; there is also the highly specialized historical approach to painting. Specialism is interchangeable, not with natural science, but with the method of science, the method which abstracts material from its context and handles it in complete isolation. The reward of scientific method is the utmost degree of precision and exactness. But, as we have seen, specialism as an educational force has its own limitations; it does not usually provide an insight into general relationships.

A further point is worth noting. The impact of specialism has been felt not only in those phases of education which are necessarily and rightly specialistic; it has affected also the whole structure of higher and even of secondary education. Teachers, themselves products of highly technical disciplines, tend to reproduce their knowledge in class. The result is that each subject, being taught by an expert, tends to be so presented as to attract potential experts. This complaint is perhaps more keenly felt in colleges and universities, which naturally look to scholarship. The undergraduate in a college receives his teaching from professors who, in their turn, have been trained in graduate schools. And the latter are dominated by the ideal of specialization. Learning now is diversified and parceled into a myriad of specialties. Correspondingly, colleges and universities are divided into large numbers of departments, with further specialization within the departments. As a result, a student in search of a general course is commonly frustrated. Even an elementary course is devised as an introduction to a specialism within a department; it is significant only as the beginning of a series of courses of advancing complexity. In short, such introductory courses are planned for the specialist, not for the student seeking a general education. The young chemist in the course in literature and the young writer in the course in chemistry find themselves in thoroughly uncomfortable positions so long as the purpose of these courses is primarily to train experts who will go on to higher courses rather than to give some basic understanding of science as it is revealed in chemistry or of the arts as they are revealed in literature.

It is most unfortunate if we envisage general education as something formless—that is to say, the taking of one course after another; and as something negative, namely, the study of what is not in a field of concentration. Just as we regard the courses in concentration as having definite relations to one another, so should we envisage general education as an organic whole whose parts join in expounding a ruling idea and in serving a common aim. And to do so means to abandon the view that all fields and all departments are equally valuable vehicles of general education. It also implies some prescription. At the least it means abandoning the usual attitude of regarding "distribution" as a sphere in which the student exercises a virtually untrammeled freedom of choice. It may be objected that we are proposing to limit the liberty of the student in the very name of liberal education. Such an objection would only indicate an ambiguity in the conception of liberal education. We must distinguish between liberalism in education and education in liberalism. The former, based as it is on the doctrine of individualism, expresses the view that the student should be free in his choice of courses. But education in liberalism is an altogether different matter; it is education which has a pattern of its own, namely, the pattern associated with the liberal outlook. In this view, there are truths which none can be free to ignore, if one is to have that wisdom through which life can become useful. These are the truths concerning the structure of the good life and concerning the factual conditions by which it may be achieved, truths comprising the goals of the free society.

Finally, the problem of general education is one of combining fixity of aim with diversity in application. It is not a question of providing a general education which will be uniform through the same classes of all schools and colleges all over the country, even were such a thing possible in our decentralized system. It is rather to adapt general education to the needs and intentions of different groups and, so far as possible, to carry its spirit into special education. The effectiveness of teaching has always largely depended on this willingness to adapt a central unvarying purpose to varying outlooks. Such adaptation is as much in the interest of the quick as of the slow, of the bookish as of the unbookish, and is the necessary protection of each. What is wanted, then, is a general education capable at once of taking on many different forms and yet of representing in all its forms the common knowledge and the common values on which a free society depends.

Having entered college at fifteen, Stringfellow Barr (1897–) went on to Oxford as a Rhodes Scholar to study history. After serving on the faculty of University of Virginia, he joined a committee set up by Robert M. Hutchins to study the undergraduate curriculum of American colleges and universities. From 1937 to 1946 he was president of St. John's College, Annapolis, Maryland, where he revived the traditional liberal arts program as the focus of undergraduate education. Subsequently Barr became president of the Foundation for World Government. He is now a fellow of the Center for the Study of Democratic Institutions.

4

Liberal Education: A Common Adventure

STRINGFELLOW BARR

There is a specter which haunts American education and all our discussion of it. It is a question that we almost never make explicit, a question most of us have never consciously formulated: are there any intellectual skills that every member of a free society should acquire up to the extent of his native ability? Because we generally refuse to permit the question to become a conscious one, it remains spectral, and therefore confusingly haunts our discussions. If there are indeed some things that every free man should be able to do, then those things should be central to our schools and colleges.

The nearest we have come to an answer is, I imagine, our professed desire to abolish illiteracy. It is true that, while the American people are not only the richest people on earth but the richest people history records, we are not the most literate people. Nevertheless, we were the first people to make a serious attempt at universal schooling, an attempt not unconnected with our dogma, which I find many Americans now doubting, that all men are born free and equal. And I suppose that this dogma reflects an even older belief that all men are the children of God. Again, it is true that our press abounds in almost daily complaints that even those of us who are technically classed as literates, do not read very correctly and that those who might teach us to do so are being forced into other occupations because we decline to pay our teachers enough to afford them even a modestly decent living. Even if we did read correctly, it might remain true that we do not read very attentively, or imaginatively, and it certainly might remain true that difficult but important books that can be published in many countries and sold at a profit cannot be safely published here without subsidy. Millions of our college graduates are simply not well enough educated to be able to read them, or to want to read them. A very large number of them are now reading the comics instead, on the erroneous assumption that if a book is important but difficult, its reading had best be left to specialists, or at least to people who "took a course" in the subject matter the book represents.

I suggest that any people which wishes to be a free community must be able to communicate, and communicate better than animals appear to do, better even than adolescent boys do. There are many grades of communication and therefore many grades of literacy. When I was in India last year, I discovered what the reader may already know: that those citizens are classed by the census as literate who can sign their own names—or, perhaps more precisely—draw a recognizable picture of their name in one of the scripts now used in India. But there is another sense of "literate" than the literal sense of being able to read and write. There are Indian peasants who cannot do either, but who can recite hundreds or even thousands of lines of great poetry and who can frame their own thoughts with accuracy and even with nobility. While I am sure that we Americans, living in a highly technological society, must learn to read and write, beyond our own signatures, I must say I frankly envied the Indians for their great oral tradition.

Maybe we should think of literacy as an indefinitely expansible process. Maybe our ideal for each free man should be that he become as literate as possible. That ideal would involve his learning to handle the two great sets of symbols which men have used for millennia when they have sought to communicate: words and numbers. If so, language and mathematics must be the common property of a free community. Its members must be able to speak better, listen better, read better, write better, and think better than we Americans now can. How well? I know of no limit to how well it is desirable for human beings to do these things. Most of us still fall so far short of William Shakespeare that there is still room for improvement. As for the mock modesty of saying that we are not geniuses and cannot hope to communicate better than we already do, I wonder whether we can make this claim with any greater truth than we could make another: that we cannot learn to use our body more skilfully than we already do? Art is long. We are here talking about art—about what were traditionally called the liberal arts.

How are these arts of communication acquired? If we would drop our educational jargon and watch a young child learn to talk, I suspect we should have the key. Little children learn to talk by listening to people do it who already know how, and then imitating them. They can keep on learning to talk better and better by listening frequently to talkers who bear the same relation to them that grown-ups bear to children, and by imitating these superlative talkers. Again, I myself find Shakespeare one of the best talkers I get a chance to listen to—much better than any talker now alive in the town I live in, and much better than nearly any other talker whose "talk" I can listen to only in printed words across the centuries that separate us.

This, I would suppose, is why over many long centuries men have turned to books: in order to tune in on the Great Conversation that we call civilization. This is what it means to be the child of a great civilization and not a cultural bastard. But, in doing this, we should show some of the humility and some of the daring that little children habitually show. We should dare to listen attentively and humbly even to conversation that is out of our depth, provided it is good. After all, every person who ever learned to speak English learned by listening, at least so long as he was a small child, to conversation that was out of his depth. It is when the child stretches his mind to follow what seems at first like gibberish that his own command of language steadily expands. Those who want, even when they are adults, to increase their own powers to communicate, and even to commune, with other men can scarcely do better than listen to great talk out of their depth, trusting in the same unbelievable miracle that enables a child to learn to talk.

Over the centuries and throughout many lands a few men have talked magnificently, and a few of these few have transmitted to us in books what they said. We commonly call such books classics. They are so called, I believe, because they communicate with great skill ideas about matters that human experience has taught us are important, just as a painting, a statue, a sonata, or indeed a football game may achieve the rank of classic through the pre-eminent skill with which it was painted, sculpted, or played. The reasons for having even young children, and certainly college students, read such books and look at such paintings and listen to such music are that life is short; that these things are the best of their kind that civilization has salvaged; and that the best is none too good for a man.

Thousands of other books and paintings and sonatas may be ever so worth reading or hearing or seeing; but of the making of such things there is no end. Any attempt at coverage would be folly. And the second best will always be second. There may be a difference of opinion about which of man's creations belong to this top rank. Somebody has to decide; and the professional obligation to decide falls on the teacher. If he cannot make a better rough choice than his pupil, then there is a lot to be said for their changing places and for reallocating the salary accordingly—such as it now is. Patients who distrust their doctors are well advised to seek doctors they trust. Writing one's own prescriptions is at best inefficient and at worst dangerous. Those patients who develop allergies for certain medicines can always speak to their doctors about it.

For those of us who glorify "individual differences" at the expense of whatever may be the common property of educated men, there is always the student who simply doesn't "like" Shakespeare. Some men there are who cannot abide a harmless, necessary cat. But I am by no means sure that Shakespeare is quite that special: he has so often been called universal that there really may be something in it. And I should think that, while no student may be required to love Shakespeare, all students may properly be invited to listen to him. This is precisely our point of second abdication. We teachers, having first asked the student which of several subjects, none of which he knows, he thinks he would prefer, next let him drop whatever subject seems to present difficulties. I suppose these practices are akin to our practice of letting children decide which foods they will eat before they have tasted them, or at least after the first mouthful.

If our schools and colleges were now teaching all the members of the American community how to read, in the sense in which I have being using "read," I would happily exempt them from the multitude of other responsibilities they have assumed in place of that one. The information they now try to dispense can be readily found and acquired by an educated man—that is, by one who has learned to read, to use his mind imaginatively and rigorously. I have suggested that the quickest way I know of from my own teaching experience to teach people to read, and to read well, is to help them read those things most worth reading. The traditional name for such things is "the classics."

But the classics, though traditionally used for this purpose, were over the centuries used almost exclusively by a select few. Can classics be read for this purpose by everybody? Aren't some young men and women too stupid to read them, or too uninterested, or too ill prepared? I can only answer that I have myself used them with undergraduates whose previous school training branded them as stupid, uninterested, and unprepared, and I am convinced that what they gained from the classics was more than they would have gained from more trivial books. Some of these undergraduates had reached college in some sense able to read, but only in some very vague sense. Some of them arrived in college so uninterested that their eyes wore a kind of glaze. Some of them seemed to have very little ability, although in their stupefied condition it was impossible to know what their bad grades in high school meant. They had clearly never been awakened from a sort of intellectual somnambulism, and there was no earthly way of knowing what their powers were if they should ever be brought into anything like full use.

The difference between what such undergraduates got out of the classics and what their abler, or more interested, or better prepared classmates got was a wider gap than one sees in most classrooms, precisely because one of the most magical properties of a true classic is that it can be read on many levels. When I was eight, my father gave me for my birthday a copy of *Macbeth* and told me he would give me other plays of Shakespeare as fast as I could read them. That is exactly fifty years ago, and I cannot reconstruct precisely what I got out of that first reading of *Macbeth*. But I infer that it was very little, since my favorite character was King Duncan and since I muttered his lines while striding across the floor with my dressing-gown trailing behind me as I had reason to believe his kingly robes must have trailed. When I was eleven, I witnessed my first performance of a Shakespearean play—and it was *Macbeth*. I was amazed by meanings I saw in the play which had evaded me in my King Duncan period. I was sixteen the next time I read the play, and I was surprised by how little I had understood the play when I had seen it performed five years before. Every time I have seen it performed since, or even read it, this surprise has been repeated. But I loved the play when I was eight, as many children have; and at eleven I was mad about it. Not, of course, for precisely the same reasons that I read it now. In between each reading, I have been experiencing my own life—partly in the light of my last previous reading—and it is not surprising that

I see things in *Macbeth* that I had no real way of seeing the time before.

I ask the reader's pardon for this autobiographical note, but sometimes a homely illustration can jar us "educators" out of our jargon and our self-imposed mystification about matters every good teacher knows. One of these matters is that thousands of young boys have taken their Homer straight and reveled in him. Those who read him without reveling often get the point from discussing what happened on the plain of Troy with those who have managed to be transported there. As for those who prefer other types of reading, this is a matter of taste, and fortunately for mankind tastes change, sometimes for the better, but only by further tasting of things we at first do not much like. The teacher's job is not to discover the restricted and transient tastes of an immature mind nor to protect it from other tastes, but to help it acquire other tastes.

The true classic is, I believe, highly communicable, and can be read on many levels, by the stupid and the brilliant alike. It is written about important matters, matters that remain important in their essence, so that the classics which treat of them retain the flavor of the contemporary book, with its immediacy and relevance, for successive generations of men: in short, they endure. But, even so, the author's way of treating important matters varies from time to time and from place to place. There is high discipline in experiencing these "translations" of a basic problem from country to country and from century to century. I think, therefore, there is every reason for a faculty to choose first-rate books from many times and places. A choice I was myself once involved in ran from Homer to contemporary authors. It is true that the list of books we used, a list that grew out of a famous list the American Library Association had once published, included only Western classics, and there are strong arguments both for and against including the classics of the Oriental tradition.

But just as there are good reasons for not confining one's choice of the best and greatest products of the human mind to one country or one century, so there are, I believe, equally compelling reasons for not confining oneself to one, or to a few, "fields." Graduate work properly concentrates on a field of knowledge which it has deliberately abstracted out of man's intellectual experience as a whole. But in the last analysis fields are for cattle, not for the human mind. "That is not in my field" never exonerates a human mind from inquiry. The atomic bomb has dramatized, as it had never before been so dazzlingly dramatized in my lifetime, what happens when we cultivate one field hard and leave the others to lie fallow. It is a postwar cliché that mankind simply cannot afford to know so much more about nuclear physics than it does about the moral and political problems which the atom raises.

One suspects therefore that the most profitable use of classics involves the reading of classics in all the major areas that man's mind has entered. The last lecture that Sir William Osler gave before his death deplored the fact that Oxford's famous Literae Humaniores included such things as the great Greek and Latin monuments in philosophy, in history, in poetry, but not the imposing monuments the Greeks and Romans left in mathematics and the natural sciences. What that brilliant modern scientist then said should be pondered afresh. What he did not say about Greek scientific treatises was: "*Nous avons changé tout cela.*"

If an educated faculty selects a list of books it thinks worthwhile for students to chew on, instead of leaving it to the students who have come to college for help in getting educated to choose the books for themselves, the same faculty has to retain the right and duty to revise the list whenever it changes its mind or finds that a given book releases its students' powers even more than another and slightly "better" book. The faculty of St. John's College in Annapolis was shocked to find that, when the college catalogue included "A List of a Hundred Great Books," newspapers tended to translate the caption into "The Hundred Best Books." It is an important shift.

The books really are "to chew on," not to master. The idea that a schoolboy or even a college undergraduate is going to "master" Plato's *Republic* seems to me to be lacking in a sense of humor. Let us pass over in courteous silence any claim his professor may make that he himself really has mastered Plato. The reason students have for many centuries read books of this sort as a means of practicing the liberal arts on worthwhile material was not to master the books. The reason a puppy may wisely be given a large bone to gnaw on is not so that he can chew it up and swallow it but so that he can sharpen his teeth trying to. A well-read man is one who has sharpened his intellectual teeth on many such books. But the bones will not be serviceable tooth-sharpeners unless they exemplify an author in the act of practicing the liberal arts, the arts of communication, of "readin' an' writin'," in an eminent degree. And the author is unlikely to do that on trivial subject matter. At this point our bone metaphor creaks pretty badly. For the fact is that our undergraduate, when he lives for several years with the classics, trying to comprehend them to the limit of his developing powers, not only learns to practice the liberal arts himself but he lives among the ennobling images and deals with the great and permanent ideas that the great poets' imaginations have caught and the great philosophers have identified and grasped. He becomes familiar with the great questions, including those which perhaps no man has answered. They tell the story that when Gertrude Stein lay dying, with the faithful Alice B. Toklas at her bedside, Miss Stein asked: "Alice, what is the answer?" Miss Toklas is reported to have answered: "Gertrude, there is no answer." Whereupon, the great Gertrude parried with: "Alice, what is the question?" and turned over and died. If an undergraduate can learn from the great classics always to seek the problem before offering a pat solution, he will have learned more than have most of his contemporaries.

If over the centuries "the classics" have nurtured and disciplined and rendered supple and subtle the minds of men, if even in our pioneering, scrambling young republic they nourished many of our leaders and formed the basis of college studies until less than a century ago, why did we abandon them—since they really have been all but abandoned? We cannot, I believe, safely infer that we abandoned them because we found they did not really nourish or that what we teach now has been demonstrated to nourish more. I believe the historical evidence points to two principal reasons for our current suspicion of them. First, the way the classics were taught had robbed them of their function; and the most nourishing food can be ruined by a cook until it is both unpalatable and indigestible. So the classics were thrown out. Secondly, the failure of the college of liberal arts to assimilate to its intellectual tradition the brilliant achievements of natural science doomed the very phrase "liberal arts" to mean useless but ornamental learning. Whereupon science, technology, and the industrial culture which they have created, swept the classics aside. These two causes for the decline of liberal education in America will bear closer scrutiny.

By the time my generation reached school and college, "the classics" had turned into courses in Latin and Greek: Cæsar-Cicero-Virgil and perhaps Xenophon-Herodotus-Homer. There was a pronounced tendency to "take" sixty lines a day. We did not read and discuss such authors; we studied and recited on them. Not William Shakespeare himself, not even King Duncan, can survive the sixty-lines-a-day treatment. And although I am more grateful for the Greek I learned as an undergraduate than for anything else I learned at the time, I must confess that I did not really "read" the Greeks and the Romans until I was a grown man and read them in English translation. As a matter of fact, many of the Greek and Roman classics that I would want an undergraduate to read today did not exist in English when I was young or existed only in very expensive editions. Today cheap and good translations abound, and at paperbound prices.

There are few more powerful exercises in the liberal arts than putting into the best English one can muster, the best things written in Greek or Latin. And there are few better ways of learning how to write English. But, when all this has been granted, the fact remains that he who reads the classics at the rate of sixty lines a day is doing a dreadful thing, and he will eventually die of boredom, or revolt. Our scholars and undergraduates revolted; Greek has largely died out in our colleges, and in most places Latin is busy dying. The books which a few of our forefathers read (knowing enough Greek or Latin) and found inspiring, are shrinking now to excerpts or appear as subjects of discussion in textbooks or are studied in some "fields" out of their total context and as specialized knowledge. Whether the classics— Greek, Roman, or those written in later tongues—play a vital role again will depend, I suspect, on whether we read them in English and read them straight through in the way we read, or ought to read, other books worth reading. Many people are beginning to do this, especially those who have finished college and are still hungry for something they feel they somehow missed.

We owe a great deal to the followers of John Dewey, and to "progressive education" in general, for backing up the revolt against the sixty lines a day, the sadistic grammatical drill, the mnemonic doggerel verses, the pedantry, the false claims that Hellenist and Latinist resorted to when they had lost their purpose and redoubled their effort. Greek and Latin studies had lost their liberal arts content: now they were not merely difficult, but dull and irrelevant. A curricular revolution all but liquidated them—instead of rediscovering their proper use as media peculiarly adapted to the practice of the liberal arts. Revolutions have a way of throwing out the baby with the bath. But the guilt for depriving generations of students of the classics rests more on the head of the confused classicist than on the head of his unconvinced colleagues. The time has come to recover the bruised baby without bothering about the bath-water.

If and when we recover the liberal arts, we ought to do so with the mature knowledge that, being human arts, they are always subject to decay and misuse. That is one reason historians talk of civilization and barbarism, of Renaissances and Dark Ages. The liberal arts, the arts of "reading," have often been revived and we could revive them again.

I have tried to suggest that the classics, or some of them, can be read with joy and profit by children, but at some point they should be read as a sort of final inoculation for the long educational process called Life, an inoculation that Europe tried to give a few youngsters in its British "public school," its French *lycée*, its German *Gymnasium*; and America gave in its "academies." And for this inoculation, for this "general education," which a modern democracy needs to give to as many of its citizen-rulers as possible, it is not necessary to wait until what we call "college age."

I would certainly plump for fifteen rather than the seventeen at which the average American matriculates today, remembering always that while a fifteen-year-old will "get less out of" such books than his elder brother, the problem is not primarily to get stuff out of the books and into the human head but to initiate a certain kind of intellectual growth in the student as early as that sort of process can be initiated. Then he will have both the ability and the desire to "get something out of the books" during the period that extends from his graduation until his death. They are worth that much of a man's time. Graduation should certify merely to a successful inoculation and to the formation of certain habits of mind. I know of few college curricula today that can certify to so much.

If my guess is correct—and it is at least based on some direct personal teaching experience—four-year liberal arts colleges could be graduating people at nineteen instead of twenty-one, more able than our present college graduates are to study law or medicine or to enter practical affairs. I find an amazing proportion of business executives and teachers in graduate and professional schools who agree with these judgments, but few teachers in schools or undergraduate colleges willing to consider so drastic a shift. Anything less drastic will, I suggest, prove less than enough. But if we cannot face reorganizing our colleges for a different age level, at least let us try to achieve basic education by twenty-one.

In addition to reading and discussing the classics under competent guidance, the undergraduate ought to translate portions of them too if he is to learn how to use his mother tongue well. Nearly any language that contains a classic will do for this purpose. For that matter, "translating" an English writer like Gibbon into contemporary English, or even into current slang, will help. But, at the risk of appearing blindly conservative, I would plump for Greek or Latin. My reason is simple: Greek and Latin are highly inflected tongues, which force attention on the precise meaning of a sentence. Their inner structure is such that the bones show more clearly than in French or German, and they do not breed the contempt and inattention that our own familiar English breeds. What they say has to be dug out, and the digging process poses neatly some basic problems of language in general, English included. Even sixty-lines-a-day can be tolerated if backed up by an exciting program of reading in English translation.

In addition to translating into English what some man like Sophocles said so well in Greek, the student of the liberal arts ought to translate what Euclid said about quadratic equations in geometrical form into what can be said about them in modern algebra. The growing fear of mathematics in our schools and colleges would be frightening in any sort of society. In a society based on a complicated technology, it is completely terrifying. It poses the problem of whether a community of button-pushers, who do not know what happens when they push buttons except for the final result, can hope to retain both the community's economic base and its freedom of political and moral choice. In terms of its daily problems, it is today quite simply too ignorant to retain both.

Mathematics leads us naturally into the second reason I posited for our surrender of the classics in the college of liberal arts: the refusal of our grandfathers and our fathers to incorporate into the liberal arts the intellectual process we call modern science. Modern science has had its revenge of Academe. After having been considered in the late nineteenth century the intellectual kitchen of the campus which young gentlemen trod, it created a new material environment that left the humanities stranded in their own snobbery and preciosity, until at last the "social sciences" and even the philological course in language began to ape the scientist's methods, methods which he had evolved for the specific purposes for which he used them—the investigation of the behavior of matter. The results have often been grotesque, and nobody has been more horrified by those results than the leading natural scientists.

The protection against this ironical comedy, this typical idolatry, this minor blasphemy lay in admitting to start with that the laboratory experiment can be a classic too. It lay also in doing what no second-rate scientist wants to tolerate: the study of the great classics of scientific thought, regardless of whether later experimentation and improved instruments have forced a revision of the hypothesis. The average scientist today would not know any more than the average scholar in "the humanities," why Osler thought Greek scientific masterpieces were worth reading and understanding.

It would presumably be perverse to study the great crucial experiments in natural science merely out of books, no matter how wonderful these books may be as products of the human intellect, while not bothering to set up the experiments the books are based on in a college laboratory. The art, as well as the science, incorporated in those experiments is precisely the art our immediate ancestors so grudgingly admitted to sacred Academe. Nor had we better stop at laboratories: workshops can play a role too. The manual arts support the liberal arts. The liberal arts, when seriously pursued in all the areas where man's mind has roamed, can put machine oil on a man's hands and grease in his hair. There has never been anything dandy-esque or upper-class about the liberal arts, although a leisure class has often tried to make them so.

And who will teach the classics in the sort of context I have just described? Ah, there's the rub. Most professors are suffering acutely from intellectual agoraphobia, and the special aspect of a specialized subject matter has been their protection against being caught out intellectually, as it has been their best hope of promotion and recognition. Moreover, we professors did not ourselves receive the sort of education I have been describing, except where we have picked it up as best we could. Frequently, we are not even very much interested in teaching, certainly not in teaching undergraduates, and most certainly not in helping to prepare people for college. We are interested in "publishing," although only the most hopeful of us can attach much importance to the bulk of what we are publishing. To teach the liberal arts in the manner I have tried to describe would involve entering again into our mother's womb or at least studying things we long ago decided never to look at again—such, let us say, as mathematics. Or, according to the particular case, language. We have lost our amateur standing, and we prefer to think that this sort of teaching, as against the sort we do daily, would be intellectual charlatanry.

Yet the classics are still there. We even pay them lip service. With their exuberant intellectual vitality they could bring us back to life, rid us of our academic false modesty and our ill-concealed anti-intellectualism, and revive our people's vision of the common good. If such things happened, there might be what men call a revival of learning.

*Born in St. Louis and educated
at Harvard, T. S. Eliot (1888–
1965) left for London in 1914.
In 1927 he became a British
citizen and in 1928 announced
himself a ". . . classicist in
literature, royalist in politics,
and Anglo-Catholic in religion."
Author of "The Love Song of
J. Alfred Prufrock" and "The
Waste Land," and perhaps the
most influential modern poet-
critic writing in English, he
received the Nobel Prize for
literature in 1948. Religious conversion and pressures of world
affairs increasingly drew Eliot's
attention from purely literary
topics to politics, economics,
theology, and education. This
essay was published in 1936.*

5

Modern Education and the Classics

T. S. ELIOT

Questions of education are frequently discussed as if they bore no relation to the social system in which and for which the education is carried on. This is one of the commonest reasons for the unsatisfactoriness of the answers. It is only within a particular social system that a system of education has any meaning. If education today seems to deteriorate, if it seems to become more and more chaotic and meaningless, it is primarily because we have no settled and satisfactory arrangement of society, and because we have both vague and diverse opinions about the kind of society we want. Education is a subject which cannot be discussed in a void: our questions raise other questions, social, economic, financial, political. And the bearings are on more ultimate problems even than these: to know what we want in education we must know what we want in general, we must derive our theory of education from our philosophy of life. The problem turns out to be a religious problem.

One might almost speak of a *crisis* of education. There are particular problems for each country, for each civilization, just as there are particular problems for each parent; but there is also a general problem for the whole civilized world, and for the uncivilized so far as it is being taught by its civilized superiors; a problem which may be as acute in Japan, in China or in India as in Britain or Europe or America. The progress (I do not mean the extension) of education for several centuries has been from one aspect a drift, from another aspect a push; for it has tended to be dominated by the idea of *getting on.* The individual wants more education, not as an aid to the acquisition of wisdom but in order to get on; the nation wants more in order to get the better of other nations, the class wants it to get the better of other classes, or at least to hold its own against them. Education is associated therefore with technical efficiency on the one hand, and with rising in society on the other. Education becomes something to which everybody has a "right," even irrespective of his capacity; and when everyone gets it—by that time, of course, in a diluted and adulterated form—then we naturally discover that education is no longer an infallible means of getting on, and people turn to another fallacy: that of "education for leisure"—without having revised their notions of "leisure." As soon as this precious motive of snobbery evaporates, the zest has gone out of education; if it is not going to mean more money, or more power over others, or a better social position, or at least a steady and respectable job, few people are going to take the trouble to acquire education. For deteriorate it as you may, education is still going to demand a good deal of drudgery. And the majority of people are incapable of enjoying leisure—that is, unemployment *plus* an income and a status of respectability—in any but pretty simple forms—such as balls propelled by hand, by foot, and by engines or tools of various types; in playing cards; or in watching dogs, horses or other men engage in feats of speed or skill. The uneducated man with an empty mind, if he be free from financial anxiety or narrow limitation, and can obtain access to golf-clubs, dance halls, etc., is, for all I can see, as well equipped to fill his leisure contentedly as is the educated man.

The inadequacy of most people's notions of education is revealed whenever there is any public discussion on the subject of raising the school age. To dismiss as irrelevant the miserable stop-gap idea that raising the school-leaving age will diminish unemployment—a mere confession of inability to solve a different problem—it is assumed by most people (and there are always a great many people ready to discuss the problem) that more education—that is to say, more years of education—would be a good thing "if the nation could afford it." Of course the nation could afford it, if it is such a good thing as all that. But no one stops to consider what is this education of which no one can have too much; or whether the society in which more of this education is a good thing is necessarily a good society. If, for instance, the "nation," or the people composing it, have only a little money, should we not assure ourselves first that our elementary education is already so good that no money could improve it, before we attempt a more ambitious programme? (Anyone who has taught children even for a few weeks knows that the size of a class makes an immense difference to the amount you can teach. Fifteen is an ideal number; twenty is the maximum; with thirty much less can be done; with more than thirty most teachers' first concern is simply to keep order, and the clever children creep at the pace of the backward.)

The first task of anyone who might be imagined as occupying a dictatorial position in the education of a country should obviously be to see that elementary education is as good as it can be made; and then proceeding forward make sure that no one received *too much* education, limiting the numbers treated to "higher education" to a third (let us say) of those receiving that treatment today. (I do not want a dictator even in education, but it is sometimes convenient to employ a hypothetical dictator in illustration.) For one of the potential causes of deterioration of the universities is the deterioration lower down. The universities have to teach what they can to the material they can get: nowadays they even teach *English* in England. American universities, ever since Charles William Eliot and his contemporary "educators," have tried to make themselves as big as possible in a mad competition for numbers: it is very much easier to turn a little university into a big one than to reduce the size of one that has grown too big. And after Eliot had taught America that a university should be as big as possible (and I have seen one that boasted an enrolment of 18,000 students—including, I must explain, evening classes) America grew very rich—that is to say, it produced a considerable number of millionaires, and the next generation set itself to an equally mad programme of building, erecting within a short time a great variety of imposing, though in some places rather hastily-built, halls and dormitories and even chapels. And when you have sunk so much money in plant and equipment, when you have a very large (though not always well-paid) staff of men who are mostly married and have a few children, when you are turning out from your graduate schools more and more men who have been trained to become teachers in other universities, and who will probably want to marry and have children too; when your whole national system of higher education is designed for an age of expansion, for a country which is going indefinitely to increase its population, grow rich, and build more universities—then you will find it very difficult to retract.

What happens in America is not so irrelevant to British affairs as it is commonly taken to be. For, as I have already said, what we have to recognize is a crisis of education not in one country but in all, a crisis which has its common features everywhere. What has happened in American universities can happen in provincial universities in England; and what happens in provincial universities exerts influence on what happens in Oxford and Cambridge. We are well advanced in an age of great social changes. I do not object to that; but I think that if we admit that social change inevitably means change in our system of education, in our conceptions of *who* should be educated, and *how*, and of the still more neglected question, *why*, we shall be better able to give intelligent direction, instead of leaving education to take care of itself.

It is against this shifting vast background, very important for my picture, that I would set the question of the place of the classics in modern education. We discern three tendencies in education as in politics, the *liberal*, the *radical*, and what I am tempted to call, perhaps simply because it is my own, the *orthodox*. In using these terms about tendencies in education I do not wish to draw any close political parallel, because in politics there is no pure breed of any kind.

The *liberal* attitude towards education is that with which we are the most familiar. It is apt to maintain the apparently unobjectionable view that education is not a mere acquisition of facts, but a training of the mind as an instrument, to deal with any class of facts, to reason, and to apply the training obtained in one department in dealing with new ones. The inference is drawn that one subject is as good, for education, as another; that the student should follow his own bent, and pursue whatever subject happens most to interest him. The student who applies himself to geology, and he who applies himself to languages, may both in the end find themselves in trade: it is assumed that if they both have made the most of their opportunities, and have equal abilities, they will both be equally fitted for their vocation, and for "life." I think that the theory that the mind can be trained equally well upon any subject, and that the choice of the class of facts to acquire is indifferent, can be pushed too far. There are two kinds of subject which, at an early stage, provide but poor training for the mind. One is the subject which is concerned more with theories, and the history of theories, than with the storing of the mind with such information and knowledge as theories are built upon: such a subject, and a very popular one, is *economics*, which consists of a number of complicated and contradictory theories, a subject by no means proved to be a science, usually based on illicit assumptions, the bastard progeny of a parent it disowns, *ethics*. Even *philosophy*, when divorced from *theology* and from the knowledge of life and of ascertainable facts, is but a famishing pabulum, or a draught stimulating for a moment, leaving behind drought and disillusion. The other kind of subject which provides indifferent training is that which is too minute and particular, the relation of which to the general business of living is not made evident. And there is a third subject, equally bad as training, which does not fall into either of these classes, but which is bad for reasons of its own: the study of *English Literature* or, to be more comprehensive, the literature of one's own language.

Another fallacy of liberal education is that the student who advances to the university should take up the study that interests him most. For a small number of students this is in the main right. Even at a very early stage of school life, we can identify a few individuals with a definite inclination towards one group of studies or another. The danger for these fortunate ones is that if left to themselves they will overspecialize, they will be wholly ignorant of the general interests of human beings. We are all in one way or another naturally lazy, and it is much easier to confine ourselves to the study of subjects in which we excel. But the great majority of the people who are to be educated have no very strong inclination to specialize, because they have no definite gifts or tastes. Those who have more lively and curious minds will tend to smatter. No one can become really educated without having pursued some study in which he took no interest—for it is a part of education to *learn to interest ourselves* in subjects for which we have no aptitude.

The doctrine of studying the subject we like (and for many youths in the process of development this is often only what they like at the moment) is most disastrous for those whose interests lie in the field of modern languages or in that of history, and worst of all for those who fancy that they will become writers. For it is these people —and there are many of them—for whom the deficiency of Latin and Greek is most unfortunate. Those who have a real genius for acquiring these dead languages are few, and they are pretty likely of their own accord to devote themselves to the Classics—if they are given the opportunity. But there are many more of us who have gifts for modern languages, or for our own language, or for history, who have only a modest capacity for mastering Latin and Greek. We can hardly be expected to realize, during adolescence, that without a foundation of Latin and Greek we remain limited in our power over these other subjects.

Now while *liberalism* committed the folly of pretending that one subject is as good as another for study, and that Latin and Greek are simply *no better* than a great many others, *radicalism* (the offspring of liberalism) discards this attitude of universal toleration and pronounces Latin and Greek to be subjects of little import. Liberalism had excited superficial curiosity. Never before had so much miscellaneous information been made available to everybody, in degrees of simplification adapted to everyone's capacity for assimilation. The entertaining epitomes of Mr. H. G. Wells bear witness in their popularity; new discoveries are made known to the whole world at once; and everyone knows that the universe is expanding or else it is contracting. In dissipated curiosity about such novelties great numbers of people, many of them poor and deserving, think that they are improving their minds, or passing their leisure in a praiseworthy occupation. Radicalism then proceeds to organize the "vital issues," and reject what is not vital. A modern literary critic, who has gained considerable publicity by Marxist criticism of literature, has told us that the real men of our time are such as the Lenins, Trotskys, Gorkys and Stalins; also the Einsteins, Plancks and Hunt Morgans. To this critic *knowledge* means "primarily scientific knowledge of the world about us and of ourselves." This statement might be given a respectable interpretation; but I am afraid that the critic meant only what the man in the street means. By "scientific knowledge of the world about us" he does *not* mean understanding of life. By scientific knowledge of ourselves he does *not* mean self-knowledge. In short, while liberalism did not know what it wanted of education, radicalism does know; and it wants the wrong thing.

Radicalism is, however, to be applauded for wanting something. It is to be applauded for wanting to select and eliminate, even if it wants to select and to eliminate the wrong things. If you have a definite ideal for society, then you are right to cultivate what is useful for the development and maintenance of that society, and discourage what is useless and distracting. And we have been too long without an ideal. It is a commonplace nowadays that Russian communism is a religion. Then its rulers must educate the young in the tenets of that religion. I am trying to indicate now the *fundamental* defence of Latin and Greek, not merely give you a collection of excellent reasons for studying them, reasons which you can think of for yourselves. There are two and only two finally tenable hypotheses about life: the Catholic and the materialistic. The defence of the study of the classical languages must ultimately rest upon their association with the former, as must the defence of the primacy of the contemplative over the active life. To associate the Classics with a sentimental Toryism, combination-rooms, classical quotations in the House of Commons, is to give them a flimsy justification, but hardly more flimsy than to defend them by a philosophy of humanism—that is, by a tardy rearguard action which attempts to arrest the progress of liberalism just before the end of its march: an action, besides, which is being fought by troops which are already half liberalized themselves. It is high time that the defence of the Classics should be dissociated from objects which, however excellent under certain conditions and in a certain environment, are of only relative importance—a traditional public-school system, a traditional university system, a decaying social order—and permanently associated where they belong, with something permanent: the historical Christian Faith.

I do not ignore the great value which negative and obstructive forces can have. The longer the better schools and the older universities in this country (for they have pretty well given up the struggle in America) can maintain some standard of classical education, the better for those who look to the future with an active desire for reform and an intelligent acceptance of change. But to expect from our educational institutions any more positive contribution to the future would be vain. As only the Catholic and the communist know, *all* education must be ultimately religious education. I do not mean that education should be confined to postulants for the priesthood or for the higher ranks of Soviet bureaucracy; I mean that the hierarchy of education should be a religious hierarchy. The universities are too far gone in secularization, they have too long lost any common fundamental assumption as to what education is for, and they are too big. It might be hoped that they would eventually follow, or else be relegated to preservation as curious architectural remains; but they cannot be expected to lead.

It is quite possible, of course, that the future may bring neither a Christian nor a materialistic civilization. It is quite possible that the future may bring nothing but chaos or torpor. In that event, I am not interested in the future; I am only interested in the two alternatives which seem to me worthy of interest. I am only here concerned with readers who are prepared to prefer a Christian civilization, if a choice is forced upon them; and it is only upon readers who wish to see a Christian civilization survive and develop that I am urging the importance of the study of Latin and Greek. If Christianity is not to survive, I shall not mind if the texts of the Latin and Greek languages became more obscure and forgotten than those of the language of the Etruscans. And the only hope that I can see for the study of Latin and Greek, in their proper place and for the right reasons, lies in the revival and expansion of monastic teaching orders. There are other reasons, and of the greatest weight, for desiring to see a revival of the monastic life in its variety, but the maintenance of Christian education is not the least. The first educational task of the communities should be the *preservation* of education within the cloister, uncontaminated by the deluge of barbarism outside; their second, the provision of education for the laity, which should be something more than education for a place in the Civil Service, or for technical efficiency, or for social or public success. It would not be that tawdry adornment, "education for leisure." As the world at large becomes more completely secularized, the need becomes more urgent that professedly Christian people should have a Christian education, which should be an education both for this world and for the life of prayer in this world.

PART II

The Contemporary Situation in Perspective

A mong the demands of student and faculty activists on American
campuses today, one of the most frequently heard insists that
the university disengage itself from "the military-industrial complex." That phrase has come to represent what many consider
the single most insidious force in higher education today: the
constellation of Pentagon and business influence which, in its
support of what it considers valuable research and in its on-campus
recruitment of graduating seniors, is accused of performing what
one writer has spoken of as the rape of Alma Mater. It is not
clear whether most of the activists object to outside influences
in principle, or merely to those of whose purposes they disap-
prove. Other and perhaps more deeply radical critics of outside
influence maintain that the university should not be the handmaiden of society, waiting upon its every pleasure, nor should
university administrators become panderers, seeking popular approval by catering to society's every whim. These critics say that
when the university becomes the servant of the government,
business, or any group representing outside interests, it gives up
its proper function as an institution in but not of society, removed
from the fray of pressure groups, and free to contemplate and
above all to criticize the world around it.

Such an attitude is, in fact, a traditional view of the ideal of
the university. It finds expression here in "The Meaning of a
University" by Howard Mumford Jones, which opens Part II.
The American university's readiness to accede to the pressures
of society has, he says, violated ". . . the pure idea of a university as a house of intellect."

There is undoubted value in our holding before ourselves a vision of what a Utopian university might be like. But we may also ask how fully the ideal of an autonomous university dedicated to the disinterested pursuit of truth has ever been realized.

In fact, there has been a perennial tension between society's demands on the university and the common desires of students and teachers for freedom from such extramural pressures. Schools and colleges have not generally appeared spontaneously; they have been founded, most frequently by the church and the state. In creating those institutions their patrons have generally structured them to reflect and transmit the values they held to be important. Significantly, the term "university" had its origin in the name applied to groups of students and teachers who banded together in medieval Europe to pursue their work free from excessive manipulation by church officials and local authorities. Complete freedom, however, was never achieved.

Of course, Professor Jones is himself aware that his ideal of higher education has never been quite the reality in America. Our nation's first colleges were chartered by the state and supported by various churches and, thus, were directly responsible to two groups. While the churches underwrote colleges to train ministers and to provide a suitable spiritual climate for the secular studies of laymen, the state was concerned with higher education in order to ensure a citizenry capable of participating in a democratic society. As A. Whitney Griswold documents compellingly in "Liberal Education and the Democratic Ideal," to the minds of the founding fathers, education was prerequisite to good citizenship and vital leadership for our new nation.

The longest essay in this section, John S. Brubacher's "The Autonomy of the University," explores the history of accommodation between the community of students and scholars within the university walls, seeking to preserve their autonomy, and the larger community outside, seeking some influence on the activities of the university. In practice if not in theory, Brubacher argues, one of the most persuasive arguments for some public influence on education is, "They pay for it." As parents and college administrators are well aware, higher education is a costly enterprise. Tuition receipts can barely begin to meet the expenses of a university; supplementary money must be obtained from public and private sources. Moreover, hardly any colleges are without benefit of such governmental subsidy as the subtle but important benefit of relief from many forms of taxation.

It is, at the least, unrealistic to expect government or private donors to continue their support of institutions which subvert the achieving of those benefactors' goals. If colleges and universities are to continue to operate on the large and often luxurious scale that many of them now enjoy, they can hardly afford to alienate their sources of vital financial support. "Goodwill," says Professor Jones, "is one of the obscuring forces in academic life." But it is difficult to imagine the survival of the university as we know it today without continued goodwill, and concomitant financial support, from beyond the walls.

The unfortunate implications of some academic cooperation with the so-called "military-industrial complex" have become all too clear in the last several years. One can justly question whether the university can serve two masters, truth on the one hand and immediate social necessity on the other. But one may also ask whether teachers and students can afford to divorce themselves from contemporary realities in a single-minded pursuit of truth. Can a scholar conscientiously devote himself exclusively to the study of literature, when all around him values espoused by that literature, such as the dignity of human life, are being violated? This is, of course, not a new situation, though it is perhaps new to regard it as a problem. If a scientist develops a weapon, perhaps as a by-product of his quest for truth, should he be unconcerned about the use to which it is put? And could a university community, whose very existence may depend upon the survival of the nation in which it has its being, fail to respond when that nation is endangered?

Clearly there are some circumstances in which university involvement in the world is necessary and proper. Historical, practical, and even moral considerations militate against complete autonomy for the university. Lines must be drawn, however, between appropriate and inappropriate instances of such engagement. The essays in this book ask us to consider the proper positions of such lines.

In putting the contemporary situation in perspective, one must look to the future as well as the past. Alvin C. Eurich's "Higher

Education in the 21st Century" takes us ahead to the year 2000 and describes both new pressures and new resources with which educators will be working. Among the latter are improved technological devices for teaching and improved means of communication and transportation to facilitate cooperation among schools. Outstanding among the former is the pressure of still greater numbers of students who want and deserve higher education.

The lessons of history and the prospect of the future combine to deny the possibility of any single, static definition of the goals of higher education or the nature of the college and university. That which is dead permits such precise, unchanging description. The living does not. But it is important that the continuing redefinition of these terms, which takes place in each generation, be informed by the meanings they have held in the past.

A *distinguished author and educator, Howard Mumford Jones
(1892–   ) taught in the department of English at Harvard
University, ultimately as
Lawrence Lowell Professor of
Humanities, until his retirement
in 1962. A specialist in American literature, Jones received a
Pulitzer Prize in 1964 for his
book* O Strange New World.
*From 1944 to 1951 he served as
president of the prestigious
American Academy of Arts and
Sciences. Numerous universities
have recognized his contributions to American humanistic
studies by awarding him
honorary degrees.*

The Meaning of a University

HOWARD MUMFORD JONES

The Americans have never quite understood the theory of a university. The first source of ambiguity is that since the seventeenth century we have seldom or never used the word "university" in any consistent sense. Thus Harvard College, oldest of all American academic institutions, was through the Colonial period and into the nineteenth century referred to as Harvard College or as the university in Cambridge. Ambitious makers of state constitutions in new commonwealths or of new pieces of legislation designed to bring a state swiftly into cultural maturity bestowed the word "university" upon a paper organization or upon actual institutions that were often no more than indifferent high schools or academies. The term is still so loosely employed that I have heard of a university of cosmetology.

One might think that with the maturing of the nation, the creation of the Johns Hopkins University in 1876 and the University of Chicago in 1893, the word would have been clearly understood. Not at all. The semantic confusion is now worse than ever. A common verbal syndrome follows this pattern: a normal school sheds that name and becomes a teachers college; the teachers college sheds that name and becomes a state college; the state college sheds that name and becomes a state university without making any perceptible attempt to discover what the proper function and necessary equipment of a university should be. A parallel case is the present tendency to turn honest agricultural schools or some agricultural and mechanical colleges, titles that indicate honorable functions, into state universities. Thus there are both the University of Kansas and Kansas State University, both the University of Colorado and Colorado State University. Or a complex of colleges, as in the state of New York, is transformed without any clear central purpose into a "university" supported by the state, and the four city colleges in New York City sprout an indeterminate something called the University of the City of New York. Confusion is increased by the existence of New York University, a privately endowed institution, and the Regents of the University of the State of New York, which is simply the state board of education. Transformation in most cases has been dictated by a desire for status to impress the legislature, the alumni, donors, and the community. The great schools of technology are among the few institutions that have resisted this facile renaming.

A second source of confusion is historical. American universities, however defined, differ from Old World universities in being the creation of the state, not of the church or of a guild of learned men. This has been true since the Great and General Court of Massachusetts Bay granted a charter creating Harvard College. Creation may be by charter or by organic law. The charter, without which no college or university can grant degrees, is (or was) a grant of power by the sovereignty of the colony, the state, or the federal government. Charters were necessary for private institutions. State colleges or universities were created by the state constitution or by public law. In any case, the legislature also created a small body of men charged with the duty of bringing a university into being.

In the first case, this body is commonly called the board of trustees; in the second, the board of regents; in almost every case it is either self-perpetuating or appointed by the governor or constituted of members *ex officiis*, together with appointed or (more rarely) elected members. In Europe, universities often preceded the state, at least in modern terms; in America, the state precedes the university. In point of law, therefore, the trustees or the agents *are* the university. Seldom chosen for learning, these boards usually begin by securing real estate. Then they hire as their agent a president, whose duty it is to devise a curriculum and find a faculty to teach it.

In other cultures universities are self-governing bodies with a minimum of state supervision except in fascist or Communist countries. If by a university one means primarily a group of scholarly experts, no American university is self-governing. The faculty are employees. Few boards of trustees or regents admit a representative or representatives of the faculty regularly as members of the board, and many do not admit a representative of the faculty to be present at their meetings except in unusual circumstances. Few include the president as a member. The president is usually the agent of the board as well as the only agent of lawful communication between the body of scholars and the nonacademic board. The situation is further complicated by the fact that nowadays the American university president is usually chosen either for his name value or his presumed managerial potentiality. If he has been a scholar, he gives up that profession.

No American university faculty is empowered either to choose a president or to depose him; and though faculty members may be formally or informally consulted by members of the board when a new president is to be chosen, the board is under no obligation to accept the recommendation of the faculty or a committee thereof, these recommendations being in fact often ignored or overruled. Most of the nineteenth century and much of the twentieth has been spent in working out a proper *modus vivendi* between a nonprofessional board, members of which incline to look upon the university as an odd sort of baffling business enterprise, and the body of professional scholars, who, unlike their European counterparts, have little or no responsibility for the financing of the university.

In older American institutions, public or private, a long record of trial and error has resulted in rough definitions and limitations of responsibility. In such universities the board is now commonly content to leave the courses, the modes of teaching, the direction to be taken by research, and the granting of degrees to the president, his academic aides (the deans of the several faculties or colleges making up the university), and the faculty. The vexed question of university finance, which necessarily determines academic policies, lies in a sort of undistributed middle that involves investments, appropriations, salaries, government contracts, fees, fellowships, promotions, and so on. Obviously the financial situation profoundly affects the nature of any university. Obviously the faculty has, at best, only an indirect, sometimes only a remote, relation to financial policy. A board may be so negligent as to permit a university president to bankrupt his institution; or it may be so fussily intrusive as to enforce standards and values that have more relation to popular trends than to the pursuit of truth and excellence.

Since all legal authority rests in the board, its members may abolish or alter parts of a university or invent new ones with or without the knowledge or consent of the faculty. With or without the advice of the faculty the board may also promulgate rules governing the lives of students and of faculty members that may or may not be consonant with the real purpose of the institution. Of course, with experience, boards tend to leave this sort of thing more and more to the "administration," but the recent turmoil at Berkeley illustrates the confusion that results when the distribution of responsibility among the board, the administration, the faculty, and the students is not clear.

The American university is further distinguished from its Old World counterpart by a confusion of aims and responsibility between undergraduate (and vocational) and graduate (and professional) education. The American college of arts and sciences is unique in the world. American graduate schools developed out of existing colleges of arts and sciences in this country late in our educational history. The graduate school of arts and sciences therefore did not, like a law school or a medical school, come into being for a unitary purpose. Indeed, in one sense there is no graduate school of arts and sciences but only departments that offer graduate work. The common denominator that makes the concept of a graduate school of arts and sciences possible is a mild uniformity in entrance requirements for graduate work (the entrant must have a bachelor's degree) and an equally mild uniformity about the mode of granting advanced degrees—the M.A. and the Ph.D. A dean of a law school heads a professional body devoted to teaching law; a dean of a graduate school of arts and sciences heads ten, twenty, thirty, forty separate professional units, part of whose time is devoted to teaching students not in the graduate school and part of whose time is devoted to teaching graduate courses. Without a graduate school there can be no university, but the graduate school of arts and sciences rests upon the unstable foundation of shifting departmental interests as the school of medicine does not.

In creating Cornell University, the founder said he wanted to establish an institution in which anybody could study anything. This dictum has been widely accepted as a sound definition of university work. Consequently, television programs sending out news broadcasts, information, and domestic science courses for future housewives, the teaching of advertising layouts and the training of future football coaches, "short course" instruction in agriculture, and adult education classes for retired businessmen are offered by the "university" along with advanced research in atomic physics, abstruse work in higher mathematics, chemical studies of the sun's corona, metaphysical speculation about the nature of metaphysical speculation, and a seminar in the economic background of the First Crusade. This need not obscure, but in most cases it certainly straitens, the pure idea of a university as a house of intellect. Goodwill is one of the obscuring forces in academic life.

The American university is also expected to assume responsibility for the housing, feeding, medical and psychiatric care, amusement, and in some cases religious instruction of youngsters just out of the secondary school, and has permitted itself to be surrounded by an amiable jungle of fraternity and sorority houses, religious institutions especially directed to keeping student faith alive, student journalism, intercollegiate athletics, intercollegiate debating, student dramatics, ROTC units, musical enterprises ranging from jazz to Beethoven, cooperative housing, bookstores, alumni offices and organizations, responsibility for extension courses, responsibility for nonacademic conferences on business, social, sociological, political, or international problems, alumni reunions at commencement, and so on, until the original aim of the university has disappeared.

One of the latest, most praised, and in some ways most disastrous new functions assumed by the university is the encouragement of "creativity." Creativity is not scholarship and not science, but a surrogate for them. Creativity is not research, which is an act of the controlled intellect, but as practiced on most American campuses, an emotional outlet. Courses in creative writing, creative dancing, creative painting, creative music, creative play-making, and creative folk singing abound. In the nature of the case, these activities cannot be judged by the severe intellectual standards basic to research, nor can they be judged by the harsh, if differing, standards of professional excellence. They lie in a kind of no-man's-land more distinguished for sentiment than for severity, and the existence of this no-man's-land is one of the principal reasons for our current confusion between the "creative" arts and humane learning. If these activities are proper to college instruction, they should remain collegiate. If the intent is to be professional, they should be referred to such professional institutions as a conservatory of music. As universities are lauded for supporting a quartet in residence, a tame painter, a writers' conference, a school of the theater, or a studio for dancing or painting or sculpture, the original concept of the university becomes more and more blurred, and the public comes more and more to believe that a university fails of its true purpose (the frayed phrase about an "ivory tower" commonly appears at this point) if it does not nourish the arts.

What, then, is a university? In the Continental sense it is a collection of professional faculties—the faculty of the humanities, the faculty of science, the faculty of law, the faculty of medicine, the faculty of theology, for examples—empowered to offer mature instruction in their several professions and to grant "advanced" degrees when the student has demonstrated his ability to go it alone. In the British sense a traditional university is a collection of colleges that, taken separately, house and teach students, and taken collectively, offer general advanced instruction (the lectures) and grant degrees. In the American sense, at least as defined by the Office of Education, a university is an institution of higher learning comprising a college of arts and sciences or its equivalent, a graduate school of arts and sciences, and one or more professional schools—for example, law, medicine, or theology. A college of liberal arts and sciences may grant a bachelor's or a master's degree. Only a university can grant a Ph.D. degree, though in certain cases (again the confusion of American nomenclature!) established colleges grant the doctor's degree and so-called universities do not, the reason being that they do not have either the proper faculty or the proper facilities for advanced professional work.

I trust I shall not be considered mystical if I put the matter another way. A college is, or should be, concerned with the elements of knowledge, a university with bringing these elements into professional fruition. In this sense, therefore, a university is more especially an act or product of intellect. It is an institution created for the critical examination by professional minds of tenets, principles, laws, dogmas, and ideas that make up the ever varying body of truth. It preserves truth by perpetually subjecting conventional assumptions to critical analysis, discarding fallacies, and retaining as valid only the information or the general statements that pass severe, impersonal, and professional testing; and it extends truth by pushing forward, into the unknown, task forces of professionally trained persons who are skilled in distinguishing fact from assumption. The university climate of opinion is therefore critical. When a given group of professionally competent scholars approve of something they have thoroughly examined, be it a biblical text or a new discovery about the chemistry of meteorites, their findings circulate freely among other professional men all over the world.

The faculty of a university, however organized into schools or colleges, is a group of men and women dedicated to the assumption that there is an intellectual order in life, that they participate, however imperfectly, in that order, and that they can make this intellectual order clear, whether it be in literary history or non-Euclidean geometry, to younger scholars who can carry on learning and research in a particular field. The faculty of a university is the only body competent to determine what general knowledge and what specialized education are necessary for a continuation of professional knowledge and professional skill.

The university may develop other functions, many of them laudable in themselves, and in America they have done so, but if these other functions are not kept subordinate to the central idea of university education and university work, they can overwhelm the university idea by their very multitudinousness. The university then disappears in a smog of sentimentality, "school spirit," vocationalism, pseudo-parental responsibility, experiments in living, and fallacious political activity.

Three observations seem to me pertinent. The first is that the present amiable tendency to confuse college with university, "creativity" with scholarship, vocational training with professional education, and extension courses for high school teachers with a mature philosophy of education must somehow be subdued or clarified. We need universities as universities. The necessity for a clear definition of university work is evident in the fact that whereas fifty years ago a Ph.D. was the mark of professional education, those in charge of research in many fields are now, in despair, talking about the need of postdoctoral education to accomplish what the university was originally established to do. There is nothing shameful about being an excellent teachers college or a good agricultural school, but the highest needs of the nation are in a sense betrayed when the teachers college or the agricultural school becomes a pseudo-university granting a third-rate Ph.D.

The second is our need for a stern insistence upon the truth that university education is a privilege for the competent, not a right to be claimed by the many. American parents seem to feel that some "university" somewhere somehow should be required to accept their children upon demand. Legislatures sometimes pass laws requiring a state university to admit virtually any high school graduate. The result is general confusion, waste of funds, futile teaching, and the creation of special undergraduate "colleges" for the mentally indigent. Why do mediocre high school graduates have to go to universities? Our need, as John Gardner has said, is for excellence, not for mediocrity. If universities are overcrowded, this is only in part a result of population pressures. A more disturbing reason is the incapacity of boards and presidents to insist that a university is, precisely, *not* an institution in which anybody can study anything, but an institution for mature professional education.

Finally, the student being admitted to the high privilege of a university must be taught, if he does not know them (commonly he does not), his rights, duties, and responsibilities as a member of the great traditional republic of learning. Much has been talked about the indifference of one student generation to political issues and about the rebellion of another student generation against university regulations. No one questions the idealism of young men and women who go to Selma or Bogalusa or join the Peace Corps. No one wants to deny the student the right to express his political opinion. But the student, by becoming a student, has lost something and gained something. He has lost the opportunity of embracing anarchy, and he has gained the more durable possibility of becoming a mature citizen in both the political republic and the republic of learning. If more and more students spend more and more time in public demonstrations against this and that, they inevitably spend less and less time in scholarly pursuits, their avowed purpose in asking to be admitted to the university. In other countries the university function of an institution of higher learning was destroyed when the campus became an arena for political action as the principal manifestation of intellectual life. The American problem has not yet been thought carefully through.

The sixteenth president of Yale
University, A. Whitney
Griswold (1906–1963) was distinguished both as a scholar
and an administrator. Having
received both his bachelor's degree and doctorate at Yale,
Griswold remained there to
teach in the departments of history and political science. An
eloquent defender of academic
freedom, he was also a severe
critic of many aspects of American education. This selection is
the title essay of a collection of
his speeches and writings on
educational matters.

7

Liberal Education and the Democratic Ideal

A. WHITNEY GRISWOLD

The ideal of liberal education lies at the very roots of
American history. For centuries this type of education
had been esteemed throughout
western civilization as the
education of the ideal citizen.
But the political and social
structure of that civilization
had denied access to such
education to all but a privileged few. To uphold an ideal
of citizenship and then deny
citizens the means of attain-
ing it was difficult to justify
in logic and impossible in
democratic philosophy. Even
if such attainment could not
be guaranteed to all citizens,
it should at least be the op-

portunity of all. The educational route to ideal citizenship should be open to all who were able to travel it; and all who showed such promise should be encouraged to strike out upon it and proceed as far as native intelligence and industry could carry them.

Such was the educational philosophy of the founders of our country. "The Puritans," John Adams wrote in his *Dissertation on the Canon and Feudal Law* in 1765, "transmitted to their posterity . . . a hereditary ardor for liberty and thirst for knowledge. They were convinced, by their knowledge of human nature, derived from history and their own experience, that nothing could preserve their posterity from the encroachments of the two systems of tyranny, in opposition to which, as has been observed already, they erected their government in church and state, but knowledge diffused generally through the whole body of the people. Their civil and religious principles, therefore, conspired to prompt them to use every measure and take every precaution in their power to propagate and perpetuate knowledge. For this purpose they laid very early the foundations of colleges, and invested them with ample privileges and emoluments; and it is remarkable that they have left among their posterity so universal an affection and veneration for those seminaries, and for liberal education, that the meanest of the people contribute cheerfully to the support and maintenance of them every year, and that nothing is more generally popular than projections for the honor, reputation, and advantage of those seats of learning. But the wisdom and benevolence of our fathers rested not here. They made an early provision by law that every town consisting of so many families should be always furnished with a grammar school. They made it a crime for such a town to be destitute of a grammar schoolmaster for a few months, and subjected it to a heavy penalty. So that the education of all ranks of people was made the care and expense of the public, in a manner that I believe has been unknown to any other people ancient or modern."

"Laws for the liberal education of youth," concluded Adams in his influential *Thoughts on Government* in 1776, "especially of the lower class of people, are so extremely wise and useful, that, to a humane and generous mind, no expense for this purpose would be thought extravagant."

Adams' thoughts on education were shared by Madison, who has been called Father of the Constitution, and by Jefferson, his tutor. All three men, whose combined influence upon the shaping of our government was so great and in whose several works one finds the most comprehensive exposition of the theory and meaning of that government, saw in education not merely the corollary to democracy but the key, the *sine qua non.* In their system of education all three assigned the paramount role to liberal education. What did they mean by the term? One has but to read John Adams' letter recommending his son John Quincy Adams for admission to Harvard, or Jefferson's educational advices to his nephew, Peter Carr, to discover that they meant exactly what we mean by it.

They did not regard it as a panacea to be forced down unwilling throats or consumed by all in equal doses with identical results. They thought of it, and wrote of it, as part of a comprehensive system that began with reading, writing, and arithmetic for all, included vocational training, and progressed through the most advanced phases of higher learning. At each successive stage high standards were to be met, and progressively higher and more exalted labors awaited the survivors. This is how Jefferson described the system in a letter to Adams in 1813:

At the first session of our legislature after the Declaration of Independence, we passed a law abolishing entails. And this was followed by one abolishing the privilege of primogeniture, and dividing the lands of intestates equally among all their children, or other representatives. These laws, drawn by myself, laid the axe to the foot of pseudo-aristocracy. And had another which I prepared been adopted by the legislature, our work would have been complete. It was a bill for the more general diffusion of learning. This proposed to divide every county into wards of five or six miles square, like your townships; to establish in each ward a free school for reading, writing and common arithmetic; to provide for the annual selection of the best subjects from these schools, who might receive, at the public expense, a higher degree of education at a district school; and from these district schools to select a certain number of the most promising subjects to be completed at an University, where all the useful sciences should be taught. Worth and genius would thus have been sought out from every condition of life, and completely prepared by education for defeating the competition of wealth and birth for public trusts.

By such means, said Jefferson, in his *Notes on Virginia,* the "best geniuses" would be "raked from the rubbish," and society would be provided with "an education adapted to the years, to the capacity, and the condition of everyone, and directed to their freedom and happiness."

The political context of these educational ideas is particularly significant. A highly selective educational system appears side by side with laws abolishing primogeniture and entail, not as an exception to them, but as their fulfillment. Raking genius from the rubbish was a means of laying the axe to pseudo-aristocracy. The whole system, with its ultimate aims of a general diffusion of knowledge and the freedom and happiness of everyone, revolved around the principle of seeking out "worth and genius . . . from every condition of life" and preparing it "by education . . . for public trusts."

Here was no dogmatic leveling or rationalizing of privilege in the name of "leadership." Worth and genius were just as vital to democracy as to any other type of society. To the extent that power and responsibility are diffused in a democracy, they were more vital. Unless democracy was prepared to renounce their accomplishments—which, of course, it was not—it must find its own way of producing them. Far from stifling or retarding worth and genius, it must devise truly democratic means of discovering them and capitalizing their powers for the benefit of society.

Liberal education supplied these means. No one should be denied access to it because of his condition of life. None who gained access should be retarded because of someone else's condition of mentality. There was no distinction between public and private responsibility in this regard. Those who could afford to pay their way through school and university were to do so, those who could not were to be carried at public expense, both being subject to the same educational qualifications. The important thing was the educational process. This was democracy's answer to a universal need, the best answer any nation had given so far, the best and surest any has given to date.

The role of liberal education is defined in the preamble to Jefferson's *Bill for the More General Diffusion of Knowledge* as follows:

And whereas it is generally true that people will be happiest whose laws are best, and are best administered, and that laws will be wisely formed, and honestly administered, in proportion as those who form and administer them are wise and honest; whence it becomes expedient for promoting the publick happiness that those persons, whom nature hath endowed with genius and virtue, should be rendered by liberal education worthy to receive, and able to guard the sacred deposit of the rights and liberties of their fellow citizens, and that they should be called to that charge without regard to wealth, birth or other accidental condition or circumstance . . .

The bill goes on to provide that the books used to teach children reading and writing in elementary schools should be "such as will at the same time make them acquainted with Graecian, Roman, English, and American history"; and that students in secondary (or as Jefferson called them, grammar) schools should "be taught the Latin and Greek languages, English grammar, geography and the higher part of numerical arithmetick, to wit, vulgar and decimal fractions, and the extraction of the square and cube roots."

It is hardly necessary to cite further evidence of the importance Jefferson attached to liberal education. It was perhaps the principal inspiration of his life. It runs as a major theme through all his works—his public papers and his private correspondence—informing and prompting him at every stage of his career. It is reflected in his omnivorous reading, his love of learning in every field, and the ingenuity and versatility with which he turned it to practical account. "Nothing could be sounder than your view of the importance of laying a broad foundation in other branches of knowledge whereon to raise the superstructure of any particular science which one would chuse to profess with credit and usefulness," he wrote one of his friends in the fullness of his experience, in 1811. Jefferson's life was a monument to that principle. He not only preached liberal education; he personified it.

One could wish for a more general knowledge of these facts in the United States today. There appears to be a disposition to regard high educational standards as undemocratic, and liberal education as either useless or beyond our intellectual competence. It is hard to understand how anyone acquainted with the mind and spirit of the founders of our country could entertain such views. There is no country that owes so much of its very existence to liberal education as the United States.

*John S. Brubacher (1898–   ),
one of the leading American
historians of education, has
written and edited a number
of books on educational issues.
Having received an A.B. from
Yale, a law degree from Harvard,
and a Ph.D. from Columbia,
he taught at Yale before going
in 1960 to the University of
Michigan, where he is now professor at the Center for the
Study of Higher Education.
From 1942 to 1946 he served as
president of the Philosophy of
Education Society.*

8

The Autonomy of the University

How Independent Is the Republic of Scholars?

JOHN S. BRUBACHER

Nostalgia often leads people to refer to the university
as a republic of scholars. Thus
faculties may long for the
time when the university had
larger scope as a self-governing
body than it has today. But
the longing seems forlorn. If
anything, the university's autonomy appears to be diminishing rather than increasing
or even holding its own. On
the one hand, political, ecclesiastical, and economic interests press against its perimeter;
and on the other, professors
themselves seem bent on compromising it by issuing forth
from the quiet groves of academe into the hurly-burly of
public affairs. The resulting

situation is confusing, to say the least. Some think the outlines of autonomy should be sharply defined and ruggedly defended. Others assert that university autonomy is anachronistic or obsolescent.[1] Certainly, before we concede the second claim, we should take a penetrating look at what is happening.

If the republic of scholars is currently in some disarray, it is in part because the basic issue over the autonomy of the university is not clearly stated. The underlying issue, it seems to me, concerns the proper relation between the layman and the expert in determining the policies of higher education. Each has recognized interests, but it is the claim of the expert (faculty) to an exclusive interest that is partly responsible for strife and confusion. To what extent is this claim warranted?

The idea of an independent republic of scholars is of long standing. A medieval and a nineteenth-century reference will show its perennial appeal. The medieval university began to take shape when teachers and taught first came together and formed societies or guilds. These associations were autonomous as well as spontaneous, since their formation did not need acquiescence of the Roman law. Their nearest modern counterpart would probably be the "free universities" which are currently springing up here and there in protest against contemporary conventional universities. Since the early guilds had little or no property, they were highly mobile and could go from city to city to take advantage of the circumstances most favorable to their academic purposes. This mobility was obviously a very effective weapon for repelling any interference that might threaten their autonomy.

Inasmuch as the autonomy of the medieval guild of scholars was unquestioned, no one took occasion at the time to make an outright claim to it. Such a claim, however, was made for the German university of the nineteenth century. Its prototype, of course, was the University of Berlin. The intellectual progress of this university was thought to depend on the indefinite perfectibility of the human race. Once professors steeped in their learning and students suitably prepared to study under them were gathered in its halls, the university

---

[1] Clark Kerr, *The Uses of the University.* Cambridge, Massachusetts: Harvard University Press, 1963, pp. 97–99.

could be allowed to continue independently. "If . . . a university is to achieve its purpose and be what it really pretends to be," said the great German patriot, philosopher, and educator, Johann Gottlieb Fichte, in his inaugural address as rector of the University of Berlin, "it must be left to itself thenceforward; it needs, and rightly demands, complete external freedom . . . ." [2] In making this assertion, Fichte was repeating what the Marquis de Condorcet had said at the end of the preceding century. Writing, ironically from jail, during the French Revolution, he proclaimed, "No branch of the government should have the authority, or even the means, of preventing the teaching of new truths or the development of theories contrary to its special policies or its momentary interests." [3]

More important, now, is the theoretical justification for giving such sweeping autonomy to the university. A clue may be found in a statement by James Morgan Hart, one of the many Americans who returned to the United States from study abroad. He succinctly commended the German university to his fellow countrymen as a "detached organism . . . growing in accordance with its own laws." [4] What these laws were, he did not say, but we may readily formulate them ourselves. The law of the university's self-development is to be found in the canons by which it assays the truth. These are come by only through prolonged technical training in handling the sources of truth. As experts in determining truth and error, faculties demand the autonomy characteristic of professionals. Such autonomy is necessary because only experts can judge experts.

What we have been describing here is essentially the professional ethic of the scholar. If the professors are the sole judges of their own expertise, they owe the layman extra assurance that they are exercising their expertise—"mystery," the medievalists would have called it—in his best interests. This they do by pursuing the truth objectively,

---

[2] G. H. Trumbull, *The Educational Theory of Fichte*. London: Hodder and Stoughton, Ltd., 1926, pp. 264–65.

[3] François de La Fontainerie, *French Liberalism and Education in the Eighteenth Century*. New York: McGraw-Hill Book Company, Inc., 1932, pp. 326–27.

[4] *German Universities: A Narrative of Personal Experience.* New York: G. P. Putnam's Sons, 1874, p. 252.

esoterically, and disinterestedly. To be able to do that, the university must be detached; that is, free from extraneous and irrelevant considerations in its search for the truth.

At no point is detachment or autonomy more important than in the scholar's academic freedom. If his findings are not his own but are bent or warped by forces that have self-interest to promote, they will never win credibility. Thus the university cannot become an arm of the state, the handmaiden of the church, or the servant of industry without threatening its autonomy, indeed its status as a university. To assure his independence, the expert or professor must have tenure so that he can be indifferent to both blandishments and threats. Indeed, the American Association of University Professors and the American Civil Liberties Union insist on this "detachment" whether the professor is exercising his expertise or his civil liberties.

In marking out the area in which the university claims autonomy in being the judge of its expertise, we must include certain matters concerning the curriculum. Thus the university should have exclusive control over the degree requirements by which new experts are recruited. It must have similar jurisdiction in accrediting higher institutions of learning and determining whether they meet academic standards.

The foregoing is, roughly, the maximum case for an autonomous republic of scholars. If it is accepted, then it is unwarranted trespass for laymen to cross the boundaries of the republic. At least, that is the theory. As a matter of historical fact, however, laymen seem never to have done with trespassing on the academic precincts. From inside the republic it seems like constant encroachment. From outside it probably seems like the proper assertion of a public interest in what goes on within. In either case, hardly had guilds of students and professors made their appearance before lay forces began to assert themselves. One instance concerned the internal management of the university, and a second its external relations. We will proceed with the case of internal infringement first.

In the beginning, as already stated, guilds of students and professors were truly autonomous. Then the lay board of control was established. Although it has often been thought that this was an American innovation, the colonies had European models to imitate or adapt. Two models may be noted. In the earlier one, Florentine professors, trying to escape the tyranny of student guilds, appealed to the local town authorities for relief. Sympathizing with the professors, the town authorities set up a lay board of curators to administer financial subsidies to them and thus make them independent of the students. The later model was the one Calvin imposed on his university in Geneva. There control was placed in the hands of the four executive officers of the "small" council which governed the city. To be sure, these laymen worked in co-operation with a committee of professors on the internal affairs of the university, but nevertheless the essential control was theirs. What is notable in both models is that in sharing the control of academic affairs with laymen, the university surrendered, or at least compromised, some of its former autonomy.[5]

As nearly everyone knows, the colonial colleges in America started with lay boards of control, usually on the Calvinist model. It was not long before stresses and strains developed between these boards and college faculties. At once the integrity of the republic of scholars was at stake. The issue was most notably raised at Harvard in the early eighteenth century. In Harvard's bicameral form of organization, the lower body, or Corporation, was composed of the president and fellows. By long-established custom deriving from Europe, fellows were understood to be resident tutors or instructors. On the occasion in question, an eligible tutor who was passed over in favor of a layman in filling a vacancy on the Corporation objected strenuously but to no avail. His argument was that, being on the grounds, he understood the educational complexities of the College better than an absentee layman could. The appointing authorities thought the College needed lay rather than professional advice, and so the faculty lost the first round of a struggle to defend its expertise against lay encroachment.

A hundred years later, in the early part of the nineteenth century, a

---

[5] William H. Cowley, "Presidents, Professors, and Trustees" (unpublished manuscript, cited with permission of the author).

second round was fought over the identical issue. The outcome was the same. Indeed, with one exception, laymen controlled the Corporation from that day forward. In spite of this defeat, the faculty did seem to salvage some part of its autonomy. After the struggle had terminated, the Harvard Overseers published new statutes for the governance of the College which recognized an important distinction between its external and internal control. External control concerned the formation of policy and the allocation of financial resources to carry it out. Internal control concerned the discipline of students and the direction of instruction. If the faculty had lost the battle for external control, it had won a victory for internal control.

In yet another hundred years the issue flared up once more at Harvard. This time the president, A. Lawrence Lowell, met it head on in more theoretical terms. Since a college or university is supposed to be a self-governing guild of scholars, he asked, does it need a lay board of governors at all? And if it does, should ultimate authority lie with this lay board? Lowell answered both questions in the affirmative.[6] In answer to the first question, he held that the management of higher education needed both lay and expert personnel. Without the expert, higher education might become ineffectual, and without the layman it might in time become narrow and inharmonious with the public interest. Yet necessary as both were, they should not be intermingled. Thus Lowell advised against the practice of assigning experts to sit on lay boards and of permitting lay boards to try to direct experts in the management of their expertise.

In regard to the second question, he held that since higher education over the years had been vested with a public interest, final authority must be lodged with the lay board. Not only were larger and larger allocations of national income going to higher education, but higher education was assuming greater and greater leadership in public affairs. In fact, the time was long past when the college was a quiet, cloistered retreat regulated by the tolling of the chapel bell and removed from the highway of life.

[6] *At War with Academic Traditions.* Cambridge, Massachusetts: Harvard University Press, 1934, pp. 50–51.

With the diminution of faculty autonomy and the coincident rise of public or lay interest in the university has come a decided change in the legal status of the professor. As a member of a self-governing guild, he originally held a freehold in his position in the university. Thus he could not be separated from the university except for cause. With the rise of lay control, the professor has become just an employee on contract. The American Association of University Professors has euphemistically tried to put a different face on this situation by claiming that the professor is not an employee but an appointee. The implication is that the professor, if on tenure, can be removed only for cause. This may mean that as "academic due process," in contrast to legal due process, gains recognition, the professor may again become as well off as he was when he possessed a freehold.

There has been a clear advance, then, of lay interest in the internal relations of the university and a partial retreat of the expert so far as his autonomy is concerned. But if there have been advance and retreat, the lines between the two have become fairly well stabilized. In external relations, to which we now turn, the battle has been fought along the same lines but to a less conclusive outcome.

At an early stage and almost imperceptibly at first, lay forces infiltrated the autonomy of the university. One of the principal activities over which academic guilds exercised their autonomy was the *jus docendi*, the right to teach. No one could enjoy this right unless he was recognized as competent by the republic of scholars. At first the *jus docendi* was a purely local right which extended no further than custom and reputation made it effective. Naturally, in the course of time the *jus docendi* awarded by great seats of learning like Bologna and Paris received much wider recognition than when it was conferred by lesser universities. Consequently, it became customary for distinguished institutions to award the *jus ubique docendi*, the right to teach anywhere. Obviously, the autonomous power to award such a far-reaching right was a professional asset of tremendous worth.

In the long course of transmitting the traditions of higher education to American shores, two events occurred which have compromised this ancient autonomy. In the first place, when lords, temporal and spiritual, began founding universities by royal edict or papal bull, they conferred the *jus ubique docendi* at the very inception of the charter. These institutions, therefore, did not have to earn respect for their degrees carrying the right to teach. The immediate respect accorded them proceeded from that accorded the original grantor on other grounds, usually political or ecclesiastical. So prestigious was this respect that before long institutions, which were awarding degrees by prescription and custom, sought royal or papal approval for their own degrees. Advantageous as this may have been, it set a doubtful precedent. In exchange for undoubted prestige, the universities made themselves dependent on the sovereign and thereby yielded a measure of their autonomy.

Perhaps at the time, universities were not fully aware of the risk they were running, because they still enjoyed so large a measure of their original autonomy. Attesting this is the outcome of the struggle which the University of Paris waged with the Chancellor of the Cathedral over the awarding of degrees. On an appeal to Rome, Pope Gregory IX not only sided with the university but issued a papal bull, *Parens Scientiarum*, which has been referred to ever since as the *magna charta* of the university. According to its provisions the Pope recognized the right of the faculty to modify its own constitution, a not inconsiderable concession to academic autonomy. Yet even the need to appeal to an external power was, again, a subtle compromise of autonomy.

Skipping over many intervening details, we may note that when our colonial colleges were founded the tradition of autonomy they inherited was something less than that of the first republic of scholars. By this time, all institutions of higher education had come to be dependent on the lay sovereign for their constitutions or charters. In spite of this dependency, incorporators tried to obtain as favorable terms of self-government as possible. But just how far did these charters legally protect the faculty as an autonomous guild?

The main confrontation of the state and higher education in America took place toward the end of the eighteenth century. Carried along on the rising tide of democracy in this period were a number of men who wished to make the colleges of the day responsive to public wishes. On the other hand, the colleges, which were nearly all private, resisted the idea. Many of them ultimately composed their differences with the state by admitting *ex officio* representatives of the state to their governing boards. One college, however, Dartmouth, did not flinch but carried the question of its autonomy to the highest court of the land.

Briefly, the facts in this case were the following. A main provision of the charter which Dartmouth had originally obtained from King George III of England called for a self-perpetuating board of trustees. By this device the college hoped to protect its autonomy against interference by the King, who might have been inclined to tamper with it because his religion was different from that of the colonists. In the course of time Dartmouth became a stronghold of Congregationalism in religion and Federalism in politics. By the second decade of the nineteenth century, however, the Congregational-Federalist axis no longer represented the majority of the people of New Hampshire. Encouraged by a Jeffersonian Republican majority, the state legislature attempted to turn Dartmouth into a state university. The device employed to achieve this end was enlargement of the number of trustees to create a majority in favor of the change. The self-perpetuating board of trustees naturally resisted, contending it was a violation of the original charter. And so a case was made for the courts.

A number of issues were argued, but the one which concerns us most was whether Dartmouth was to be considered a public or a private corporation; that is, whether higher education was vested with a public interest. The supreme court of New Hampshire held that it was. Make the trustees of the college independent or autonomous and, the state court feared, they would forget their office was a public trust and manage the college in their own class interests. And the court warned that even if their motives were entirely pure and those of the lay public wrong, private status would be of little avail to them in the face of popular jealousy and mistrust.[7]

<hr>

[7] *Dartmouth College* v. *Woodward*, 1 N.H. 111, 136.

On appeal to the United States Supreme Court, John Marshall overruled the New Hampshire court, holding that the Dartmouth charter was not vested with a public interest. In support of this position, it is more interesting to note the argument of Daniel Webster on behalf of his alma mater than the involved legal reasoning of the Chief Justice. Webster argued that it would be dangerous to the autonomy of higher education to make colleges and universities dependent upon the rise and fall of popular majorities. If the charter could be amended or revoked by legislative enactment, then the property of the institution could also be confiscated or perverted to other ends than those benefactors might have had in mind. Moreover, college halls would resound to the clash of political opinions rather than to the arguments of learned men.[8]

And so the case went down in history as a great victory for the autonomy of higher education. Chancellor Kent, renowned commentator on American law, popularized this view, maintaining that the Dartmouth College case gave "solidity and inviolability to the literary . . . institutions of our Country." [9] And Sir Henry Maine, the illustrious English legal scholar, appraising the case from a greater distance, referred to it as "the bulwark of American individualism against democratic impatience and Socialistic fantasy." [10] Thomas Jefferson, as one might expect, took a contrary view. Writing to Governor William Plumer of New Hampshire, he said,

> The idea that institutions established for the use of the nation cannot be touched or modified, even to make them answer their end, because of rights gratuitously supposed in those employed to manage them in trust for the public, may perhaps be a salutary provision against the abuses of a monarch, but it is most absurd against the nation itself.[11]

[8] *Dartmouth College v. Woodward*, 17 U.S. (4 Wheat.) 518.

[9] Leon Burr Richardson, *History of Dartmouth College*. Hanover, New Hampshire: Dartmouth College, 1932, Vol. I, p. 344.

[10] *Popular Government: Four Essays*. New York: Henry Holt and Company, 1886, p. 248.

[11] See letter from Jefferson to Plumer, July 21, 1816, in *The Dartmouth College Causes and the Supreme Court of the United States*, by John M. Shirley. St. Louis: G. I. Jones and Company, 1879, p. 107.

While the Dartmouth case has never been overruled judicially, legislatively it suffered a backlash. Warned by the case, state legislatures have been wary of incorporating new institutions of higher education. On the one hand, they accelerated the founding of state universities under their own control; on the other, they revised their general laws of incorporation to make private institutions subject to periodic review by the state. Yet even though the locus of authority in external relations is clearly with the lay state, the state tends to permit private institutions considerably more autonomy than public ones.

Instances drawn from both Europe and the United States show that the advancement of lay interests, far from threatening expertise, is often a desirable corrective to the congenital defects of inbreeding in colleges and universities. In nineteenth-century England it became obvious that even such famous seats of learning as Oxford and Cambridge were failing to serve the public interest. Widespread as was this conviction, the largely self-governing faculties of these two institutions were unable to rouse themselves to correct the situation. Hence it was finally necessary for Parliament to step in and do what the universities could not do for themselves. Again, when the great liberal, Von Humboldt, was setting up the University of Berlin, he left the appointment of faculty in the hands of the ministry of education. It may seem odd that a man who struggled valiantly to establish the autonomy of the higher learning should have done this. He did it because, even more than the abridgment of autonomy, he feared professional intrigue if faculties were allowed to be completely in charge of filling vacancies.

Too zealous oversight by the state, on the other hand, has also had potential dangers, as Daniel Webster warned. There are several notable examples. Michigan is an excellent instance. In its early years the state university was not as thriving as the older institutions on the eastern seaboard. Analyzing the difficulty, the people of the state concluded it was because the legislature was keeping the university tethered to its apron strings. To free it, Michigan gave the university constitutional status in 1850. The legislature, however, continued to tamper with the university until a Michigan court decreed that the constitutional autonomy of the university amounted to a virtual fourth branch of state government. Even so, the legislature still indirectly threatened its autonomy by its control of the purse strings.

In another issue involving university autonomy, centralization in the administration of higher education, states have found it advantageous to exercise their control with restraint. Confusion and conflict often occur where states support more than one institution of higher education and each tries to act autonomously. If the state seeks efficiency through imposing some measure of order, it risks the blight of uniformity. The state has learned that to preserve initiative, flexibility, and diversity, it must guard the autonomy of each institution. Central boards of higher education exist, not to curtail autonomy, but to maximize it by co-ordinated planning.

The initiative for co-ordinating institutions of higher learning has come from the universities themselves as well as from the state. Whereas the university once thought it could explore the unity of knowledge independently, today it realizes that only as it subordinates autonomy to co-operation can it maintain excellence in the face of the chain explosion of knowledge. Thus it may specialize in segments rather than in the whole of knowledge, or enter into a consortium of universities to distribute the expense of new equipment—a multi-million-dollar synchrotron, for instance. Furthermore, universities realize today that the necessity for increasing outside management of such educational activities as testing, planning, and innovating makes co-operation, rather than autonomy, the ruling spirit of the contemporary university.[12]

Finally, there is one set of circumstances in which the state curtails the autonomy of the university regretfully and the university accepts the curtailment reluctantly but understandingly. The situation I have in mind arises from conditions created by the Cold War. The university does important research in some sensitive area and then finds that the results are "classified information." Ordinarily it is part of the ethics of scholarship, to say nothing of an aspect of academic freedom, to publish the results of research. Hence the scholar is torn between obligation to country and obligation to scholarship. Neither state nor

[12] James A. Perkins, *The University in Transition*. Princeton, New Jersey: Princeton University Press, 1966, p. 64.

university likes to curtail autonomy in this situation, but both agree on its necessity.[13]

Our discussion commenced with the thesis that the university has a clear claim to autonomy, both theoretically and historically. While the university seemed to derive some gain in its earliest days from surrendering a measure of its autonomy to laymen, it has since been fighting a series of rear-guard actions to defend what remains of its independence. If the line of internal and external authority between laymen and expert has been blurred, it is because of the aggressions of the laity. We proceed now to an era and an area wherein the line of autonomy has been obscured with the connivance, if not the approval, of the university: public service. This function of the university is beset with ambiguities. While the service function seems at first glance to nourish expertise, in the end it often diverts the university from its main purpose. For this reason, the German university had the greatest contempt for studies whose outcome might be swayed by practical results and thus stop short of the truth. In eighteenth-century Germany, professional studies had held the top rank in higher education because the state set the university's aim as the training of successful practical men. But in the nineteenth century the higher learning, carried on in a spirit of free rational inquiry, far outranked professional education. And by right it should, many thought, because the scope and significance of theoretical studies dwarfs those narrowed to practical applications.

Americans who attended German universities were trained in this tradition, but when they brought it to American shores it underwent a subtle transformation. A frontier country, such as the United States had been, was almost of necessity pragmatic. It is small wonder that the American people, beset by the exigencies of the frontier, looked to their universities for practical ways of solving their problems. Thus the Morrill Act, establishing "A & M" (agricultural and mechanical arts)

---

[13] Russell Kirk, *Academic Freedom*. Chicago: Henry Regnery Company, 1955, pp. 3–4, 17–18.

colleges, marked the inception of a policy which was to blur the status of the university as a "detached organism."

Nowhere was this better illustrated than at the University of Wisconsin in the early part of the twentieth century. A progressive governor of the state called on the university faculty frequently for advice in formulating new types of social legislation. The university gave generously of both time and talent. Indeed, the relation between the government and the university became so close, a wit quipped that whereas other states had state universities, Wisconsin had a university state. Blurring the line between scholarship and partisanship was advantageous, perhaps, so long as harmony reigned on both sides of the line. But eventually the line would have to be clearly drawn, as President Gilmore of the University of Iowa was to say in his inaugural address, if the autonomy of the university was not to be impaired.[14]

The American who protested most vociferously against this trend of events and who tried hardest to preserve the German idea of independence from lay economic as well as lay political power was Thorstein Veblen. In his zeal to protect the autonomy of the university, he went so far as to advocate the exclusion of professional and technological schools from the campus. The motivation of such schools was "worldly wisdom," whereas that of the higher learning was "idle curiosity." By "idle" Veblen meant the search for knowledge "apart from any ulterior use of the knowledge . . . gained." [15] This search runs grave risk of failure if carried on under the subtle influences of a commercial economy. However salutary the logic of the "price system" is in everyday affairs, it must not be permitted to leave its mark on the aims, methods, and standards of scholarship.

Without acceding to the radical surgery recommended by Veblen, Robert M. Hutchins nevertheless diagnosed the ambivalence of the university in much the same terms. His complaint was that the uni-

---

[14] Norman Foerster, *The American State University*. Chapel Hill, North Carolina: University of North Carolina Press, 1937, p. 165.
[15] *The Higher Learning in America: A Memorandum on the Conduct of Universities by Business Men.* New York: B. W. Heubsch, 1918, p. 5.

versity was losing sight of its main aim because of its "love of money." [16] What Hutchins had in mind was the willingness of the university to do research on almost any project for which industry or the government would give it a subsidy. He had no quarrel with subsidies for basic research; the trouble was that so many commissions the university undertook were intended to solve practical problems of the day. Instead of setting its own ends, the university was tethering itself to the ends of others. This was obviously contrary to the idea of a "detached organism . . . growing in accordance with its own laws."

As the university was gradually sucked into the vortex of public service, especially in mid-century after the Second World War, more and more educators expressed the fear that the university was allowing its services to the public to encroach on the functions that entitled it to independence. Jacques Barzun put the matter succinctly when he said he did not mind regarding the university as a "service station" so long as people remembered that the university's unique service was to assay truth. And his colleague at Columbia, Nobel Prize-winner Polykarp Kusch, commented even more pointedly, "A university ought not to do chores for anyone." Quite the opposite, "Research ought to be generated by curiosity and imagination, not by quasi-scientific problems that are essentially political." [17]

In spite of the valiant efforts of Veblen, Hutchins, Barzun, and Kusch to emancipate the American university from the "service" conception, this conception waxed rather than waned. Indeed there were those who thought the university could perform both scholarly and service functions and still maintain its autonomy. No less a pundit than Walter Lippmann recently asked his fellow citizens to look to the university as never before for leadership in *both* areas. The modern age, he claims, is marked by the "dissolution of the ancestral order, the erosion of established authority." In the past we have relied on generals, priests, statesmen, and businessmen to solve our problems, but the times are still sadly out of joint. In the complex world in which we live, our only

[16] *The Higher Learning in America.* New Haven, Connecticut: Yale University Press, 1936, p. 11.
[17] *New York Times,* March 28, 1962, Sec. 2, p. 35.

recourse is to seek help from the "ancient and universal company of scholars." Professors are not infallible—far from it—but they are the most dependable court of last resort in the field of truth and error.

> When the scholar finds that two and two make four, no policeman, no judge, no governor, no legislator, no trustee, no rich alumnus, has any right to ordain that two and two make five. Only other scholars who have gone through a mathematical training equivalent to his, and are in one way or another qualified as his peers, can challenge his findings that two and two make four. Here, it is the community of scholars who are the court of last resort.[18]

Lippmann is not content, however, with asserting the university's right to autonomy in matters of truth and error. The university must go further, he says, and take the leadership in that subtle process of transmuting knowledge into wisdom. But wisdom demands sound judgment about values as well as facts. The professor may be the court of last resort in matters of fact, but is he in matters of value as well? Wise as professors are, their wisdom is hardly incontestable in the estimation of governors, legislators, and trustees. If professors become partisans, will they not seriously jeopardize their autonomy?

The German professor struck a bargain with the state. If the state kept its nose out of his expertise, he in turn agreed not to meddle in politics. The American professor has been unwilling to restrict his activities similarly. Often a pragmatist, he has believed that the ivory tower was a too restricted assay room for truth. He has been impelled to try his theories out in life, in order to test them by their consequences. By doing so he has undoubtedly become a partisan, but, if the paradox is credible, a disinterested one. His partisanship has at least been born of scholarship. Thus, laymen will do well to accord him privileged status, one in which the immunity of tenure will hold for determining wisdom as well as knowledge. If this happens, the university, far from becoming obsolescent, will reach full flower again as an independent republic of scholars.

[18] "The University," *New Republic*, CLIV (May 28, 1966), p. 18. Cf. George S. Counts, *Dare the School Build a New Social Order?* New York: John Day Company, 1932.

To summarize the discussion, we might state the following conclusions: (1) We can logically make a tight case for the autonomy of the university on the ground that, in a guild of scholars or experts, only experts can judge expertise. If we are to have expertise—and who can doubt its need in the modern complex world—there must be no interference with experts; they must be left alone to fulfill their unique function. (2) Expertise does, however, concern the lay public. They pay for it, and it guides their affairs, directly or indirectly. In no uncertain terms, therefore, they have let the university know that it is ultimately subject to lay control. Just as Premier Clemenceau said during the First World War that war was too important to leave to the generals, so we may say that higher education is too important to leave to the professors. (3) Yet, in conceding ultimate control to the lay public, we must fervently hope that it will exercise its power with restraint. The public has the power to crush the university if it wishes. In ancient times it put Socrates to death, and even in this century it reduced the university to a tool of state policy under the Nazis. To avoid repeating such crimes, the democratic state must constantly remember that its moral worth lies in exalting the autonomy of the university.

Some think that if lay governing bodies are not restrained by a higher authority than man's, the autonomy of the university cannot be secure.[19] These governing bodies must understand that the learned man, like Socrates, is a servant of God wholly and God only. They can crush him, to be sure; they can disregard the divine conviction which prompts his teaching; but they cannot suppress that intellectual freedom which is part of the natural and unalterable order of things. Others doubt that an absolutistic metaphysic will seriously deter autocratic laymen from warping the university to fit their own narrow purposes. Rather, they conceive the autonomy of the university as the outgrowth of custom and prescription. In a democracy, intellectual freedom is something that must be learned as an indispensable part of the culture.

[19] Kirk, *Academic Freedom*. (*loc. cit.*)

Formerly president of the State University of New York, academic vice-president of Stanford University, and executive director of the education division of the Ford Foundation, Alvin C. Eurich (1902–   ) has been involved in many developments that have revolutionized higher education in America. He received a Ph.D. from the University of Minnesota where he was also professor of educational psychology. Recently, he edited Campus 1980: The Shape of the Future in American Higher Education. *Here, writing from the imaginary perspective of the year 2000, he looks back at today's colleges and universities and forward to institutions of the twenty-first century.*

9

Higher Education in the 21st Century

ALVIN C. EURICH

As we turn into the new century we find a world very different from what our parents knew in the 1960s. Travel time to Europe has shrunk to only an hour or so. Television and radio are on a worldwide basis; computers translate languages automatically and instantaneously; satellites give us very accurate weather predictions; and we are on the verge of controlling typhoons and hurricanes.

We continue to avoid a

Third World War. In the 1960s, when Russia and the United States were the two major world powers, we twice came precariously close to a nuclear holocaust, once when that atomic bomb was accidentally detonated in the Sahara. Fortunately there were few casualties, and fateful retaliation was avoided. The crater still stands as a tourist attraction and a warning.

Our population has expanded far beyond the optimistic estimates of forty years ago, when we numbered only 186 million people. Today we are approaching 350 million. Our rapid population growth forced many changes. During the first half of the twentieth century we established universal elementary and secondary education. During the second half we made education compulsory through the age of twenty. We needed the additional skills, and we had to protect the labor market, which no longer had jobs for untrained young people. In the process we rebuilt the structure of our educational system. Many of our former liberal arts colleges—there were once sixty-two in the state of Pennsylvania alone—were unable to solve their financial problems. Since their facilities were urgently needed, local communities transformed them into junior colleges. The result is that a two-year college within commuting distance from home is now available for every young man and woman.

These colleges prepare some students for more advanced college and university work; they also train most of the technicians essential to the professions. Half a century ago the Rochester Institute of Technology, under Mark Ellingson's presidency, set the pace. In the late 1960s the institute moved to a new $53 million campus. Now, after several periods of expansion, it enrolls more than 50,000 students. Its graduates have played important roles in developing the photographic computer systems which translate written messages. The institute's cooperative work-study program was, with Antioch's, among the first in the nation.

During the quarter century following World War II, teachers colleges disappeared completely from the American scene. Their place has been taken by multipurpose institutions which, together with the strong liberal arts colleges and the universities, have discontinued the first two years of higher education, since these now come almost wholly within the province of the junior colleges. The transition was accomplished with surprising smoothness. California and Florida took the lead, and, in the East, one remembers the pioneering of the University of Pittsburgh under Chancellor Litchfield.

The new multipurpose institutions, following the pattern set by Florida Atlantic University under its first president, Kenneth R. Williams, now admit qualified graduates from the junior colleges and offer three-year programs, culminating in the master's degree. During the last quarter of the century, there were heated debates at meetings of the Association of American Colleges on the question of whether the baccalaureate degree should be granted at the end of junior college work. The traditionalists won; the junior colleges continued to award the Associate of Arts or Associate of Science degree, while the baccalaureate of arts or science fell into disuse because students going beyond junior college pursued a program leading directly to the master's degree or a professional degree.

The largest universities, with their clusters of professional and graduate schools and research institutions, have now become virtually self-contained cities. Some, like New York University, enroll more than 200,000 students. We continue to wonder whether these institutions are getting too big.

During the past half century, the content of education at all levels was profoundly strengthened in two ways: we became much clearer about the objectives of education; and leading university scholars from various disciplines became so alarmed about our soft education that they produced, in cooperation with schoolteachers and administrators, new curricula extending from the kindergarten through the graduate and professional schools.

Our economy of abundance and a better system of distribution have made us less concerned with the strictly professional or vocational aims of education. Even in the sixties students were ceasing to value a college degree by the additional earning power it conferred. We now minimize the time spent on acquiring practical skills and factual knowledge. Instead, we place more emphasis on developing wisdom about major ideas, as in the course on great issues which President Dickey inaugurated in his first years at Dartmouth. Our employment of knowledge, as of leisure, is more satisfying than it was in the early days of the affluent society, when men were consumed, to the point of boredom, with strictly materialistic pleasures. We recognize the truth expressed by Mark Van Doren fifty years ago: "Freedom to use the mind is the greatest happiness."

The revival of philosophy and of the humanities emerged gradually. By the late sixties it had become clear that a spiritual malaise afflicted American life. Studies of the national character seemed to indicate that America had "run out of gas"; individuals felt dominated by the vastness of their own social institutions and by a national style of conformity also referred to as "other-directedness." Conservatism gripped the nation, and the question arose whether America had "any more great business to conduct." People of all ages had difficulty adjusting themselves to the twenty-four-hour work week, and they began to question if the zealous accumulation of creature comforts had not reached a point of diminishing returns.

College students became impatient with vocational preparation and a general smattering of culture. Through such organizations as the "Challenge" symposia and the various groups concerned with civil rights, the movement gathered strength for the redesign of higher education. Graduate students rebelled against the sterile but exhausting competition for degrees; it was they who forced a revival of humanistic thought, so that even our great technical institutions, led by the Massachusetts Institution of Technology, sought a better balance in their curriculum through a renewed emphasis on the humanities.

Scientists, furthermore, had succeeded in creating life, so that human evolution need no longer be left to chance. This discovery intensified the philosophical search for better answers to the age-old question about the ultimate destiny of man.

We are just now beginning to take seriously Ortega y Gasset's insight set down years ago in his *Mission of the University:* "The need to create sound syntheses and systematization of knowledge, to be taught in the 'Faculty of Culture,' will call out a kind of scientific genius which hitherto has existed only as an aberration, the genius for integration." At Brown University, President Barnaby Keeney was one of the first to initiate an Institute for the Synthesis of Knowledge.

The most radical difference between today's colleges and those of fifty years ago, however, is not in the curriculum but in the use of learning resources. The use of television as an educational medium in colleges developed swiftly after it was introduced in the 1950s. Educators resisted, but demonstration after demonstration, such as those carried on at Pennsylvania State University, established the truth that televised instruction was educationally effective and economically feasible. In 1962 some 30,000 courses were given over television in the United States. But more years were to elapse before colleges recognized that television had made the standard lecture obsolete and the conventional laboratory demonstration inadequate and costly.

The objections to the use of television were essentially the same as those raised at Oxford and Cambridge in the latter part of the nineteenth century when the "university lectures" were proposed. At that time the Oxbridge dons predicted that the innovation would reduce the separate colleges to mere appendages. What actually happened was that the colleges became far more vital when professors were relieved of the responsibility for lecturing and could devote themselves to probing the minds of the students, individually or in small groups. The students, of course, were enabled to hear only the very best lecturers in each field.

So, too, with television. The first glimmer of this came in 1958–1959 when a basic college physics course was offered over a national network under the direction of Professor Harvey E. White of the University of California, one of the nation's best physics teachers. During the year, seven Nobel Prize winners—Brattain, Kusch, Rabi, Block, Seaborg, Anderson, and McMillan—and other distinguished scientists helped to teach the course. They represented an array of talent that no single university could possibly have afforded. The following year, a chemistry course was similarly offered, by Professor John Baxter of the University of Florida, an outstanding teacher. He, too, was aided by eminent chemists from academic, industrial, and governmental laboratories. Other courses in biology, government, economics, and the humanities followed in rapid succession, first on national networks and then, with the success of Telstar, across national boundaries.

Now, fortunately, lectures by some of the greatest scholars are available on electronic tapes. Because it was not until the middle of the 1960s that we began systematically to record the leading scholars of the world, we missed many great men who lived in the twentieth century, such as Enrico Fermi, Henri Bergson, and Sigmund Freud. Under our present system, the senior faculty members, having been spared the drudgery of repeating over and over the basic substance of their fields, are in fresher mind to work with students on advanced topics. Moreover, the students themselves have a firmer grasp of the subject matter, because they have studied the taped lectures at their own rate of comprehension, reviewing them on kinescopes as often as necessary. Television has, in short, provided us with the technology we needed to build a genuine system of mass education, one in which each student has an equal opportunity to learn, no matter where his college is located or what its resources are.

We have also made enormous strides in the teaching of the individual student. Here the most exciting developments have been in independent study, honors work, programmed learning, and language laboratories. Programmed learning, so common today, was hardly known fifty years ago. True, Professor Sidney Pressey at Ohio State University invented the first teaching machine in the 1920s—a device which is now permanently on exhibit at the Smithsonian Institution. But it was not until the 1950s, when Professor Skinner developed another machine and carried on his experiments at Harvard, that programmed learning began to attract attention. After various experiments in the sixties at Harvard, Hamilton College, and numerous secondary schools had clearly demonstrated that students learned faster with programmed materials than with conventional texts and lectures, this scheme of instruction developed into one of the most effective resources for adjusting instruction to the individual student's rate of learning.

The resistance to programming was different from that which had confronted television. Educators knew what television was, but, perhaps because the commercial programming was so vulgar, they refused to grasp its pedagogical implications. In the case of programmed learning, though, most college teachers and administrators did not even know what the new technique was; they only knew that, because of its unfortunate linkage with teaching machines, they did not like it.

As we can now see so clearly, television and programmed learning, both introduced into education in the 1950s, defined the limits of a spectrum of instructional resources. Television provided the medium for mass instruction; programmed learning provided the ultimate in individualized instruction. Within this range, including other devices and procedures, such as motion pictures, filmstrips, language laboratories, and increased scope for independent study, a new diversity was added to the educator's repertoire. These resources enabled us to break the ancient framework that for so long had held college education in a rigid pattern. No longer do we have to divide the school day into fixed fifty-minute periods; no longer do we measure a student's progress by the number of credit hours he has banked; no longer do we march all students through the same series of lectures and classes.

Today, flexibility and adjustment to individual differences are axiomatic. Each student progresses at his own rate. Much of the time he studies on his own, or with fellow students, but always with instant access to the complete range of learning resources: taped lectures, programmed course materials, language audio-tapes, bibliographies, and original documents on microfilm.

Cooperative arrangements among colleges and universities provided another means of bringing the most competent faculty members and learning resources to more students. This, too, developed slowly at first. In the 1930s President Lotus D. Coffman of the University of Minnesota urged the Midwestern universities to share their library resources, but it took a full half century before institutions of higher learning saw the folly of competing with each other by trying to build up *all* academic disciplines. Dr. Coffman urged uniqueness and strength rather than standardization and mediocrity. The University of Minnesota, he rightly observed, was distinguished in Scandinavian literature. Why should other universities try to be equally strong in this area? Within its W. L. Clements Library, the University of Michigan possessed a rare collection of books and documents in American history. Why not send advanced students to Michigan rather than try to duplicate this resource? Some years after Coffman's death, his dream was partly realized with the construction in Chicago of the Midwest Inter-Library Center.

Seeing the major advantages of pooling library resources, the Midwestern universities moved forward quickly and cooperatively in other areas. Their Committee on Institutional Cooperation gave graduate students the opportunity to move freely from one institution to another on a short-term basis to take advantage of special opportunities—Purdue's bionucleonic laboratory, or star scholars, such as those in Egyptology at Chicago. Under the leadership of presidents Herman Wells of Indiana and Frederick Hovde of Purdue, a cooperative instructional program was further extended over a closed-circuit television system tying together the campuses at Lafayette and Bloomington and including the centers in Indianapolis, Fort Wayne, and Evansville. With the success of the Midwest Airborne television instruction of over five million school-children and the invention of multichannel electronic tapes for broadcasting, basic courses in the sciences and humanities were offered to students in all the major universities in Ohio, Indiana, Kentucky, Illinois, Michigan, Wisconsin, and Ontario. These courses supplemented the instructional program offered over Telstar on an international basis.

The universities also recognized the economy of combining their purchasing power. An Inter-University Authority now purchases and distributes supplies and equipment required on the various campuses. The need for such an operation was obvious in the 1970s, when very expensive computer systems for all types of activities became essential on every campus.

The smaller colleges were profoundly affected by all these cooperative arrangements. Their own initial efforts included groupings such as the

Claremont Colleges, the Richmond (Virginia) Center, and the Connecticut Valley Colleges, involving Amherst, Mt. Holyoke, Smith, and the University of Massachusetts. For a long time, such simple matters as not having a common academic calendar prevented students from crossing campus lines in their programs of courses. But during the latter part of the twentieth century the colleges found that they were still competing too much and duplicating their instruction. Renewed efforts were made until there was hardly a college left that was not a member of a cluster of institutions sharing facilities and programs. Each group is affiliated with one or more universities, an arrangement which first became dramatically visible in 1963, when seven faculty members from the University of Chicago personally offered a course on Civilizations from South Asia to a hundred students from Swarthmore, Bryn Mawr, and Haverford colleges, with one of these faculty members flying to Philadelphia each week. This is another way by which students gained access to the educational resources of a widespread academic community instead of being limited to the offerings of a small institution. In the process, too, the advantages of a smaller group have been preserved.

Even more drastic are the changes in our libraries. As a result of research carried on not only in the United States but also in Japan, India, Belgium, Holland, France, and England, we have revolutionized the techniques of storing and transmitting information. Most of our documents are now reduced to pinpoint size and stored on film. We have established the National Research Library, which, as John Kemeny of the Dartmouth mathematics department predicted some years ago, has reached more than 300 million volumes in miniaturized form. Through a multichannel cable, we can instantly transmit information from these volumes to reading units on campuses throughout the country. The space previously used for storing books has been freed for faculty study, reading rooms, and independent work.

Even the architecture of our campuses reflects the innovations in teaching techniques. Iowa State University, the University of Miami in Florida, with its visual communication building, and Stephens College, with its comprehensive learning center, pioneered in constructing academic facilities that make the maximum use of diverse learning aids.

For the lectures over television, students now quite generally listen to portable television sets in their own rooms. These lectures are followed by small group discussions in dormitories, patterned after the "House Plan" first tried out some years ago by Stephens College. The programmed learning laboratories are open twenty-four hours every day, and students may study whenever they desire to do so.

Along with the clarification of objectives, the upgrading and updating of the curriculum, the use of a variety of devices and procedures for learning, and the new library system, we have also vastly improved the process by which students are admitted to the colleges and universities, and the way in which they progress through the course of study. Questions like these inspired reforms:

If students learn at different rates of speed, couldn't some of them achieve the goal in three years, or two, while others worked at it for five or six? Would it not be wise to tell the student what is expected of him, what the end result of his liberal education should be, and then let the student decide, with such guidance as John Finley used to give his students at Eliot House, Harvard, how he can best make use of the university's resources?

To answer these questions, the colleges had to define more precisely the goals they were striving for in the liberal education of students. Whereas under the old system the administration could lean heavily on the accumulation of credit hours as evidence that the student was acquiring an education, the new system required the colleges to devise adequate measures of achievement.

The important point was that students began to progress with complete flexibility. The principles of early admission and admission with advanced standing, which did so much to facilitate the transition from high school to college fifty years ago, were applied as well to the transition from college to graduate work. Standard measures of achievement in each basic subject were devised. But students could meet these standards at their own rate of learning and in a variety of ways.

The system which emerged was pioneered in California under a plan initially worked out by a commission headed by President Arthur Coons of Occidental and strongly supported by President Clark Kerr of the

University of California. Virtually all California students progressed at their own rate from high school to a junior college. The top third of these students, plus some who entered advanced vocational programs, went on to college. From college, approximately the top 12 percent advanced to the university.

During the latter half of the century we also made great strides in the use of the educational plant and facilities. With the crowding of students on the campuses there was neither time nor money enough to build the necessary classrooms, laboratories, and dormitories. In the 1960s the idea of using the campus on a year-round basis caught on, and administrators discovered that existing facilities could accommodate at least 25 percent more students. Now it would be unthinkable to permit buildings to remain idle for three summer months.

Nor do we any longer tolerate such luxurious use of academic facilities as we did during the academic years of the first half of the twentieth century. Then, except for a very few metropolitan universities, we occupied our classrooms primarily in the morning and our laboratories in the afternoon. With the large federal student-aid program for veterans following World War II, some universities changed their practices. Stanford University, for example, was among the first to do so. Dr. Donald B. Tresidder, who was then president, appointed a director of planning—the first position of this kind to be created in any university. An analysis of plant use during the last pre-war year showed that with better use of available space the enrollment could be doubled.

To make maximum use of land, President Tresidder planned an industrial park. And to attract to the area industries whose research interests related to a university, he created the Stanford Research Institute. During the last half of the century, this compound of a first-rate university, the Research Institute, industries with broad research interests, and government projects such as the two-mile-long linear accelerator has set a pattern followed in most university centers of the country.

As we look back over the progress of higher education in recent decades, we may wonder when the major changes began to develop. It is difficult to fix an exact date, but I believe a turning point occurred in the mid-1950s and 1960s. First we were spurred by Sputnik; then, in the years 1964, 1965, and 1966, the colleges felt most keenly the increase in the demand for higher education. The college population nearly trebled during the sixties and seventies, with the most acute increases taking place in the mid-sixties.

It was this tremendous increase, I think, which galvanized the leading colleges and universities into action. Through such relatively simple reforms as year-round operation, control over proliferating courses, and better use of independent study, many colleges found they could enroll up to one third more students without any significant increase in costs.

Now, here we stand in the year 2000, at the dawn of another century. During the past forty years colleges and universities, like society itself, have moved farther and faster than in all previous history. But as Oliver Wendell Holmes once said, "The great thing in the world is not so much where we stand as in what direction we are moving." We are a long way from a system of higher education that cultivates the full potentialities of man, regardless of race, color, creed, or economic status. But an orderly world of rationally free men can settle for no less.

PART III

Colleges
and
Universities

M any great men in the past have educated themselves brilliantly without formal collegiate instruction; for Herman Melville, "A whale ship was my Yale College and my Harvard." With such developments as the increased use of television and teaching machines, it may well be that in the future education will take place in living rooms rather than classrooms. Currently, however, higher education is largely a matter of formal instruction in colleges and universities; and the extent to which the goals of education are realized, however those goals might be defined, is primarily a function of the success or failure of those institutions. The noted contemporary philosopher and theologian, Karl Jaspers, makes this point succinctly:

> The university exists only to the extent that it is institutionalized. The idea becomes concrete in the institution. The extent to which it does this determines the quality of the university. Stripped of its ideal the university loses all value. Yet "institution" necessarily implies compromises. The idea is never perfectly realized. Because of this a permanent state of tension exists at the university between the idea and the shortcomings of the institutional and corporate reality.

Many colleges and universities have been founded as a result of the idealism of men whose concern for their religion, their profession, or their state or community inspired in them a vision of the contribution that a place of higher learning could make to their special interest. Almost invariably, however, the institutionalization of those interests has necessitated compromising that idealism. As two of our most discerning observers on higher education, David Riesman and Christopher Jencks, have observed:

> This is what it means to speak of a college as an institution: that, once it is established, those nominally in charge become more interested in the college's survival than in the welfare and contentment of the interest groups that fathered it.

Collected in Part III are essays concerning the nature of the university as an institution written by several men who hold various views on the ends of education. Each discusses some of the compromises that in practice are necessary in negotiating between the inspiring vision of education as it might be and the realities that often militate against the fulfillment of that vision. For the most part, the age of the self-educated man has passed, and the time in which machines replace human teachers has not yet arrived. There is implicit agreement in these essays regarding the necessity and propriety of institutionalizing higher education in the form of college and universities.

Alfred North Whitehead's selection, "Universities and Their Function," eloquently discusses the ideal university's distinctive character as a community of teachers and students working together under the inspiration of imagination. He goes on, however, to consider some of the problems that arise to challenge such an ideal: the growth in the number, size, and complexity of institutions; the uncertainty regarding the proper means for the university to act "in the service of a nation;" and even the pressure of faculty publication. The same problems that Whitehead described in 1927 would still beset the university decades later. Many of the subsequent essays endeavor to offer solutions to the dilemmas Whitehead identified nearly half a century ago. Significantly however, none proposes the single-minded dedication to a guiding principle that Whitehead does. The problems of contemporary colleges and universities allow no simple answers.

In "The College of *Liberal* Arts and Sciences," Arthur Bestor recalls the theme of liberal education, central to the Part I readings. Like the writers there, he manifests a profound belief in the importance of community, both in the academy and the world at large; in the importance of the student's grasping fundamental modes of thought as well as quantities of knowledge; and in the place of the generalist as well as the specialist in our increasingly fragmented world. He speaks of the four-year, liberal arts college as the appropriate home of such an education as would fulfill these goals, and traditionally it has been so. If today the university is inheriting from the small, liberal arts college the dominant role in American higher education, it is appropriate to consider how well a college of arts and sciences within a major university can achieve Bestor's ends.

The difficulty of fulfilling the ideal of liberal education in the modern college is not to be underestimated. Not the least of the pressures on the liberal ideal come from within the educational establishment itself. On the one hand, secondary schools are appropriating courses of study that formerly belonged only to higher education, as witness the growing advanced placement program. On the other hand, some graduate and professional schools call for specialization to begin during the undergraduate years. The consequence, as Jacques Barzun suggests in "College to University —And After," may be the elimination of the conventional liberal arts program and, perhaps, the obsolescence of the purely undergraduate college, which traditionally has been built around such a program. The implications of such a development will be disquieting to many.

Two authors intimately acquainted with the situation in contemporary higher education by virtue of their service as presidents of major universities, Clark Kerr and James Perkins, take for granted the necessity for radical changes in the shape of our colleges and universities. From their essays, "The Frantic Race to Remain Contemporary" and "The Search for Internal Coherence," it is clear that they do not underestimate the difficulties of the problems which must be faced. But, equally, there is an air of confidence in their approach which suggests not only that the problems can be met and solved, but also that the university will be a healthier, more vital place because of the growing pains it is currently experiencing. As Kerr insists at the opening of his essay, traditional conceptions of the purpose and function of the university will no longer serve. If the American university is to achieve maturity and speak to the unique character of its society, it must define for itself what its nature and purpose will be.

President Perkins' essay pursues many of the issues raised by

116

Kerr, even including his allusion to the analogy between the university and the dinosaur. Suggesting some general principles that might govern the growth of the university which Kerr describes, Perkins also offers a number of concrete proposals regarding courses and distribution of power within the new university which, as an institution, has come of age.

All of the articles reprinted in Part III acknowledge the difficult challenges facing higher education in the twentieth century. But between Whitehead's proposal of a guiding principle for the university (imagination) and Perkins' (internal coherence) lies a considerable difference in emphasis. From its early center in the small community of the liberal arts college to its present home in the dinosaurian university, the institutional form of higher education in America has changed, and in the foreseeable future will continue to change, dramatically. Finally, in "The Squeeze on the Liberal University," J. Douglas Brown, reminds us again of some of the losses which such "progress" has occasioned and urges that the adjective "liberal" could be as appropriate for universities as for colleges. The desirability and possibility of maintaining the liberal educational ideal in our colleges and universities may be determined within our lifetime.

Alfred North Whitehead (1861–1947), was one of the leading mathematicians and philosophers of his day. Born and reared in England, Whitehead taught mathematics at Cambridge, where Bertrand Russell was his most distinguished pupil and, later, his collaborator on the monumental Principia Mathematica *(1910–1913). In 1910 he moved to the University of London, and in 1924 he accepted the chair in philosophy at Harvard University. He remained in America until his death at the age of eighty-six. He delivered this address before the American Association of the Collegiate Schools of Business in 1927.*

10

Universities and Their Function

ALFRED NORTH WHITEHEAD

I

The expansion of universities is one marked feature of the social life in the present age. All countries have shared in this movement, but more especially America, which thereby occupies a position of honor. It is, however, possible to be overwhelmed even by the gifts of good fortune; and this growth of universities, in number of institutions, in size, and in internal complexity of organization, discloses some danger of destroying the very

118

sources of their usefulness, in the absence of a widespread understanding of the primary functions which universities should perform in the service of a nation. These remarks, as to the necessity for reconsideration of the function of universities, apply to all the more developed countries. They are only more especially applicable to America, because this country has taken the lead in a development which, under wise guidance, may prove to be one of the most fortunate forward steps which civilisation has yet taken.

This article will only deal with the most general principles, though the special problems of the various departments in any university are, of course, innumerable. But generalities require illustration, and for this purpose I choose the business school of a university. This choice is dictated by the fact that business schools represent one of the newer developments of university activity. They are also more particularly relevant to the dominant social activities of modern nations, and for that reason are good examples of the way in which the national life should be affected by the activities of its universities. Also at Harvard, where I have the honour to hold office, the new foundation of a business school on a scale amounting to magnificence has just reached its completion.

There is a certain novelty in the provision of such a school of training, on this scale of magnitude, in one of the few leading universities of the world. It marks the culmination of a movement which for many years past has introduced analogous departments throughout American universities. This is a new fact in the university world; and it alone would justify some general reflections upon the purpose of a university education, and upon the proved importance of that purpose for the welfare of the social organism.

The novelty of business schools must not be exaggerated. At no time have universities been restricted to pure abstract learning. The University of Salerno in Italy, the earliest of European universities, was devoted to medicine. In England, at Cambridge, in the year 1316, a college was founded for the special purpose of providing 'clerks for the King's service.' Universities have trained clergy, medical men, lawyers, engineers. Business is now a highly intellectualized vocation, so it well fits into the series. There is, however, this novelty: the curriculum suitable for a business school, and the various modes of activity of such a school, are still in the experimental stage. Hence the peculiar importance of recurrence to general principles in connection with the moulding of these schools. It would, however, be an act of presumption on my part if I were to enter upon any consideration of details, or even upon types of policy affecting the balance of the whole training. Upon such questions I have no special knowledge, and therefore have no word of advice.

II

The universities are schools of education, and schools of research. But the primary reason for their existence is not to be found either in the mere knowledge conveyed to the students or in the mere opportunities for research afforded to the members of the faculty.

Both these functions could be performed at a cheaper rate, apart from these very expensive institutions. Books are cheap, and the system of apprenticeship is well understood. So far as the mere imparting of information is concerned, no university has had any justification for existence since the popularisation of printing in the fifteenth century. Yet the chief impetus to the foundation of universities came after that date, and in more recent times has even increased.

The justification for a university is that it preserves the connection between knowledge and the zest of life, by uniting the young and the old in the imaginative consideration of learning. The university imparts information, but it imparts it imaginatively. At least, this is the function which it should perform for society. A university which fails in this respect has no reason for existence. This atmosphere of excitement, arising from imaginative consideration, transforms knowledge. A fact is no longer a bare fact: it is invested with all its possibilities. It is no longer a burden on the memory: it is energising as the poet of our dreams, and as the architect of our purposes.

Imagination is not to be divorced from the facts: it is a way of illuminating the facts. It works by eliciting the general principles which apply to the facts, as they exist, and then by an intellectual survey of alternative possibilities which are consistent with those principles. It enables men to construct an intellectual vision of a new world, and it preserves the zest of life by the suggestion of satisfying purposes.

Youth is imaginative, and if the imagination be strengthened by discipline this energy of imagination can in great measure be preserved through life. The tragedy of the world is that those who are imaginative have but slight experience, and those who are experienced have feeble imaginations. Fools act on imagination without knowledge; pedants act on knowledge without imagination. The task of a university is to weld together imagination and experience.

The initial discipline of imagination in its period of youthful vigour requires that there be no responsibility for immediate action. The habit of unbiased thought, whereby the ideal variety of exemplifications is discerned in its derivation from general principles, cannot be acquired when there is the daily task of preserving a concrete organisation. You must be free to think rightly and wrongly, and free to appreciate the variousness of the universe undisturbed by its perils.

These reflections upon the general functions of a university can be at once translated in terms of the particular functions of a business school. We need not flinch from the assertion that the main function of such a school is to produce men with a greater zest for business. It is a libel upon human nature to conceive that zest for life is the product of pedestrian purposes directed toward the narrow routine of material comforts. Mankind by its pioneering instinct, and in a hundred other ways, proclaims the falsehood of that lie.

In the modern complex social organism, the adventure of life cannot be disjoined from intellectual adventure. Amid simpler circumstances, the pioneer can follow the urge of his instinct, directed toward the scene of his vision from the mountain top. But in the complex organisations of modern business the intellectual adventure of analysis, and of imaginative reconstruction, must precede any successful reorganisation. In a simpler world, business relations were simpler, being based on the immediate contact of man with man and on immediate confrontation with all relevant material circumstances. To-day business organisation requires an imaginative grasp of the psychologies of populations engaged in differing modes of occupation; of populations scattered through cities, through mountains, through plains; of populations on the ocean, and of populations in mines, and of populations in forests. It requires an imaginative grasp of conditions in the tropics, and of conditions in temperate zones. It requires an imaginative grasp of the interlocking interests of great organisations, and of the reactions of the whole complex to any change in one of its elements. It requires an imaginative understanding of laws of political economy, not merely in the abstract, but also with the power to construe them in terms of the particular circumstances of a concrete business. It requires some knowledge of the habits of government, and of the variations of those habits under diverse conditions. It requires an imaginative vision of the binding forces of any human organization, a sympathetic vision of the limits of human nature and of the conditions which evoke loyalty of service. It requires some knowledge of the laws of health, and of the laws of fatigue, and of the conditions for sustained reliability. It requires an imaginative understanding of the social effects of the conditions of factories. It requires a sufficient conception of the rôle of applied science in modern society. It requires that discipline of character which can say 'yes' and 'no' to other men, not by reason of blind obstinacy, but with firmness derived from a conscious evaluation of relevant alternatives.

The universities have trained the intellectual pioneers of our civilisation—the priests, the lawyers, the statesmen, the doctors, the men of science, and the men of letters. They have been the home of those ideals which lead men to confront the confusion of their present times. The Pilgrim Fathers left England to found a state of society according to the ideals of their religious faith; and one of their earlier acts was the foundation of Harvard University in Cambridge, named after that ancient mother of ideals in England, to which so many of them owed their training. The conduct of business now requires intellectual imagination of the same type as that which in former times has mainly passed into those other occupations; and the universities are the organisations which have supplied this type of mentality for the service of the progress of the European races.

In early mediæval history the origin of universities was obscure and almost unnoticed. They were a gradual and natural growth. But their existence is the reason for the sustained, rapid progressiveness of European life in so many fields of activity. By their agency the adventure of action met the adventure of thought. It would not have been possible antecedently to have divined that such organisations would have been successful. Even now, amid the imperfections of all things human, it is sometimes difficult to understand how they succeed in their work. Of course there is much failure in the work of universities. But, if we take a broad view of history, their success has been remarkable and almost uniform. The cultural histories of Italy, of France, of Germany, of Holland, of Scotland, of England, of the United States, bear witness to the influence of universities. By 'cultural history' I am not chiefly thinking of the lives of scholars; I mean the energising of the lives of those men who gave to France, to Germany, and to other countries that impress of types of human achievement which, by their addition to the zest of life, form the foundation of our patriotism. We love to be members of a society which can do those things.

There is one great difficulty which hampers all the higher types of human endeavor. In modern times this difficulty has even increased in its possibilities for evil. In any large organisation the younger men, who are novices, must be set to jobs which consist in carrying out fixed duties in obedience to orders. No president of a large corporation meets his youngest employee at his office door with the offer of the most responsible job which the work of that corporation includes. The young men are set to work at a fixed routine, and only occasionally even see the president as he passes in and out of the building. Such work is a great discipline. It imparts knowledge, and it produces reliability of character; also it is the only work for which the young men, in that novice stage, are fit, and it is the work for which they are hired. There can be no criticism of the custom, but there may be an unfortunate effect—prolonged routine work dulls the imagination.

The result is that qualities essential at a later stage of a career are apt to be stamped out in an earlier stage. This is only an instance of the more general fact, that necessary technical excellence can only be acquired by a training which is apt to damage those energies of mind which should direct the technical skill. This is the key fact in education, and the reason for most of its difficulties.

The way in which a university should function in the preparation for an intellectual career, such as modern business or one of the older professions, is by promoting the imaginative consideration of the various general principles underlying that career. Its students thus pass into their period of technical apprenticeship with their imaginations already practised in connecting details with general principles. The routine then receives its meaning, and also illuminates the principles which give it that meaning. Hence, instead of a drudgery issuing in a blind rule of thumb, the properly trained man has some hope of obtaining an imagination disciplined by detailed facts and by necessary habits.

Thus the proper function of a university is the imaginative acquisition of knowledge. Apart from this importance of the imagination, there is no reason why business men, and other professional men, should not pick up their facts bit by bit as they want them for particular occasions. A university is imaginative or it is nothing—at least nothing useful.

III

Imagination is a contagious disease. It cannot be measured by the yard, or weighed by the pound, and then delivered to the students by members of the faculty. It can only be communicated by a faculty whose members themselves wear their learning with imagination. In saying this, I am only repeating one of the oldest of observations. More than two thousand years ago the ancients symbolised learning by a torch passing from hand to hand down the generations. That lighted torch is the imagination of which I speak. The whole art in the organisation of a university is the provision of a faculty whose learning is lighted up with imagination. This is the problem of problems in university education; and unless we are careful the recent vast extension of universities in number of students and in variety of activities—of which we are so justly proud—will fail in producing its proper results, by the mishandling of this problem.

The combination of imagination and learning normally requires some leisure, freedom from restraint, freedom from harassing worry, some variety of experiences, and the stimulation of other minds diverse in opinion and diverse in equipment. Also there is required the excitement of curiosity, and the self-confidence derived from pride in the achievements of the surrounding society in procuring the advance of knowledge. Imagination cannot be acquired once and for all, and then kept indefinitely in an ice box to be produced periodically in stated quantities. The learned and imaginative life is a way of living, and is not an article of commerce.

It is in respect to the provision and utilisation of these conditions for an efficient faculty that the two functions of education and research meet together in a university. Do you want your teachers to be imaginative? Then encourage them to research. Do you want your researchers to be imaginative? Then bring them into intellectual sympathy with the young at the most eager, imaginative period of life, when intellects are just entering upon their mature discipline. Make your researchers explain themselves to active minds, plastic and with the world before them; make your young students crown their period of intellectual acquisition by some contact with minds gifted with experience of intellectual adventure. Education is discipline for the adventure of life; research is intellectual adventure; and the universities should be homes of adventure shared in common by young and old. For successful education there must always be a certain freshness in the knowledge dealt with. It must either be new in itself or it must be invested with some novelty of application to the new world of new times. Knowledge does not keep any better than fish. You may be dealing with knowledge of the old species, with some old truth; but somehow or other it must come to the students, as it were, just drawn out of the sea and with the freshness of its immediate importance.

It is the function of the scholar to evoke into life wisdom and beauty which, apart from his magic, would remain lost in the past. A progressive society depends upon its inclusion of three groups—scholars, discoverers, inventors. Its progress also depends upon the fact that its educated masses are composed of members each with a tinge of scholarship, a tinge of discovery, and a tinge of invention. I am here using the term 'discovery' to mean the progress of knowledge in respect to truths of some high generality, and the term 'invention' to mean the progress of knowledge in respect to the application of general truths in particular ways subservient to present needs. It is evident that these three groups merge into each other, and also that men engaged in practical affairs are properly to be called inventors so far as they contribute to the progress of society. But any one individual has his own limitation of function, and his own peculiar needs. What is important for a nation is that there shall be a very close relation between all types of its progressive elements, so that the study may influence the market place, and the market place the study. Universities are the chief agencies for this fusion of progressive activities into an effective instrument of progress. Of course they are not the only agencies, but it is a fact that to-day the progressive nations are those in which universities flourish.

It must not be supposed that the output of a university in the form of original ideas is solely to be measured by printed papers and books labeled with the names of their authors. Mankind is as individual in its mode of output as in the substance of its thoughts. For some of the most fertile minds composition in writing, or in a form reducible to writing, seems to be an impossibility. In every faculty you will find that some of the more brilliant teachers are not among those who publish. Their originality requires for its expression direct intercourse with their pupils in the form of lectures, or of personal discussion. Such men exercise an immense influence; and yet, after the generation of their pupils has passed away, they sleep among the innumerable unthanked benefactors of humanity. Fortunately, one of them is immortal—Socrates.

Thus it would be the greatest mistake to estimate the value of each member of a faculty by the printed work signed with his name. There is at the present day some tendency to fall into this error; and an emphatic protest is necessary against an attitude on the part of authorities which is damaging to efficiency and unjust to unselfish zeal.

But, when all such allowances have been made, one good test for the general efficiency of a faculty is that as a whole it shall be producing in published form its quota of contributions of thought. Such a quota is to be estimated in weight of thought, and not in number of words.

This survey shows that the management of a university faculty has no analogy to that of a business organisation. The public opinion of the faculty, and a common zeal for the purposes of the university, form the only effective safeguards for the high level of university work. The faculty should be a band of scholars, stimulating each other, and freely determining their various activities. You can secure certain formal requirements, that lectures are given at stated times and that instructors and students are in attendance. But the heart of the matter lies beyond all regulation.

The question of justice to the teachers has very little to do with the case. It is perfectly just to hire a man to perform any legal services under any legal conditions as to times and salary. No one need accept the post unless he so desires.

The sole question is, What sort of conditions will produce the type of faculty which will run a successful university? The danger is that it is quite easy to produce a faculty entirely unfit—a faculty of very efficient pedants and dullards. The general public will only detect the difference after the university has stunted the promise of youth for scores of years.

The modern university system in the great democratic countries will only be successful if the ultimate authorities exercise singular restraint, so as to remember that universities cannot be dealt with according to the rules and policies which apply to the familiar business corporations. Business schools are no exception to this law of university life. There is really nothing to add to what the presidents of many American universities have recently said in public on this topic. But whether the effective portion of the general public, in America or other countries, will follow their advice appears to be doubtful. The whole point of a university, on its educational side, is to bring the young under the intellectual influence of a band of imaginative scholars. There can be no escape from proper attention to the conditions which—as experience has shown—will produce such a band.

IV

The two premier universities of Europe, in age and in dignity, are the University of Paris and the University of Oxford. I will speak of my own country because I know it best. The University of Oxford may have sinned in many ways. But, for all her deficiencies, she has throughout the ages preserved one supreme merit, beside which all failures in detail are as dust in the balance: for century after century, throughout the long course of her existence, she has produced bands of scholars who treated learning imaginatively. For that service alone, no one who loves culture can think of her without emotion.

But it is quite unnecessary for me to cross the ocean for my examples. The author of the Declaration of Independence, Mr. Jefferson, has some claim to be the greatest American. The perfection of his various achievements certainly places him among the few great men of all ages. He founded a university, and devoted one side of his complex genius to placing that university amid every circumstance which could stimulate the imagination—beauty of buildings, of situation, and every other stimulation of equipment and organization.

There are many other universities in America which can point my moral, but my final example shall be Harvard—the representative university of the Puritan movement. The New England Puritans of the seventeenth and eighteenth centuries were the most intensely imaginative people, restrained in their outward expression, and fearful of symbolism by physical beauty, but, as it were, racked with the intensity of spiritual truths intellectually imagined. The Puritan faculties of those centuries must have been imaginative indeed, and they produced great men whose names have gone round the world. In later times Puritanism softened, and, in the golden age of literary New England, Emerson, Lowell, and Longfellow set their mark upon Harvard. The modern scientific age then gradually supervenes, and again in William James we fined the typical imaginative scholar.

To-day business comes to Harvard; and the gift which the University has to offer is the old one of imagination, the lighted torch which passes from hand to hand. It is a dangerous gift, which has started many a conflagration. If we are timid as to that danger, the proper course is to shut down our universities. Imagination is a gift which has often been associated with great commercial peoples—with Greece, with Florence, with Venice, with the learning of Holland, and with the poetry of England. Commerce and imagination thrive together. It is a gift which all must pray for their country who desire for it that abiding greatness achieved by Athens:—

> Her citizens, imperial spirits,
> Rule the present from the past.

For American education no smaller ideal can suffice.

*Professionally a distinguished
student of American history,
Arthur Bestor (1908–   ) has
received broader popular recognition for his controversial
criticisms of contemporary
American education. After undergraduate and graduate studies
at Yale, he went on to teach at
Columbia, Stanford, Illinois,
Oxford, and the University of
Washington where he is now
professor of history. His book*
Educational Wastelands *(1953)
was followed by* The Restoration of Learning: A Program for
Redeeming the Unfulfilled
Promises of American Education *(1956), in which this essay
appeared as a chapter.*

11

The College of *Liberal* Arts and Sciences

ARTHUR BESTOR

The four-year liberal-arts college is a distinctive feature of the English and the American educational systems, and it has made a distinctive contribution to the public life of Great Britain and the United States. The nature of the liberal-arts college ought to be better understood than it is, for we are in danger of losing a uniquely precious part of our educational heritage through sheer inattention to its essential characteristics.

To compare the educational systems of different countries accurately is an exceedingly difficult task, and to offer generalizations concerning their theoretical (let alone their actual) structure is a rash proceeding. Nevertheless, such a generalization must be hazarded here. The actual standards and performance of the educational systems of other countries need not be examined at this time. Our present concern is with the theoretical relationship between secondary and higher education, or, more accurately, the way in which responsibility for secondary and higher education is theoretically apportioned among institutions of different levels. And, for purposes of this discussion, we are interested only in the student who proceeds through all the levels.

Secondary education, for such a student, is conceived of in all countries (if we except some of the American heresies that I have already discussed) as rigorous training in the fundamentals of the various fields of learning—languages, sciences, mathematics, history, and the rest. Secondary-school instruction differs from higher education (in the theory of most systems) in that it is carried out methodically, in a pattern of courses that are largely prescribed, with relatively little expectation that the student will engage in independent, wide-ranging investigations of his own. At the opposite pole is the educational scheme of the Continental university, and of those portions of English and American universities which are not embraced within the undergraduate college. University work, in this sense, is highly specialized. It is concerned with training for research or for one of the learned professions. Independent reading and original investigation are generally more important than course work. Students are largely on their own. The schoolmaster is gone, and in his place is the professor, interested not in what the student does day by day, but in the results he can demonstrate at the end of his academic career through examinations and a written thesis.

Here are two diametrically opposed educational procedures. On the Continent of Europe the student proceeds directly from the first to the second. Secondary education (in the *Gymnasium* or *lycée*) is more prolonged than with us; university work is from the beginning more independent and more specialized. The undergraduate college of England and America is interpolated, as it were, into this scheme. It is a transitional institution, in the sense that it partakes of the qualities of both the secondary school and the university, and it covers the years that on the Continent are divided between the two.

But the liberal-arts college is a great deal more than a mere transitional institution. It has a unique character of its own. And its distinctive features have had much to do, I am convinced, with producing among the educated classes of the United States (as also of England) the kind of mutual understanding that underlies our success in maintaining national unity and harmony in the midst of social and political changes as drastic as those that have rent the societies of Continental Europe apart.

What characteristics of the liberal-arts college can justify such a sweeping assertion? To put the matter simply, the liberal-arts college permits students to complete their fundamental intellectual training in an atmosphere of greater freedom than the secondary school can allow. And in the liberal-arts college, students move gradually toward specialization, mingling the while and exchanging ideas with comrades whose intellectual paths are beginning to diverge. A sense of sharing in a common intellectual life is produced by the liberal-arts college as it is not produced by any institution in the Continental educational system.

The secondary school, of course, provides a unity of background, but this is an enforced and even regimented unity. When freedom of choice is suddenly granted, in the Continental university, the sense of unity in intellectual life disappears in the pursuit of intensively specialized scholarly and professional training. Under this system, unity is associated with intellectual immaturity; mature intellectual life is compartmentalized, divided, self-consciously specialized. The English and American conception is different. As students approach intellectual maturity, the methodical preceptorial methods of the schoolroom are gradually relaxed, and a study of the fundamental intellectual disciplines is continued under conditions of freedom and individual responsibility that approximate those of the university. A free exchange of ideas among fellow students, at the level of intellectual maturity, increases and is encouraged. And as these students progress toward greater specialization, they explore among themselves the interrelations between their various fields, thus cultivating the habit of discussion and mutual understanding. They are preparing themselves for the kind of public life in which a fundamental unity of purpose and principle underlies even the most striking differences, thus permitting honest compromise. The liberal-arts college exemplifies, and prepares for the realization of, the motto inscribed upon our Great Seal: *E pluribus unum.*

Theory of course is very imperfectly carried out in practice. The contrasts I have made are admittedly too sharp, and the generalizations too sweeping. Nevertheless they help to make clear, I believe, the features of liberal education which we need to safeguard and strengthen in our colleges, if these are to serve, as they have served in the past, as the bulwarks of enlightened, harmonious, democratic public life.

The ideal of the college of liberal arts and sciences is to raise up a body of men and women who understand in common the fundamentals of intellectual life in its various branches, and who are able to apply to their own problems not one, but a choice of powerful intellectual techniques over which they have achieved some measure of disciplined control. The crucial problem is how to encourage young men and women to range freely over the various fields of knowledge and yet to maintain that unified comprehension which will enable them to understand and co-operate in one another's intellectual pursuits.

The kind of unity we require in intellectual life is the kind that comes when educated men are able to command several, not merely one, of the distinctive ways of thinking that are central in the modern world. There is no genuine unity of intellectual life if men have merely learned the same sets of facts from so-called "subject-matter" fields. There is merely a specious unity if men have been taught to think in their respective disciplines alone and have been offered merely a smattering of information *about* other ways of thinking. And there is only a narrow and shackled unity if one way of thinking has been exalted above all others and made the *sine qua non* of education.[1]

Men need to know a fair number of the crucial ways of thinking upon which modern intellectual life is based. This implies that the truly distinctive ways of thinking are reasonably limited in number, and that there is a recognizable hierarchy of importance among them. The implications of this must be squarely faced. Educational reform must begin with a courageous assertion that all the various subjects and disciplines in the curriculum are *not* of equal value. Some disciplines are fundamental, in the sense that they represent essential ways of thinking, which can be generalized and applied to a wide range of intellectual problems. Other disciplines, though equal in intellectual potency, are somewhat less central to the purposes of liberal education, either because they can be studied only after the fundamental disciplines are mastered, or because they represent highly specialized intellectual techniques, restricted in their range of applicability. Other courses in the modern curriculum do not represent disciplines at all, but offer professional preparation, or training in mechanical skills, or helpful hints on vocational and personal matters. Still other courses, alas, offer nothing at all, save collections of more or less interesting facts, opinions, or fallacies.

When we have the courage to specify which disciplines belong in the first category—that is, which ones are truly fundamental—then, and only then, can we begin to restore intellectual unity to the curricula of our schools and colleges. The decision may not be as difficult as it seems, for we are talking about disciplines, or ways of thinking, not about "subject-matter" fields. The basically different ways of thinking are few compared with the number of factual areas within which they can be applied. The method of controlled experimentation, for example, is one sort of disciplined thinking, and it underlies several different physical sciences. Mathematics is another

---

[1] Despite its many strong points, the so-called "great books" program seems to me at fault in this respect. It tends to emphasize dialectical argument at the expense of all those intellectual processes that call upon men to sift multifarious evidence and draw conclusions from it.

distinctive way of thinking, historical investigation is a third, philosophical criticism a fourth. One can go on, but one cannot go on far without exhausting the ways of thinking that are genuinely fundamental, that are clearly distinctive, and that are susceptible of being introduced at the elementary- or high-school level and carried forward systematically in college. All choices have something of the arbitrary about them, but a decision that certain disciplines are fundamental and others not can be made on reasonable and judicious grounds.

Once these premises are accepted—and not merely accepted, but believed with the kind of conviction that will lead to action—then some plan for genuinely liberal education appropriate to the mid-twentieth century becomes possible. Such a plan must provide for specialization. It must also establish standards and prerequisites that will permit an orderly progress from introductory to advanced work. It must consider the nature of the courses that are best adapted to the instruction of the non-specialist. It must develop a philosophy for guiding the student in his quest for intellectual breadth. And it must set up a final test for achievement in terms of knowledge and skill acquired, not of credits accumulated. These various points will be taken up in order in the remainder of this chapter.

Intellectual training is so laborious and time-consuming that it tends to become specialized education in *a* discipline rather than liberal education in *the* disciplines. Given the complexity of modern knowledge, a high degree of specialization is an inescapable thing. In point of fact genuine specialization is not in itself an evil. It is false specialization that we need to fear and avoid.

One kind of false specialization is exemplified by the man who imagines that he will be able to solve important problems by using only one set of mental tools. No intellectual activity is ever so specialized that it involves only a single way of thinking. If a specialist is to solve new problems in his own field he must be prepared to draw upon ways of thinking that have never yet been applied to the problem. The greater his achievement as a specialist, the broader must be his fund of general knowledge and the wider his acquaintance with other ways of thinking. Specialization that is false because of its narrowness is also self-defeating. Genuine specialization always involves the careful study of related fields.

A second type of false specialization in intellectual life is more insidious. It arises from the failure to discriminate between an intellectual discipline defined as a way of thinking and a field of study defined in some other way—defined, say, as the body of practical information connected with some specified vocation. Now, vocational training, as an earlier chapter has shown, is perfectly compatible with liberal education, but it is not the same thing. The *liberal* part of the training for any profession or trade is the part devoted to the scientific and scholarly disciplines that underlie the profession or trade. The *vocational* or *professional* aspect of the training is something added to liberal education. It should not be reckoned a *part* of liberal education at all.

A man's vocational or professional training is necessarily specialized. The liberal education upon which it is based need not be, but if it is, the specialization that is considered part of his liberal education can only be in one of the intellectual disciplines. There is no place in genuinely liberal education for a major in journalism, or home economics, or pedagogy, even though courses in these vocational subjects may be taken as supplements to a program in liberal education.

Because both specialization and the quest for intellectual breadth are recognized aims of the liberal-arts college, a problem arises over the proper grading of courses. In his special field an upperclassman or a graduate student will be pursuing advanced courses, but at the same time he may be receiving his first introduction to some other field. American colleges customarily assign different sets of numbers to courses of different levels. This is entirely reasonable. But they usually take another step, the logic of which is utterly specious. Thinking to uphold standards, they are apt to forbid a graduate student or even an upperclassman to enroll for full credit in a course the number of which indicates that it is on the introductory level. This is absurd. Where, may one ask, should a student be introduced to a new subject if not in an introductory course?

The consequence of this mechanical way of treating advanced credit is that the student enrolls in an advanced course without knowing anything of the fundamental processes of thought involved. An advanced student in history may need to commence the study of economics as a supporting discipline, but he is likely to find that to secure full credit he must enroll in an advanced course in the subject, though he has never mastered the introductory material. Not one student does so, but scores, and the instructor is forced to adjust his teaching to the situation. He cannot assume that his students possess a common fund of knowledge in the field or a command of certain clearly defined intellectual skills of a specialized nature. The supposedly advanced course becomes partly an introductory one. The compromise is unsatisfactory to all concerned. Thoroughly prepared students do not advance in disciplined thinking as far or as fast as they should, and new students are not initiated into disciplined thinking as systematically or as thoroughly as they ought to be.

If the introductory course is a really rigorous one, there is no reason why it should not be elected for full credit by upperclassmen and graduate students. Only in this way can advanced courses become and remain truly advanced ones, and a rational system of prerequisites be maintained. The difference between an introductory course and an advanced one has almost nothing to do with the chronological age of the student or his academic status. No one can vault lightly over the difficulties involved in learning the elements of an intellectual discipline merely because he happens to be a senior or a graduate student. He may learn a little faster, it is true, but he does not learn differently. In particular, he cannot skip essential steps in a process of thought. Knowledge, after all, *is* cumulative, and intellectual processes do advance through clearly defined stages of increasing complexity.

Once the difference between introductory and advanced courses is firmly established, we can deal more intelligently with the harder question of the kind of course that a student should be offered in a discipline outside the field of his special interest and effort. What, for example, does a student majoring in the discipline of history need to know of mathematical reasoning, of scientific investigation, of philosophical criticism, of literary expression, of æsthetic comprehension?

The answer is that he needs to know the things represented by the nouns or gerunds in the phrases above—that is to say, the nature of reasoning, investigation, criticism, expression, and comprehension, as these appear in their various special forms. He does not need to know all the different lines of inquiry pursued in a given field, but he needs to know its particular way of thinking well enough to grasp its special power and applicability.

Liberal education is training in thinking. It is not the mere communication of facts. What every student—specialist or non-specialist—should gain from a course is command, even if only limited command, of the processes of thought employed in the discipline he is studying. Far less than the specialist does the student from another field need to fix in his mind a multitude of facts already discovered and verified. These facts and formulas may be necessary parts of the equipment that a specialist requires for further work in the field; hence to him they are important in themselves. To a non-specialist, however, the facts and formulas are significant as examples, as the fruits of successful inquiry, as tests of the validity of some process of reasoning. Few are so important that they must be remembered for their own sakes.

To have solved a quadratic equation is the vital thing if one wishes to grasp the nature of algebraic reasoning. Whether to memorize the general formula of solution depends entirely on one's future use for it. Similarly, to have weighed historical evidence in order to reach a conclusion and to have explored the problems of historical causality are the crucial matters. The number of specific historical facts that the student remembers is of secondary importance. Actually a student will remember a great many facts without special effort if he has really entered into the process of investigation which produced them. His score on a factual test is thus an indirect, nor a direct, measure of what he has learned. It can be a fairly reliable test (if not abused by the get-rich-quick technique of factual "cramming"), because the student who has thought a lot will remember a lot, and the student who remembers nothing has probably never thought at all. Memory and disciplined thinking do go hand in hand, but we must never forget that it is the latter that really counts.

So far as "general" education is concerned, these considerations lead to a conclusion the opposite of the one ordinarily accepted. The course for the non-specialist should emphasize theoretical reasoning to an even greater extent than the course for the specialist. The latter needs to know—and hence should be drilled to remember—facts, conclusions, and formulas for which the non-specialist has little use once he has grasped the reasoning involved. In practice, colleges and universities have acted upon a contrary premise. Courses originally planned for specialists have been adapted for general students by eliminating or reducing the discussion of methodology and theory, and crowding in as much purely factual information as possible. Such courses advance neither intellectual discipline nor mutual understanding among educated men.

If this reasoning is correct, the proper introduction to each of the great areas of knowledge is a rigorous course, emphasizing intellectual processes, in one of the fundamental disciplines lying within the area. In certain fields it may be desirable to create for the non-specialist a course somewhat different in structure and emphasis from that offered to the future specialist. In the sciences, for example, it is possible that a study of crucial principles in the historical order of their discovery (as President Conant has suggested) might be more effective for the non-specialist than the study of them in the systematic order in which they need to be known by the man who is to do research in the field. Two courses, equally rigorous and equally thorough in their use of laboratory techniques, are a possibility here. Needless to say, when alternative courses are offered, there ought never to be a qualitative difference between them. Every course must discipline the mind of every student who enrolls in it. In actual fact, however, separate courses in most fields are quite unnecessary. The typical introductory course in college would serve the needs of both specialists and non-specialists more effectively if it were reorganized in such a way as to pay *more* attention than at present to methodology, to rigorous thinking, and to abstract theory. If, however, classes for non-specialists seem necessary, the instructors in charge should eschew the encyclopedic approach, should select with care the topics that exemplify basic methodological and theoretical questions, and should concentrate upon making perfectly clear the kinds of thinking involved.[2]

Courses alone, even though properly organized for the non-specialist, will not guarantee breadth of intellectual understanding. A plan of study outside the field of specialization is needed. And American colleges are only gradually emerging from an era of complete planlessness. The free-elective system has long since proved a faulty answer to the questions raised for education by the increasing complexity of modern knowledge. It did not solve the problem of integrating the new disciplines into an ordered structure of learning; it simply dodged the problem. Under the free-elective system, two programs of study might contain no element whatever in common. Worse than that, the very mechanics of the free-elective system put all subjects on a par with one another, and tended even to treat advanced courses as if they were quantitatively equivalent to elementary ones. It fostered the belief that a man acquires a liberal education by adding so many hours in one classroom to so many hours in another until he has served his time in full.

American colleges have begun to put behind them the follies of the free-elective system. But at best they have usually done no more than apply palliatives to the evil. A college may force the student to make his choices in such a way that each of the broad areas of knowledge is represented somewhere and in some fashion among the array of courses he offers for the degree. Or the college may institute omnibus courses designed to "survey" each of these broad areas for the student, usually in his freshman or sophomore year. Or it may seek in some other mechanical way to produce unity by adding together disunities.

It must do a great deal more than this if it is really to restore among liberally educated men a sense of participating in and compre-

[2] The principles I have in mind are admirably exemplified by the series of *Select Problems in Historical Interpretation* prepared for use in undergraduate courses by various members of the Department of History at Yale, and by the proposals for scientific instruction embodied in James B. Conant's *On Understanding Science*.

hending the varied ways of thinking that belong to modern intellectual life. To devise an adequate scheme for that part of liberal education which aims to give a student breadth of understanding is far more difficult than to devise a scheme for that part which aims at intensive, specialized knowledge. The difficulties are not insurmountable, however, provided we make clear to ourselves exactly what we are after. We have failed, I think, to do this, and we have masked our confusions under vague and undefined terms like "general education."

The last-mentioned phrase has gained widespread currency in the United States since the end of World War II, thanks largely, I suppose, to the prestige of the Harvard report on *General Education in a Free Society* (1945). In that document, as I read its arguments, "general education" was simply a synonym for "liberal education." The report dealt with education in the basic intellectual disciplines, and it proposed various means for introducing students more effectively than before to a wider range of such disciplines. There was nothing anti-intellectual in its recommendations, but the term "general education," which was unfortunately chosen to describe them, was sufficiently ambiguous to be applied elsewhere to almost any kind of pseudo-educational program. On many campuses university administrators announced that they were following in the footsteps of Harvard, and proceeded to set up rambling, catch-all courses, geared to the meager abilities of the marginal student. In teacher-training institutions the professional educationists seized upon the term with glee and promptly introduced into the curriculum college versions of "life-adjustment" training. At one state teachers' college that I visited, a faculty member asked me in all seriousness whether a course in general education was not the proper place to teach good table manners to college students. Since "general education" has come to signify, in so many institutions, complete educational inanity, we ought to abandon the term forthwith and restore the traditional phrase "liberal education," which, despite frequent misuse, has never suffered such utter degradation as the new one.

To get back to first principles, liberal education involves three distinct kinds of intellectual training. It aims to give a student thorough, and hence creative, command of one discipline. It undertakes, in addition, to give him control over the basic and related intellectual skills that are necessary to successful work in his field of specialization. Finally, it seeks to give him breadth of intellectual understanding.

The last two of these objectives are not very clearly differentiated in most college programs. They need to be, if we are to deal effectively with the problems involved. For the sake of clarity. I should like to avail myself, in the paragraphs that follow, of a more or less arbitrary terminology. The term "major" will be given its usual meaning, the discipline in which a student specializes. The term "supporting fields" will be used to describe the work a student needs to do in the disciplines that are closely related to his "major." And the term "minor" will be used to describe the work outside the "major" and the "supporting fields"—the work, that is, which is designed to produce breadth of comprehension. This special usage needs to be borne in mind, for at present the term "minor" is used sometimes for the work in what I call the "supporting fields," and sometimes for that which I too call the "minor."

The fields that are necessary to "support" sound specialization include both the basic intellectual disciplines of general applicability, and the specialized disciplines that fall within the same general area as the "major." An adequately trained chemist, for example, requires knowledge of mathematics (one of the disciplines of general applicability) and also of physics (one of the related specialized disciplines). Similarly a well-trained historian requires knowledge of foreign languages and also of economics. For the most part the training in the disciplines of general applicability ought to be completed in the secondary school, and rigorous college entrance examinations should take care of the matter. Once minimum standards in English grammar and composition, in mathematics, and in foreign languages (at least one, and preferably two) are assured for college matriculation, the further requirements in these disciplines should be established in terms of the actual demands of each major field. Likewise, a rational plan of study in the related "supporting" disciplines needs to be worked out for each field of specialization. These requirements, it should be noted, are in the interests of sound specialization. They do not, by themselves, completely solve the problem of securing breadth of intellectual understanding.

The latter problem, indeed, is the most difficult of any that can arise in liberal education. Present-day attempts to solve it have proved, in my judgment, quite unsatisfactory. The existing "distribution" requirements of most colleges—that is, the requirements that specify work in a number of different areas—are at once too impatient, too mechanical, too ambitious, and yet too distrustful. They are too impatient because they do not take into account the time required to achieve a mature grasp of a subject. They are too mechanical because they do not go beyond scattering a student's effort. They are too ambitious because they expect an undergraduate to range over more fields than he is really capable of assimilating. And they are too distrustful because they assume no ability on the part of an individual to enlarge his range of intellectual powers through his own efforts.

It takes time to acquire a usable command of any intellectual discipline. This seems to me the most neglected fact in American educational thinking. Psychologists and physiologists make use of a concept that is relevant here. A stimulus must reach a certain intensity before it can produce a response. This critical point is called the *threshold*. Below the critical point the stimulus might as well not exist so far as any observable reaction is concerned. There is, it seems to me, such a critical point or threshold in intellectual training. The study of a foreign language, for example, if pursued for only a single school year, does not bring the knowledge of the language up to the threshold where it produces the desired response in the student—namely, a sense of being at home in the language. American colleges usually proceed on the theory that at least two college years of language study are necessary to reach this threshold. I believe, incidentally, that this figure is too low, but the important fact is that a threshold is tacitly recognized in the learning of a foreign language. My conviction is that such a critical point or threshold exists for every intellectual discipline, and that to disregard it is to doom any educational program to futility.

Unless we bring a student's command of a discipline beyond the threshold, we give him nothing that he can use for ordinary working purposes. We leave him bewildered and uncomprehending. Instead of opening a door for him, we may actually slam it shut. In the early stages of learning a new discipline, the student is mainly impressed with how much there is to be known and how unfamiliar and hence difficult the processes of reasoning are. Only when he reaches the threshold does he acquire pleasure and confidence as the reward of his labors. If we cut him off before he reaches the critical point, we frustrate the process of learning. The student carries his discouragement away with him, and usually convinces himself that he could never have mastered the discipline sufficiently well to make it a part of his own thinking. Thereafter he makes no real effort to understand it.

As a psychological compensation he is apt to convert what is actually self-distrust into active distaste for the discipline that he feels has betrayed him. If he becomes a teacher he communicates this feeling to his students, and they go through life with blindspots for certain disciplines, most of which are simply the consequence of bad teaching. The distaste of many students for mathematics, I firmly believe (and many mathematicians with me), is a measure of the number of elementary- and secondary-school teachers who are frightened of the subject because they have never been required to bring their command of it up to the threshold of genuine comprehension. And the neglect of foreign languages—one of the gravest weaknesses of our educational system—seems to me the result of a vicious circle, originating in the shame that most American teachers (including a great number of university scholars) feel, but suppress, concerning their own linguistic inadequacies.

This situation must be corrected in the elementary and secondary schools which are, with devastating success, killing off every budding intellectual interest by refusing to carry forward any disciplined study to the point where the student passes the threshold into confidence and enjoyment. In the college we must avoid the same mistake when we try to counter the evils of overspecialization. If we send a student into a multitude of courses without making sure that his knowledge of each discipline reaches the all-important critical point, we run the risk of producing not breadth but an almost neurotic narrowness of mind.

In my judgment, the college should approach the problem of producing intellectual breadth in a quite different way from the one it has customarily followed. I have already pointed out that the distinctively different ways of thinking are limited in number. There is another fact to be noted. For any given discipline there is another in which the processes of thought are of an almost opposite character. The discipline of chemistry, for example, is at an opposite pole from the discipline of literary criticism. The process of inductive generalization in history stands in the sharpest possible contrast with the process of deductive reasoning characteristic of mathematics. The college of liberal arts and sciences, I suggest, should recognize this fact and make it the principal basis of its efforts to encourage a wide-ranging comprehension on the part of students.

To be specific, I propose that the college should require each student to offer (besides his "major" and his work in its "supporting fields") a "minor" in some discipline that is as remote as possible, in its way of thinking, from the one to which his principal efforts are devoted. A physicist, for example, should choose his minor from one of the humanities; an economist from one of the biological sciences. Such a minor would not be a mere collection of courses, but a systematic program of study, which would bring the student well beyond the threshold of genuine understanding. Other plans, admittedly, disperse a student's efforts more widely, but dispersed effort is no virtue in an educational program. Dispersed effort is usually halfhearted effort. One virtue of such a minor as I have described would be that it would guarantee that all a student's work—outside his own field as well as in it—would be equally serious, equally rigorous, and equally productive of demonstrable intellectual power.

Would not such a program provide the essential basis for the intellectual breadth we are really seeking, and for the mutual understanding among educated men which we so desperately need? The danger in specialization is that a man will fail to recognize that there

are cogent ways of thinking markedly different from those he customarily employs. This realization can be brought home to him by giving
him a thorough grasp of one such divergent way of thinking. This
experience should teach him, if he is a truly thoughtful man, that
every disciplined field has its rationale and its reason for existence. It
should teach him that no field is beyond his grasp, if only he will
devote the requisite effort to understanding it. The arrogance that arises
from narrow specialization will dissolve, and real unity of intellectual
life will emerge. The liberally educated man will overcome the barriers
that now keep specialists from fruitful conversation and collaboration.
The liberally educated teacher (and all teachers should be such) will
be able to explain to students of divergent temperament the processes
of thinking in his own field because he will be able to relate them to
processes of thinking in fields of remote and opposite character.

If the college aims to give a student true breadth of understanding,
it should abandon the hopeless task of acquainting him with every
one of the disciplines. Instead it should bring the student's efforts to
a focus, first of all upon his own discipline with its related fields,
then upon some discipline far beyond the normal horizon of his specialty. We cannot (to change the metaphor) enable him to conquer
the whole world of learning in one undergraduate career. We can,
however, assist him to win a foothold on two different continents.
Thereafter we ought to be content to trust him, as an educated man,
to plant his banner in whatever province he wishes and win control
of it by his own efforts.

In the last analysis, moreover, the synthesis of knowledge must be
the student's own achievement. Only the things that he can bring together in his own mind has he really learned. Only the intellectual
skills that he can co-ordinate for his own purposes has he really mastered. It is the responsibility of the college not only to offer the courses
that might produce such intellectual powers, but also to satisfy itself
that the student has in fact acquired them. The degree should be
awarded only when the college is so satisfied. Indispensable to a sound
college program of liberal arts is a comprehensive examination at the
end. This should test the student's command not only of his own

discipline, but also, if possible, of the "supporting" fields that are a necessary part of fruitful specialization. Many colleges require such examinations; every college worthy of recognition should require them.

A way should also be found to examine the student's command of the field remote from his own that he has elected to study, lest the work there be considered by him a mere accumulation of credit hours. A comprehensive examination in this minor field of concentration, administered perhaps at the end of the sophomore or junior year, should form part of the pattern of the college which strives for genuine breadth and balance in its program. And if the work in the minor field is validated by an examination, then the field itself can safely be set up, if desired, on an interdisciplinary basis.

Liberal education—in both its specialized and its generalized aspects —can be placed on a sound basis only if we restore to the college curriculum as a whole the intellectual vitality that has so largely departed from it in recent years. We are not producing men and women with a general and liberal education by requiring students to elect specified fragments of a curriculum that has been pulverized into unrelated three-semester-hour courses, and in which the distinction between elementary and advanced work has been forgotten. We are not producing them by adding more "survey" courses. We shall not produce them until we go back to first principles and create a college curriculum which, as a whole and in its interrelated parts, provides ordered and progressive training in the various forms of disciplined thought. When we do this we shall at last train up specialists who are scholars and scientists in the highest sense, and citizens who are truly educated men. Liberal education will then become a reality, because it will introduce all men alike into that world of disciplined thought where scholars and reflective citizens meet on common ground.

*One of America's leading
scholars in the humanities,
French-born Jacques Barzun
(1907–   ) was admitted to
Columbia University at fifteen
and has been connected with the
university as student and teacher
nearly ever since. A prolific
writer, Barzun has published
books on education, art, music,
literature, and culture. In 1958
he was appointed Dean of the
Faculties and Provost at Columbia, in which capacity he
delivered this address before
a 1963 convocation celebrating
the first anniversary of Hofstra's
existence as a university.
Located at Hempstead, L.I.,
that institution had previously
been a college, since its founding in 1935.*

12

College to University— And After

JACQUES BARZUN

It is an honor and a pleasure to attend this ceremony
which marks the first year of
a notable change in the life
of an important institution.
Although everyone is clear
about the nature of that
change, one does not quite
know what to call it: one does
not want to say the "transformation" of Hofstra College
into Hofstra University, because the College remains;
one does not want to say the
"elevation" of the one into
the other, for the College

stands high and any University would be doing well to keep level with it. Finally, one does not want to say the "graduation" of the college—that metaphor is obviously the worst of all. Let us then simply say that Hofstra, following the natural course of things in American higher education, has become a university, having first proved its worth to the demanding public of our day, and received from the guardians of our state system the authority to assume the more comprehensive name.

I shall try in a moment to tell you some of the things that this new name suggests to me—and what it may mean to the country in the future. Right now, as the privileged representative of a sister institution which went through the same mutation eighty years ago, I take leave to congratulate the trustees, the faculty, the students, and the friends of Hofstra on this happy occasion. It is the culmination of many hopes, of a generous vision, of skillful management, and of much hard work, in which the efforts of teachers and students were the determining cause of success. All honor to these men and women, young and old, who for nearly a third of a century have, in the pursuit of their own work, changed the connotation of the name Hofstra from that of a public-spirited family to that of a respected seat of learning. Such an achievement is in its quiet way a victory of mind and will, daily renewed, over the forces of error and inertia, over the temptations of sloth and stupidity. It is altogether right that we should rejoice and be grateful to the makers of this spiritual edifice, in which the students now here and those to come can develop and thrive with greater ease, quite as if colleges and universities grew by a natural process, like vegetables.

What I have been saying so far expresses my feelings as an academic delegate to Hofstra University, as a colleague of its members and as a well-wisher to all its works. Now, with your permission, I should like to take a few moments to speak as a detached observer of the larger scene in which the deeds of this day are taking place. What I want to say still has to do with colleges and universities; but it should not be taken as a statement of policy by a university administrator, much less as a program for the future of your university or my own. I want

for a few minutes to impersonate the private citizen who looks about
him and forms opinions—opinions which may be wrong, but which
are at any rate free from partisanship and from professional clichés. Let
me repeat that I am not going to *do* anything in pursuance of my
remarks—neither start a campaign nor establish an association with
seven initials spelling the word Hofstra—I shall not even argue with
anyone who disagrees with me.

I have just said that I mean to talk about colleges and universities.
In casual speech we lump the two together as if they were small variations each of the other. No one here today can continue to think so:
there are between a college and a university great differences, which
justify our celebration. And we all know what the chief of these differences is: a university gives instruction in professional subjects, gives
degrees that open to a man or woman the professions of teaching,
medicine, law, business, and the rest. More professions are born every
year, for which people qualify by taking combinations of university
subjects. Whenever we speak of the country's need for experts in all
fields, we imply the existence of universities to provide the training.
Nor must we forget the growing shadow of every profession, which is
Research, and for which more and more people must be prepared, since
so many agencies, public and private, offer positions of comfort and
prestige to competent researchers.

Let me remind you that this national concern is not new or alien
to the American university. A hundred years ago, the American university was created on top of the American college to fill this same
need of national leaders in government and the professions. You can
on this point read the testimony of John W. Burgess, the founder of
the School of Political Science at Columbia, which proved to be the
first graduate faculty in the United States. Burgess wanted to prevent
through better statesmanship and a wiser public opinion a repetition
of the catastrophe of the Civil War, in which he had been caught as
a youth of seventeen. He wanted native universities so as to train well-
informed public servants—teachers, politicians, diplomats, journalists,
captains of industry. This training was to rest upon the solid base of
college instruction in what he called "universal history and general
literature."

Today, the urge to train has been enlarged by the vast complication of our technological life and the increasing numbers of our population —you know at first hand the intricate details and crushing pressure of these developments. But in all this confusion, what has happened to the American College? Well, there are more colleges than ever before, but I for one find it harder and harder to know what they do and why. There is a very fine sentence in the *Hofstra College Bulletin,* which discusses the difference between college education and university training. It states that whereas "training stresses a tangible salable skill . . . education cultivates reasoning ability, creativity, tolerance, eagerness for new ideas, a sense of history and of potentialities for the future." This is very sanguine, as it should be, but what is the reality? The reality is that the best colleges today are being invaded, not to say dispossessed, by the advance agents of the professions, by men who want to seize upon the young recruit as soon as may be and train him in a "tangible salable skill."

This at any rate is true in the colleges attached to universities. Consider the forces at work. First, it seems desirable to have the great scholar teach undergraduates, and he naturally teaches them as if they were future scholars in his own line, as professionals. Then, the young themselves want to get on as quickly as possible, and in the last two years of college they elect a major which relates directly to their future profession. If they are able, they qualify for honors work, which may be defined as premature research. An even stronger influence is that of the young teachers, all Ph.D.'s, who need to establish themselves. This they can do only in one way: by showing productivity in research. Every moment spent otherwise is wasted. Accordingly, these junior scholars decline to teach anything not related to their own specialties. As one of them said to me, they "do not want to teach second-hand subjects." First-hand subjects are necessarily narrow, and what is worse, they are treated as if everyone in the class were to become a professional, a duplicate of his own teacher.

In short, both teachers and students are responding to the spirit of the times. They are impatient with everything that is not directed at the development of talent into competence. The undergraduate who can assist his instructor in the instructor's research, the youth who can get an essay published in a journal, the senior whose program is half made up of graduate courses—these are the models for general envy and emulation. The meaning of this is plain: *the liberal arts tradition is dead or dying.* We may keep talking about the liberal ideals at Commencement but the Commencement platform is their last and only refuge. During the year, the college pursues a professional ideal; during the summer, those who can afford it accelerate. And that acceleration has only one goal—to qualify for a professional job.

Please understand that I am not objecting or criticizing, but only describing. The trend seems to me so clear that to object would be like trying to sweep back the ocean. It would be foolish to repine or try to prolong a tradition which has run its course. It is far better to understand how we come to be where we are, for at the present moment the idea of a university is as confused as the situation of the college. The reasons are evident: the great movement for General Education, which began after the First World War, has in forty years transformed our entire precollegiate schooling. The good high school now gives the historical surveys, the introductions to social science, the great books, that formed the substance of general education. What is more, the Advanced Placement Program has managed to fill in the old vacuum of the eleventh and twelfth grades with real work, so that more and more freshmen—even without Advance Placement—find the first year of college feeble and repetitious. They've had the calculus; they've had a grown-up course in American history; they've read Homer and Tolstoy—college holds for them no further revelations; it no longer marks the passage from pupil to student, from make-believe exercises to real thought. So that if we stand off and look at the silhouette of the American College—I speak of the solid and serious ones, not the shaky imitation—what we see is the thinning and flattening out of its once distinctive curriculum under pressure from above and below, the high school taking away the lower years; the graduate and professional schools the upper.

What then is happening to the beautiful notion of developing the imaginative and the reasoning powers apart from marketable skill and professional competence? What is happening to contemplation and the cultivation of sensibility and judgment? What is happening to "the four happiest years of my life"? The last boon, certainly, has vanished. If colleges were ever places of elegant leisure, they are so no longer. Look about you on the campus and all you see is anxious preoccupation. Students are married, employed, going to or returning from a conference, apprehensive about examinations, ruled by the clock like the most harried executive. They are not in cloistered halls but in the midst of life—which is why so many are also in the midst of psychiatric treatment.

But the vanishing college and the proliferation of worldly activities on its campus do not mean that the university succeeds in training happy young professionals. They are not happier or younger than they would be if they still enjoyed four years of maturing in the old atmosphere of apparently useless study. They are not younger when they find their footing, because competition forces them to go into postgraduate work—one sheepskin to one sheep is no longer enough. And they are not happier because the professional invasion of college teaching makes for dullness, poor preparation, and a new kind of pretense. No undergradute can believe that he is going to be at the same time an anthropologist, a Milton scholar, an historian, and a chemist. Yet that is what the modern teaching assumes about him in successive hours of the college day. This is bad enough for a boy; it is ridiculous for a girl. The motive to study is inevitably lacking in at least three out of four classes when so conducted, that is, when the listener is not addressed as a person or a citizen, but only as that dreadful model of our age: the useful member of society who must be clothed in qualifications and armed with licenses to practice.

Oddly enough, while the liberal arts college, abetted by the graduate school, is squeezing out the old liberal education, the chief professional schools still ask for it in their candidates for admission. The law schools want students who know some history and can read English; the medical schools want well-rounded men; and the engineering schools profess the greatest respect for the humanities and social sciences. In practice, admissions committees often betray these principles and prefer the candidate whose record shows a positive gluttony for science and mathematics. The committee may be right, although the fair words persist. The upshot is that nowadays the only true believers in the liberal arts tradition are the men of business. They *really* prefer general intelligence, literacy and adaptability. They know, in the first place, that the conditions of their work change so rapidly that no college courses can prepare for it. And they also know how often men in mid-career suddenly feel that their work is not enough to sustain their spirits. Such men turn to the arts, to disinterested reading, in a word to self-cultivation as means of keeping their souls alive. Some business firms even provide instruction of this sort to their care-worn executives —seminars in Plato and round tables on political science—in hopes of restoring the energies by feeding an organ of the soul that has been starved during the professional career. This starvation occurs not only in business but also in the other professions, which are growing more and more like business in their paper-pushing aspects.

Obviously, if starvation by routine has killed off the intellectual appetites there will be nothing to restore; and it is likely that no appetite will last very long if it is neglected from the age of sixteen, when it is just becoming aware of itself. What follows? What follows is a proposition you may cry out against, but which seems to me implied in the situation before us: sooner or later the college as we know it will find that it has no proper place in the scheme of things. It will find that the secondary school has added a year or two to its present curriculum; that the graduate school has kidnapped all the college juniors and seniors into its own departments. All that will be left in college is the dean, and he is the most expendable of creatures.

If this happens—and I ask you to remember that I shall do nothing to bring it about, but on the contrary everything to retard it; if this happens—I say, *if*: then the students and the professions and the universities and the nation will benefit in a number of ways. The cost will be emotionally great: we all feel an attachment to that unique institution, the American college. On the strength of this feeling millions "want to go to college" without quite knowing what they may expect from it. In the past, their innocent hopes were not disappointed; now it is the best colleges that disappoint the most, for the reasons I mentioned. So the first benefit of the change will be that students' natural desire for exploring the world of ideas will be fed by secondary school teachers, who still believe and practice general education, instead of deserting their charges to indulge in research.

Next, the professions and the university which trains for them will benefit in having their students' exclusive attention. Finally, that concentrated training can begin a couple of years earlier than now; therefore, the country will benefit through a fresher and larger supply of professionals. Acceleration may then become normal and calm, instead of being special and frantic. All this will occur if—I say again, if—the colleges follow, consciously or unconsciously, the tendency evident in their actions for the last dozen years. Their unrest, their sense of futility, are shown in recent proposals to cut the normal course to three years, or to add a fifth year that would bring with it a graduate degree; their impatience is visible in the programs that lead to a four years' master's degree in teaching, or to a Ph.D. in chemistry in six years, or to various other degrees more quickly by a telescoping of the upper years. This disquiet can only grow as the high schools improve and the freshman grows bored, as students begin college in the sophomore year and university work begins in the junior or senior year. At this moment, when one lends an ear, it seems as if a good many bolts were loose in the machine and even though it keeps running, the noises it makes are not reassuring.

All the more reason why we should have at hand the strongest universities we can fashion. Universities are not in any sense a substitute for the college. The mood and tenor of the liberal arts differ from professional training and purpose exactly as the *Hofstra Bulletin* says, and the liberal arts cannot be dispensed with permanently. The question is where to situate them, how to administer them, whom to entrust them to. And in these high matters a strong university which knows what its role is can assist, advise and protect. It can require and enforce the right preparation of its candidates for professional training. In a word, a clear-minded university can dispel both error and confusion. That is why today I am glad that one more university has been added to the older strongholds of learning in the country.

*In 1932 Clark Kerr (1911–   )
was one of 113 graduating
seniors at Pennsylvania's Swarthmore College. In 1967 he ended
a nine-year term as president of
the huge University of California
complex (then embracing some
87,000 students and 7,500 professors on nine campuses). A
noted labor economist, Kerr had
considerable success as a labor
mediator before he brought his
talents to the direction of the
largest university in the nation.
In 1963 he delivered a lecture
series at Harvard, published as*
The Uses of the University, *in
which he coined the term
"multiversity." This article is
adapted largely from those
lectures.*

13

The Frantic Race to Remain Contemporary

CLARK KERR

"The true American University," David Starr Jordan once observed, "lies in the future." It still does; for American universities have not yet developed their full identity, their unique theory of purpose and function. They still look to older and to foreign models, although less and less; and the day is coming when these models will no longer serve at all.

The American university is currently undergoing its second great transformation. The first occurred during roughly the last quarter of the nineteenth century, when the land grant movement and German intellectualism were together bringing extraordinary change. The current transformation will cover roughly the quarter century after World War II. The university is being called upon to educate previously unimagined numbers of students; to respond to the expanding claims of government and industry and other segments of society as never before; to adapt to and channel new intellectual currents. By the end of this period, there will be a truly American university, an institution unique in world history, an institution not looking to other models but itself serving as a model for universities in other parts of the globe. This is not said in boast. It is simply that the imperatives that are molding the American university are also at work around the world.

Each nation, at it has become influential, has tended to develop the leading intellectual institutions of its world—Greece, the Italian cities, France, Spain, England, Germany, and now the United States. The great universities have developed in the great periods of the great political entities of history. Today, more than ever, education is inextricably involved in the quality of a nation. And the university, in particular, has become in America, and in other nations as well, a prime instrument of national purpose. This is new. This is the essence of the transformation now engulfing our universities.

American universities are currently facing four great areas of related adjustments: (1) growth, (2) shifting academic emphases, (3) involvement in the life of society, and (4) response to the new federal involvement. The direction of adjustment in each of these areas is reasonably clear; the detailed arrangements and the timing are not. There are several other areas where adjustments will be necessary but where the direction of adjustment is as yet by no means clear; and four such areas will also be noted below.

GROWTH

The number of university and college students in the United States will almost double during the 1960's. This addition of three million will duplicate in one decade the growth of the three centuries since Harvard was founded. The proportion of graduate students will rise considerably, and there are already 25,000 post-doctoral students.

Existing university campuses are being enlarged and many new ones founded. The University of California, for example, now has seven campuses and a total enrollment of 65,000 students. Four of those campuses will triple or more in size in the next decade. One campus admitting undergraduates for the first time this fall, and two entirely new campuses admitting students for the first time in 1965, are being planned to accommodate ultimate enrollments of 27,500 each.

But university expansion alone cannot begin to meet the demand for some kind of education beyond the high school level. In the years before World War II, post-high school study was the exception; it is rapidly becoming the norm. In California today four out of every five high school graduates seek further education; soon it will be even more. This great shift in the pattern of American education will call for many more four-year colleges, both public and private. And a particularly large number of junior colleges will be formed as the community college movement becomes nationwide. Problems of differentiation of function will arise among public sectors of higher education—junior colleges, four-year colleges, and universities—as they compete for state support. The State of California has already met that problem through legislative adoption of a Master Plan for Higher Education, and other states are working along similar lines. However the total demand for higher education may be parceled out among the public and private institutions of varying types, one fact is clear: this will be the most unprecedented period of campus development in American history, or indeed in the history of the entire world.

To accommodate the great increase in enrollments, many academic calendars are being rearranged, particularly in state-supported institutions, to permit more nearly year-round use of physical facilities. Students will be able to accelerate their work if they wish, and general students will come and go with less reference to their "class"; more of them will drop in and drop out as suits their particular schedules and needs.

There will be some further mechanization of instruction (television, language laboratories, programmed learning) to improve quality and to save faculty time for other endeavors, including more individual work with students. The sciences will almost eagerly embrace these aids to learning. The foreign language departments will be rather reluctant, because these devices can threaten their structure of faculty employment and the recruitment and utilization of graduate students.

Because of the competition for faculty members, salaries will continue to rise; fringe benefits of all sorts will be devised to tie professors to a particular campus. In addition to competition among universities, there is also intensified competition with industry and government. This competition has obvious advantages in raising faculty income, but it has its negative aspects. As the market becomes more active, internal equity will be injured, for some disciplines are much more in demand in the market than others. Teaching loads will be competitively reduced, sometimes to zero, although more teachers are needed and students are complaining about lack of attention. The identification of the professor with his university will be generally loosened—he will become more a member of a free-floating profession. The rules regarding how much time a professor can spend away from his university assignments, and those affecting the sources of his income within the university, will continue to be in great flux.

This current phenomenon of rising salaries and benefits, however, may be of relatively short duration, lasting, perhaps, for the remainder of this decade. Faculty salaries have been catching up with incomes in other professions after a historical lag. By 1970, also, the personnel deficit of today may be turning into the surplus of tomorrow as all the new Ph.D.'s roll into the market. A new plateau of compensation may be reached in the 1970's.

In addition to the great expansion of individual institutions of higher learning, there will be an increasing tendency for university centers to cooperate and even coalesce for added strength, particularly in their graduate and research programs. Allan Nevins has put it this way: "Observers of higher education can now foresee the inexorable emergence of an entirely new landscape. It will no longer show us a nation dotted by high academic peaks with lesser hills between; it will be a landscape dominated by mountain ranges." The highest peaks of the future will rise from the highest plateaus.

One such plateau runs from Boston to Washington. At the universities and laboratories situated along this range are found 46 per cent of the American Nobel Prize winners in the sciences and 40 per cent of the members of the National Academy of Sciences. A second range with its peaks runs along the California coast. C. P. Snow has written: "And now the scientific achievement of the United States is moving at a rate we all ought to marvel at. Think of the astonishing constellation of talent, particularly in the physical sciences, all down the California coast, from Berkeley and Stanford to Pasadena and Los Angeles. There is nothing like that concentration of talent anywhere in the world. It sometimes surprises Europeans to realize how much of the pure science of the entire West is being carried out in the United States. Curiously enough, it often surprises Americans too. At a guess, the figure is something like 80 per cent and might easily be higher."

The California mountain range has 36 per cent of the Nobel laureates in science and 20 per cent of the members of the National Academy of Sciences. The Big Ten and Chicago constitute a third range of academic peaks, with 10 per cent of the Nobel laureates and 14 per cent of the members of the National Academy of Sciences. These three groupings of universities—the East Coast, California, and the Big Ten and Chicago—currently produce over three quarters of the doctorates conferred in the United States. Another range may be in the process of development in the Texas-Louisiana area.

This concentration of talent partly follows history—the location of the older private and public universities. Partly it follows industrial strengths and population centers. But it also has its own logic. No one university can cover all specialties, or cover them well enough so that there is a sufficient cluster of close intellectual colleagues. The scholar dislikes intellectual isolation, and good scholars tend to swarm together. These swarms are extraordinarily productive environments. No library can be complete, nor any graduate curriculum. Some laboratories, to be well used, must be used by more than one university. Thus the Big

Ten and Chicago, through their Committee on Institutional Cooperation, are merging their library resources, creating a "common market"
for graduate students, diversifying their research laboratories on a com-
mon-use basis, and parceling out foreign language specializations. Something similar is happening in the University of California system, and
between Berkeley and Stanford. Harvard and M.I.T., Princeton and
Pennsylvania, among others, run joint research enterprises. These clustering universities in turn have clustering around them scientifically
oriented industrial and governmental enterprises. To match the drawing
power of the great metropolis, there now arrives the Ideopolis. The
isolated mountain can no longer dominate the landscape; the constellation is greater than the single star and adds to the brightness of the sky.

The rate of growth being forced upon American universities and
colleges by the surging enrollment wave will present difficult problems.
As President Johnson said in his 1964 Commencement address at the
University of Michigan: ". . . more classrooms and more teachers are
not enough. We must seek an educational system which grows in
excellence as it grows in size." A period of rapid growth is necessarily
a period of both flexibility and ingenuity. Institutions can readily adopt
on new campuses ideas and programs that would require costly reorganization on older campuses. The University of California, for
example, is building its new Santa Cruz campus as a series of small
residential colleges, each with its own subject field orientation. The
University's new Irvine campus will explore ways of involving organized
research units in the formal process of instruction. The new San Diego
campus of the university will subdivide its ultimate enrollment of
27,500 students into a series of smaller colleges, with groups of four
such colleges constituting largely self-contained sub-campuses of varying
academic emphases. The University of the Pacific, in Stockton, California, has established a new residential college in which the entire
curriculum is conducted in Spanish. Thus the enrollment explosion
may bring unusual opportunities for colleges and universities, along
with the heavy burden of numbers.

The current surge in higher education is not, of course, unique to
the United States. In Canada the proportion of eighteen- to twenty-

one-year olds in higher education is expected to double in the decade from 1962 to 1972. In France the total enrollment in higher education is expected to soar from around 200,000 now to 500,000 by 1970. In Britain, the much-discussed Robbins Committee Report recommends doubling the number of universities by 1980. These figures reflect the rapidly growing pressures resulting from a vast increase in secondary enrollments throughout much of the world. The decade of the 1950's has seen a world increase of 81 per cent in secondary enrollments and an increase of 71 per cent in college enrollments.

The data both from this country and abroad clearly indicate that we are witnessing everywhere the demise of two long-held notions: that higher education ought to be restricted to a small elite minority, and that only a small percentage of a country's population is capable of benefiting from some kind of higher education. Growth is having quite uneven impacts on American universities. Some, and they are almost always private, are building walls around themselves as aristocratic enclaves protected from the swirling currents of the population explosion. Others, and they are mostly public, are engulfed with more than their share of accommodation to the new hordes, that do not wish to be barbarous, advancing through their gates. The aristocratic enclave offers refuge to the faculty member who wishes protection from the new invasion, and many do; but it will become a more and more isolated element within the society of the future. The university with the open door will suffer the pangs of adjustment, but it will become in the process a more central element in a dynamic society. The one will be a pleasant place to be but increasingly out of tune with the surrounding society. The other will be a less pleasant place to live but will provide a more challenging and exciting environment, and will be more a part of the evolving life around it. Each will have its place, but the places they occupy will grow farther and farther apart.

SHIFTING ACADEMIC EMPHASES

A second major factor in the changing scene for American higher education is that knowledge is exploding along with population. There is also an explosion in the need for certain skills. The university is responding to all these explosions.

The vastly increased needs for engineers, scientists, and physicians will draw great resources to these areas of the university. Also, some new professions are being born. Others are becoming more formally professional, for example, business administration and social work. The university becomes the chief port of entry for these professions. In fact a profession gains its identity by making the university the port of entry. This creates new roles for education; but it is also part of the process of freezing the structure of the occupational pyramid and assuring that the well-behaved do advance, even if the geniuses do not. The university is used as an egg-candling device; and it is, perhaps, a better one than any other that can be devised, but the process takes some of the adventure out of occupational survival, and does for some professions what the closed shop has done for some unions. The life of the universities for a thousand years has been tied into the recognized professions in the surrounding society, and the universities will continue to respond as new professions arise.

The fastest-growing intellectual field today is biology. Here there is a veritable revolution where the doctrine of evolution once reigned supreme. To the classifying efforts of the past are being added the new analytical methods of the present, often drawn from chemistry and physics. There are levels of complexity to be explored in all living structures. The "code of life" can now be read; soon it will be understood, and soon after that, used. It is an intellectual discovery of unique and staggering proportions. The secrets of the atom, much as they have changed and are changing human activity on this planet, may hold no greater significance than the secrets still hidden in the genetic code. If the first half of the twentieth century may be said to have belonged to the physical sciences, the second half may well belong to the biological. Resources within the universities will be poured into the new biology and into the resulting new medicine and agriculture, well supported though medicine and agriculture already are. Medical education and research may be, in particular, on the threshold of revolutionary change.

Another field ready to bloom is that of the creative arts, hitherto the ugly duckling or Cinderella of the academic world. America is bursting with creativity in painting, music, literature, the theater, with a vigor equaled in few other parts of the world today. Italy, France, Spain, Germany, Russia, England, the Low Countries have had great periods of cultural flowering. America is having one now. In the arts the universities have been more hospitable to the historian and the critic than to the creator; the latter has found his havens elsewhere. Yet it is the creativity of science that has given the sciences their prestige in the university. Perhaps creativity will do the same again for the humanities, though there may be less new to create than has recently been true in science, and though the tests of value are far less precise. A very important role remains for the historian of past ages of creativity and for the critic of the current productions. But the universities need to find ways also to accommodate pure creative effort if they are to have places on stage as well as in the wings and in the audience in the great drama of cultural growth now playing on the American stage.

These possibilities for expansion—in the training of engineers, scientists, physicians, and the newer professionals, in biology, and in the creative arts, among various others—raise the problem of balance. As James Bryant Conant has noted, the Western world has had for a thousand years a continuing problem of "keeping a balance between the advancement of knowledge, professional education, general education, and the demands of student life."

But the balance is always changing; this is the unbalancing reality. The balance is not equal treatment, the provision of equal time in some mechanical and eternal way between teaching and research, or between the humanities and science. The dynamics of balance did not give equal treatment to the available scientist in Padua in 1300 when Giotto was painting his chapel, or to the available artist in Padua in 1600 when Galileo was lecturing from his crude platform. Balance cannot be determined on the scales by blind justice, field versus field and activity versus activity.

The essence of balance is to match support with the intellectual creativity of subject fields; with the need for skills of the highest level; with the kinds of expert service that society currently most requires.

None of these measures is constant. Balance requires, therefore, a shifting set of judgments which relates facilities and attention to the possibilities inherent in each field, each skill, each activity at that moment of time in that environment, yet preserves for all fields their essential integrity. To know balance is to know the potential creativity, the potential productivity, the potential contribution of each competing activity in an unfolding pattern of time and an evolving landscape of environment. To know balance is to know more than anyone can ever know in advance. But decisions must nevertheless be made, and time will tell how well. The only certainly wrong decision is that the balance of today must be preserved for tomorrow. Where will the world's work and the university's work best be done? The answer to that question is the true definition of balance.

INVOLVEMENT IN THE LIFE OF SOCIETY

The third great change affecting the contemporary university is its thorough-going involvement in the nation's daily life. At the heart of this involvement is the growth of the "knowledge industry," which is coming to permeate government and business and to draw into it more and more people raised to higher and higher levels of skill. The production, distribution, and consumption of "knowledge" in all its forms is said to account for 29 per cent of the gross national product, according to Fritz Machlup's calculations; and "knowledge production" is growing at about twice the rate of the rest of the economy. Knowledge has certainly never in history been so central to the conduct of an entire society. What the railroads did for the second half of the last century and the automobile for the first half of this century may be done for the second half of this century by the knowledge industry: that is, to serve as the focal point for national growth. And the university is at the center of the knowledge process.

So the campus and society are undergoing a somewhat reluctant and cautious merger, already well advanced in some fields. M.I.T. is at least as closely related to industry and government as Iowa State ever was to agriculture. Indeed, universities have become "bait" to be dangled in front of industry, with drawing power greater than low taxes or cheap labor. Route 128 around Boston and the great developing industrial complexes in the San Francisco Bay area and southern California reflect the universities in these areas. The Gilpatric report for the Department of Defense explained that 41 per cent of defense contracts for research in the fiscal year 1961 were concentrated in California, 12 per cent in New York, and 6 per cent in Massachusetts, for a total of nearly 60 per cent, in part because these were also "centers of learning." Sterling Forest outside New York City seeks to attract industry by location next to a new university campus. In California, new industrial laboratories were located next to two new university campuses before the first building was built on either of these campuses. Sometimes industry will reach into a university laboratory to extract the newest ideas almost before they are born. Instead of waiting outside the gates, agents are working the corridors. They also work the placement offices. And the university, in turn, reaches into industry, as through the Stanford Research Institute.

The university and segments of industry are becoming more alike. As the university becomes tied into the world of work, the professor—at least in the natural and some of the social sciences—takes on the characteristics of an entrepreneur. Industry, with its scientists and technicians, learns an uncomfortable bit about academic freedom and the handling of intellectual personnel. The two worlds are merging physically and psychologically.

The rapid production of new knowledge has given new significance to university extension slogans about "life-long learning." Television makes it possible for extension to reach into literally every home; the boundaries of the university are stretched to embrace all of society. The student becomes alumnus and the alumnus continues as student; the graduate enters the outside world and the public enters the classroom and the laboratory. Knowledge has the terrifying potential of becoming popular, opening a Pandora's box.

Extension divisions are proving to be increasingly effective administrative devices for linking campus and community in the further pursuit of knowledge. Freer of traditions and rules than regular university academic departments, extension units can respond quickly and in a variety of patterns to meet society's needs for current information and training. Professional schools and colleges, in particular, are making widespread use of extension programs for "refresher" and "continuing education" courses for the active practitioners in their fields. University of California Extension, for example, now enrolls in its courses one of every three lawyers and one of every six physicians in the state. Its total enrollment now numbers some 200,000 students, and it sponsors a remarkably wide range of academic activities including workshops, resident seminars and conferences, theater groups, symposia attracting participants of world renown, and even, recently, a notable scientific expedition to the Galapagos Islands. During the summer of 1964, in response to the growing concern with problems of school integration, University Extension was able to present several short-term workshops and courses on this urgent subject. The new role for knowledge is bringing a new and potentially quite exciting role for extension divisions in American higher education.

The campus becomes a center for cultural life; it has a ready-made audience in its students and faculty and it has the physical facilities. Persons attracted by the performing and visual arts and the lectures come to live around the campus—also assorted crackpots. As the downtown area in some cities decays, the campus takes its place as the cultural center of the community. A new dimension has been added to the land grant idea of service.

The New Deal took professors to Washington from many campuses, the New Frontier from more than just one. In Wisconsin before World War I, the campus and the state house in Madison were exceptionally close. Today the campus is being drawn to the city hall and the state capital as never before. The politicians need new ideas to meet the new problems; the agencies need expert advice on how to handle the old. The professor can supply both. Keynes concluded his *General Theory* as follows: ". . . the ideas of economists and political philosophers, both when they are right and when they are wrong, are more powerful than is commonly understood. Indeed the world is ruled by little else. Practical men, who believe themselves to be quite exempt from any intellectual influences, are usually the slaves of some defunct economist. Madmen in authority, who hear voices in the air, are distilling their frenzy from some academic scribbler of a few years back. I am sure that the power of vested interests is vastly exaggerated compared with the gradual encroachment of ideas." As, for example, the ideas of Keynes.

The university must range itself on the side of intelligent solutions to sometimes unintelligent questions. These questions more and more arise from abroad as well as at home; and the quality of the answers has been made all the more crucial in a world swept by Communist and nationalist revolutions.

There are those who fear the further involvement of the university in the life of society. They fear that the university will lose its objectivity and its freedom. But society is more desirous of objectivity and more tolerant of freedom than it used to be. The university can be further ahead of the times and further behind the times, further to the left of the public and further to the right of the public—and still keep its equilibrium—than was ever the case before, although problems in this regard are not yet entirely unknown. There are those who fear that the university will be drawn too far from basic to applied research and from applied research to application itself. But the lines dividing these never have been entirely clear, and much new knowledge has been generated at the borders of basic and applied research, and even of applied knowledge and its application. Whitehead once wrote of the creative margin when the "adventure of thought" met "the adventure of action."

INVOLVEMENT WITH THE FEDERAL GOVERNMENT

Growth and shifting emphases and involvement in society all take money; and which universities get it in the largest quantities will help determine which of them excel a decade or two hence. Will federal support be spent according to merit or according to political power? Will private donors continue to do as well as they recently have done for those universities that have done well already? Will the states find new sources of revenue or will their expenditures be held under a lid of no new taxes? The answers to these questions will help predict the standings on the next rating scale of universities.

Of key importance to American universities is the role of the federal government, particularly through federal support of scientific research. This support, which received its great impetus during and after World War II, has already changed the face of the leading American universities almost as much as did the land grant program a century earlier. Federal support has today become a major factor in the total performance of many universities, and the sums involved are substantial. Higher education in 1960 received about $1.5 billion from the federal government—a hundredfold increase in twenty years. About one third of this $1.5 billion was for university-affiliated research centers; about one third for project research within universities; and about one third for other things, such as residence hall loans, scholarships, and teaching programs. This last third was expended at colleges as well as universities, but the first two thirds almost exclusively at universities, and at relatively few of them.

The $1 billion for research, though only 10 per cent of total federal support for research and development, accounted for 75 per cent of all university expenditures on research and 15 per cent of total university budgets. Clearly the shape and nature of university research are profoundly affected by federal monies. The effects of this extensive federal aid and the new problems that have arisen as a consequence are many and varied, but the more important of them might be grouped under the two general headings of "federal influence" and "balance."

(1). Federal control as a substantive issue is, as Sidney Hook has said, a "red herring." With a few exceptions—the generally necessary exception of secrecy in certain types of work, and the unnecessary exception of the disclaimer affidavit once required by the National Defense Education Act—there has been no control in any deleterious sense. The real problem is not one of federal control but of federal influence. A federal agency offers a project. A university need not accept —but, as a practical matter, it usually does. Out of this reality have followed many of the consequences of federal aid for the universities;

and they have been substantial. That they are subtle, slowly cumulative and gentlemanly makes them all the more potent.

A university's control over its own destiny has thus been substantially reduced. University funds from tuition and fees, gifts and endowments, and state sources go through the usual budget-making procedures and their assignment is subject to review in accordance with internal policy. Federal research funds, however, are usually negotiated by the individual scholar with the particular agency, and so bypass the usual review process. Thus 20 to 50 to 80 per cent of a university's expenditures may be handled outside the normal channels. These funds in turn commit some of the university's own funds; they influence the assignment of space; they determine the distribution of time between teaching and research; to a large extent they establish the areas in which the university grows the fastest. Almost imperceptibly, a university is changed.

The authority of the department chairman, the dean, the president is thereby reduced; so also is the role of faculty government. This may have its advantages. The university's internal process of distributing funds would be generally less selective and less flexible than the federal research project approach. Within a university, the tendency is to give each faculty member about the same opportunity and once having given it to keep giving it thereafter; but the project method allows more attention to exceptional merit and has the advantage that all projects may end some time. Additionally, federal agencies are more responsive to particular national needs than the universities would be, given the same amount of money to spend according to their own priority system.

There are, however, clearly detrimental effects. Some faculty members come to use the pressure of their agency contacts against their university. They may try to force the establishment of a new administrative unit or the assignment of land for their own special building, in defiance of general university policy or priorities. These pressures, of course, should be withstood; they speak well neither of the professor nor of the agency. Also, some faculty members tend to shift their identification and loyalty from their university to the agency in Washington. The agency becomes the new alma mater. There are especially acute problems when the agency insists on the tie-in sale (if we do this for you, then you must do that for us) or when it requires frequent and detailed progress reports. Then the university really is less than a free agent. It all becomes a kind of "putting-out" system with the agency taking the place of the merchant-capitalist of old.

(2). The question of "balance" in federal aid arises in relation both to support of specific fields within an institution and to distribution of support among institutions of higher learning. Among the totality of university functions, federal support has been heavily concentrated on research and on graduate and postdoctoral training in fields of national interest. Expenditures have been largely restricted to the physical and biomedical sciences, and to engineering, with only about 3 per cent for the social sciences and hardly any support for the humanities.

All this is said to have destroyed the "balance" among fields, and it is generally concluded that something should be done about it. The balance among fields, however, has never been a static thing. If it were, philosophy, theology, and the classics would still be the dominant areas of study, as they have not been for a long time. Assuming that the balance of 1942, say, was appropriate for 1942, this does not mean it would have been appropriate for 1962. It is not enough to say that the old "balance" has been destroyed. The real question is what should be the proper balance today. It is clear that the flowering of the Renaissance should have affected the "balance" in the sixteenth century. It would seem likely that the splitting of the atom and the deciphering of the genetic code should in their turn affect the balance of the twentieth century. We should expect the most money and the brightest students and the greatest prestige to follow the most exciting new ideas. By and large they have done so, and this is one way of defining the nature of balance.

The real question, it seems to me, is not one of balance in any historical or monetary sense, but rather what is most appropriate to each field in each period. "All fields are equal, only some are more equal than others." There should be no effort to do the same things in the same amounts for each field. Each should receive support in accordance with its current potentialities, and potentialities vary. There are no timeless priorities.

Federal research expenditures have also been heavily focused on relatively few institutions. If both project research and large research centers are included, six universities received 57 per cent of the funds in a recent fiscal year, and twenty universities received 79 per cent. If project research alone is considered, the figures are 28 and 54 per cent. As a percentage of total university expenditures for all purposes among the leading twenty recipients, federal funds have amounted to 20 to 50 per cent when project research alone is counted, and from 20 to over 80 per cent when the research centers are added. These twenty universities are only about one tenth of all universities in the United States. They constitute the primary "federal grant" universities.

The project approach almost automatically led to concentration of federal research effort in a relatively few universities. The universities best equipped to undertake the research were also those with the faculty and facilities to provide for the training of Ph.D's. It is no coincidence that the six universities with a little more than 25 per cent of project funds graduated about 25 per cent of the Ph.D.'s; and a similar situation prevails for the top twenty universities. If "only the best will do," this concentration of effort is inevitable. A different result would have been quite surprising.

The concentration of effort has undoubtedly strengthened the facilities and improved the quality of faculties of universities already in the front rank. It has probably widened the gap between those of the first and those of the second and third ranks. It may, in fact, have actually injured universities of the second and third ranks and some colleges by turning their potential faculty members into research personnel in the front-rank universities. The good are better; the poor may well be worse. And it has greatly accentuated the differences between colleges and universities.

The general policy of federal agencies in allocating research grants to universities for the last two decades has been one of "seeking excellence wherever it is." The period has been one of what I have called "intuitive imbalance." We are now clearly entering a new phase of federal support policy, one that might be called "bureaucratic balance."

The new balance calls for developing a larger number of outstanding centers of graduate instruction and research. The Seaborg report of 1960 suggested expansion from the present fifteen or twenty centers to thirty or forty over a fifteen-year period. The National Education Improvement Act of 1963 envisaged expansion from twenty to seventy. Teaching is being emphasized along with research. Summer refresher courses for teachers of science, improvement of science textbooks, and language laboratories are programs already established. The National Science Foundation has a large effort under way to improve and renovate equipment for undergraduate teaching in the physical sciences. Undergraduates, as well as graduate students, are being assisted by loans and scholarships. The social sciences are receiving increasing sums of money. More funds are being granted to colleges as well as to universities, and to universities of all ranks.

A particularly significant step in the direction of broadening institutional support is the new science development program announced in the spring of 1964 by the National Science Foundation. This program is specifically designed to raise the overall quality of science programs in good institutions to the level of excellent. Distinguished institutions are excluded: "institutions already recognized as being outstanding in science should continue to depend on existing programs for assistance."

Undergraduates as well as graduate institutions will be eligible, and the grants (up to $5 million per institution) may be used in any way the institution chooses to strengthen single departments or related departments, to create new departments, or to improve the entire science program. *Science* magazine, commenting on the NSF plan, said, "it is probably safe to say that the success or failure of this program is going to have a far-reaching influence on the evolution of higher education in the United States."

The approach to a university "as an institution" has interesting implications. If additional universities are to be selected to become centers of strength in research and graduate instruction, then it will be necessary for the federal government to be concerned with the "general health of the institution." This will be a notable departure from historical practice, except in agriculture. If we are to move toward federal orientation to the "total function of the university," then the University Grants Committee in Great Britain is the outstanding precedent, and one that has received some support in the United States. However, there are only about thirty universities in Great Britain, and it is clear what is and what is not a university. Additionally, the University Grants Committee has come to exercise more influence over the establishment of new programs, the cost and size and even the appearance of new buildings, the equalization of faculty salaries among institutions, and the determination of admission policies than would currently be acceptable if it came from the federal government in this country.

Some hard choices must be faced. The decentralized project approach of the last two decades has much to recommend it. It is selective on merit, flexible in accordance with quality of performance, and responsive to national goals. The universities and their scholars retain substantial freedom. But such dominant reliance on the project approach is no longer likely. It is said that support to institutions as such will "give a university the necessary autonomy" and will permit dispersion of effort and better balance in several directions. It is difficult, however, to assess the merit of a total institution as complex as a modern university. One alternative is to rely on a formula, as in the case of agriculture in the land grant institutions. Another is to be guided by political influence; and this is increasingly happening. Inter-university competition is being taken from the quasi-academic arena of the agency committee to the legislative halls.

The partnership of the federal government with higher education and particularly with the federal grant universities over the last two decades has been enormously productive in enlarging the pool of scientific ideas and skills. Now we are entering a new phase of widening and deepening relationships. This new phase can carry the American commitment to education to new heights of endeavor. It can also preserve the traditional freedom of higher education from excessive control. It can enlarge the horizons of equality of opportunity. It can maintain and even increase the margin for excellence. The challenge is to make certain it does all these things.

However this turns out, the scene of American higher education will continue to be marked by great variety, and this is one of its great strengths. The large and the small, the private and the public, the general and the specialized all add their share to overall excellence. The total system is extraordinarily flexible, decentralized, competitive —and productive. The new can be tried, the old tested with considerable skill and alacrity. Pluralism in higher education matches the pluralistic American society. The general test of higher education is not how much is done poorly, and some is; rather it is how much is done superbly, and a great deal is, to the nation's great benefit.

CHANGES STILL TO COME

But there are some problems still to be fully faced; and they are problems of consequence.

1. One is the improvement of undergraduate instruction in the university. The much-advertised conflict between teaching and research puts the problem the wrong way. The teaching of graduate students is so closely tied to research that if research is improved, graduate instruction is almost bound to be improved also. And the almost universal experience seems to be that federal research support has improved graduate instruction. At the undergraduate level, however, a "subtle discounting of the teaching process" has been aided and abetted.

The reasons for the general deterioration of undergraduate teaching are several. Teaching loads and student contact hours have been reduced. Faculty members are more frequently on leave or temporarily away from the campus; some are never more than temporarily on campus. More of the instruction falls to teachers who are not members of the regular faculty. The best graduate students prefer fellowships and research assistantships to teaching assistantships. Postdoctoral fellows who might fill the gap usually do not teach. Average class size has been increasing.

There seems to be a "point of no return" after which research, consulting, graduate instruction become so absorbing that faculty efforts can no longer be concentrated on undergraduate instruction as they once were. This process has been going on for a long time; federal research funds have intensified it. As a consequence, undergraduate education in the large university is more likely to be acceptable than outstanding; educational policy from the undergraduate point of view is largely neglected.

Improvement of undergraduate instruction will require the solution of many sub-problems: how to give adequate recognition to the teaching skill as well as to the research performance of the faculty; how to create a curriculum that serves the needs of the student as well as the research interests of the teacher; how to prepare the generalist as well as the specialist in an age of specialization looking for better generalizations; how to treat the individual student as a unique human being in the mass student body; how to make the university seem smaller even as it grows larger; how to establish a range of contact between faculty and students broader than the one-way route across the lectern or through the television screen; how to raise educational policy again to the forefront of faculty concerns.

2. Another major task is to create a more unified intellectual world. We need to make contact between the two, the three, the many cultures; to open channels of intelligent conversation across the disciplines and divisions; to close the gap between C. P. Snow's "Luddites" and scientists; to answer fragmentation with general theories and sensitivities. Even philosophy, which once was the hub of the intellectual universe, is now itself fragmented into such diverse specialities as mathematics and semantics. However, the physical sciences are drawing together as new discoveries create more basic general theories; the biological sciences may be pulled together in the process now going on; the social sciences might be unified around the study of organizations and the relations of individuals to and within them. Biochemistry and social psychology may come to be central focalizing fields. As knowledge is drawn together, if in fact it is, a faculty may again become a community of masters; but "a sense of the unity . . . of all knowledge" is still a very long way off.

3. A third problem is to relate administration more directly to individual faculty and students in the massive institution. We need to decentralize below the campus level to the operating agencies; to make the collective faculty a more vital, dynamic, progressive force as it now is only at the department level; to bridge the growing chasm between the department that does the teaching and the institute that does the research, with the faculty member torn between; to make the old departments and divisions more compatible with the new divisions of knowledge; to make it possible for an institution to see itself in totality rather than just piecemeal and in the sweep of history rather than just at a moment of time; to bring an understanding of both internal and external realities to all those intimately related to the process, so that there may be greater understanding; to see to it that administration serves and stimulates rather than rules the institution, that it is expendable when necessary and flexible all the time; to assure that the university can do better what it does best; to solve the whole range of governmental problems within the university.

4. Additionally, there is the urgent issue of how to preserve a margin for excellence in a populist society, when more and more of the money is being spent on behalf of all of the people. The great university is of necessity elitist—the elite of merit—but it operates in an environment dedicated to an egalitarian philosophy. How may the contribution of the elite be made clear to the egalitarians, and how may an aristocracy of intellect justify itself to a democracy of all men? It was equality of opportunity, not equality *per se*, that animated the founding fathers and the progress of the American system; but the forces of populist equality have never been silent, the battle between Jeffersonianism and Jacksonianism never finally settled.

George Beadle, president of the University of Chicago, once implied that the very large American university (but not his own) might be like the dinosaur which "became extinct because he grew larger and larger and then sacrificed the evolutionary flexibility he needed to meet changing conditions"; its body became too large for its brain. David Riesman has said that the leading American universities are "directionless . . . as far as major innovations are concerned"; they have run out of foreign models to imitate; they have lost their "ferment." The fact is that they are not directionless; they have been moving in clear directions and with considerable speed. These directions, however, have not been set as much by the university's visions of its destiny as by the external environment, including the federal government, the foundations, the surrounding and sometimes engulfing industry.

But the really new problems of today and tomorrow may lend themselves less to solutions by external authority; they may be inherently problems for internal resolution. And these solutions, if they are to come, are more likely to emerge on the campuses of those old, private universities which have prided themselves on control of their own destiny, and on the totally new campuses of the state universities in America (and the new public universities in Britain). The university for the twenty-first century is more likely to emerge from these environments than from any others. Out of the pride of the old and the vacuum of the new may come the means to make undergraduate life more exciting, intellectual discourse more meaningful, administration more human. And perhaps there will arise a more dynamic demonstration of how excellence makes democracy more vital and its survival more assured. Then the contemporary American university may indeed rise to "the heights of the times." Then it may demonstrate that it has a mind as well as a body.

*James A. Perkins (1911–)
like Clark Kerr, moved from
being an undergraduate in a
small college, Swarthmore, to
the presidency of a major university, and was installed in 1963
as president of Cornell. Perkins
received his M.A. and Ph.D. in
political science from Princeton.
At various times a teacher at
Princeton, a government official
in Washington, vice-president
of Swarthmore, and an executive
of the Carnegie Corporation,
Perkins has broad and intimate
acquaintance with the problems
of higher education. This essay
is the second of his three
Stafford Little lectures delivered
at Princeton in November, 1965.*

14

The Search
for
Internal
Coherence

JAMES A. PERKINS

We have discussed the at-
tributes of knowledge—its acquisition, transmission, and
application—and discovered
that they correspond to the
three missions of the modern
university: teaching, research,
and public service. We suggested that the explosive
power of knowledge might be
traceable to an interaction of
its attributes, and that in like
manner the growth and current power of the university in
the United States might derive
from the fact that it, and perhaps it alone, had fully embraced its three missions.

We also observed that, in the midst of all this, the modern university appears threatened by its own success. There are some indications that the university may, in responding to society's urgent demands that it enlarge its research, teaching, and service functions, risk the fate which size and mindlessness imposed on the dinosaurs. It is a chilling thought, but I have hinted at my optimistic belief that we can avoid such a fate by the exercise of our reason and our organizing abilities.

We shall deal here with some of the more formidable problems which the university faces internally, within its own family on campus. Many of these problems have been created by the growth of the institution and also by the vast attending explosion in knowledge itself. Many of them are wrapped up, too, in the constant debate about the university's integrity, and that may be, therefore, a good place to start.

It is popular these days to talk about the compromising of university integrity, and to decry, in the words of one critic, the weakening of the university's "capacity to fulfill its function as the corporate agent of free inquiry." Presumably, integrity is something good the university once had and is now losing with every response to the forces that would change the *status quo* or compromise intellectual chastity with new social involvement.

I think we must be very careful that we do not turn integrity into a "dry-ice" word which freezes everything it touches. Certainly, it cannot be used to solidify the *status quo* and to resist change, for change has long been the watchword of university development, and adaptation the key not only to its survival but to its enormous vitality and usefulness. Those who promulgated the Yale report of 1828 doubtless believed that to introduce engineering into the course of studies was to violate the university's integrity. If so, they were confusing the university's purposes with its traditions. Similarly, the addition of a law school to Princeton would surely not affect its integrity, whatever it might do to its traditions and its style.

University integrity, then, is involved not with preserving things as they are, but rather with maintaining the coherence of its various parts, and the harmony with which it is able to pursue its aims—whatever their specialized nature. Are the university's pursuits carried out to assure work of the highest order, with thoroughly professional standards and with clarity of purpose? Even more important, are the university's efforts in research, instruction, and public service undertaken in such a manner that each mission supports the other? We have already noted that these three missions are subtly and intricately meshed. It follows that the real integrity of the university is violated when large decisions in one area do not consider the impact on the other two. I would state it even more strongly: university integrity is compromised when decisions about any one of our three aspects of university activity fail to *strengthen* the others.

Keeping in mind these considerations which should influence the university's response to pressures for growth and change, let us look now at some of the factors which can help to inhibit the uncontrolled growth of the university—and which, to that end, can work in our favor.

With respect to research, the controlling factor is the increasing necessity for choosing among fields and areas where the university can expect to excel. Knowledge is growing so fast that no university can pretend to cover it all—at least not with any hope of maintaining high professional standards. Even a single department of physics or philosophy must decide to concentrate within its respective field. Uncontrolled growth may come, therefore, from an uncontrolled selection of areas for excellence and it follows that the university can and must choose among possibilities. The very nature of the knowledge explosion and the desire for highest standards will force choice and thus will act as a brake on uncontrolled growth.

It is wrong to say that this choice must not be influenced by outside considerations. On the contrary, there may be a pressing public need which attracts a university's attention, or an opportunity to draw superior talent to the campus, perhaps even combined with the availability of funds. Let me add quickly that the funds alone cannot be the determinant. But their availability may insure the highest standards for the activity to be financed—if it is the right activity. Whether it be in high-energy physics or comparative linguistics, if the activity fits into the university scene, the presence of funds should not be a barrier to the addition, nor its acceptance a violation of integrity. It is the casual, unreflective, opportunistic development of interests for the sole purpose of attracting funds and prestige which obviously violates integrity.

While research must operate under the restraints of choice and excellence in the disciplines, instruction must operate under the restraints of student numbers and student selection.

We must remember that the most important factor in the pressure for university growth is the increased percentage of the age group that is demanding access to higher education. The figure is now well on its way to 50 per cent. But there is a great difference of opinion as to what the trends may be in the future. Some believe 50 per cent will represent something of a plateau. Others believe that there may actually be an accelerated increase after that figure is reached as more young people move out of a minority status.

If those who predict a relatively slow growth are correct, the pressure from increasing numbers will begin to lose some of its steam in the foreseeable future. Then the system as a whole will be relieved, though the prestige universities will hardly feel it. As the Negro spiritual puts it, "No resting place down there." Such universities may find restrictions on further growth arising from student reaction to an overcrowded campus. As more colleges and universities achieve higher standards, there may well be a disposition to pass up those whose size is, from the social or even intellectual point of view, forbidding. There are already signs of such a development, aided and abetted by avowed government policy to promote geographic equality. But, alas, neither Cornell nor Princeton is large enough to be very much benefited by this prospective development either.

More important than any prospective leveling-off of enrollments, however, is the rapid emergence of alternatives to the university, primarily in private and state-supported systems of junior and four-year colleges. Certainly the absence of enough satisfactory alternatives has been responsible for some of the excessive enrollments in our universities—though we have not suffered anything like the growth of such institutions as the University of Mexico, with over 80,000 enrolled students, or Buenos Aires, with over 60,000, both of which are operating in systems where there are no alternatives at all. Now in the United States there are many alternatives—the junior and four-year colleges; courses given through educational TV, with off-campus testing programs; and various types of correspondence, radio, and taped curricula—all of which are beginning to drain off some of the demand for university attendance. Obviously, the universities have a profound stake in the successful development of these alternative measures, and for this reason they should lend their weight and prestige to assure that these measures are successful. Their own preservation will be at stake.

In its public service undertakings, the university may also find some natural restraints working to limit growth, although it is true that the demands of our fast-growing technological society are voracious and are becoming more so along the whole growing edge of social change: there is almost no problem in our society that does not increasingly require expert advice. It is also true that expert advice can be found most frequently and in greater variety in the university than in any other institution; indeed, hardly any field of knowledge in the university has not felt the heady experience of being publicly useful.

But the unique contribution of the university in all of this is knowledge, not operating skills, and this should be a limiting factor of great importance. The government and particularly the corporation have been organized in our society to get things done, and it is to these institutions that society normally looks for operational responsibility. The university social scientists can provide the economic case for a state sales tax, for example, but they should not be expected to collect the money. It is legitimate for a university engineer to design a bridge, but not to involve the university in building it. And it is often to the university's credit that its agronomists are called upon to discuss the corn-hog price ratio, but it makes no sense for the university to participate in the mechanics of that complicated business. The fact that lines can be and are drawn between advice on how to do something and assistance in doing it thus constitutes a limiting force which aids the university in its need to preserve its balance and its unity.

Turning from these factors which may impose certain general restrictions on the growth of university missions, we face a whole range of internal decision-making which affects the size and shape as well as the direction of the institution. I have already suggested that the essential criteria to guide this internal decision-making grow from the interrelatedness of the university's missions, and that the university's capability in each area must be strengthened by decisions regarding the other two. Let us see how this is so, by examining the ways in which each mission of the university must be specifically related to the others—if integrity is to be preserved.

Few would contest the proposition that research and instruction are intimately connected. Volumes have been written supporting the proposition that university-level instruction can best be accomplished by faculty members who themselves are working at the frontiers of knowledge. The teacher-researcher is the ideal. The argument is rarely over any conflict between the functions; it most generally involves questions of degree and emphasis.

But the university gives too little attention to those courses of instruction that mesh with the university's research responsibilities. If we wish the ideal professor to teach and undertake research at the same time, then it must follow that the nature of the teaching and the research must be conditioned by the fact that they are to be carried on by the same person. If the teaching and the research are not in some way coordinated, we will have faculty members who are attempting to lead coherent lives while their research is headed in one direction and their teaching in another.

Unfortunately, this is precisely what happens in most universities. The undergraduate curriculum, particularly in the first two years, is based on the familiar doctrine of general education. This theory holds that the student, irrespective of his future specialty, should be exposed early to a common body of knowledge—at the least, to an introductory course in each of the divisions of the humanities, the social sciences, and the natural or biological sciences. The emphasis is cultural and general—a preparation for life rather than a preparation for a profession or a career.

But for the faculty member, research is particular and special, and the man really living at the edge of knowledge will frequently find that participation in survey or introductory courses requires an abrupt change of gears. Small wonder that instruction for the first two years finds relatively few of the greatest scholars either willing or able to make the necessary adjustments. Introductory courses for future majors will sometimes attract them from their research lairs, but a room full of freshmen ready to fulfill a distribution requirement can be a forbidding prospect. Pressure to perform will only encourage acceptance of the next offer from a more sympathetic institution.

There have been two main answers to this problem: the first has been to separate the graduate and the undergraduate faculties. This resolves, in part, the problem of intellectual schizophrenia; no professor is expected to perform at two different levels at the same time. But the price is separation within the university—an undergraduate college whose faculty members suffer from the suspicion that they are second-class or, at best, that they are involved in a university activity at the second level of importance.

The other answer has been to maintain the single faculty, but to divide it by age—the novices for teaching and the established professors for research. Of course, the final solution must involve some compromise of these extreme positions, because there are many famous full professors who bend their backs to contribute to the improvement of undergraduate instruction. In many cases the problem is resolved by a discreet distribution of teaching loads within departments, based upon tacit assumptions of the teaching and research capabilities of individual faculty members. Sometimes there is an equally subtle distribution of teaching responsibilities among departments. History and government faculty, for example, have traditionally carried a heavier load of teaching hours than anthropology and sociology professors, because the behavioral wing of the social sciences is more scientifically oriented and less digestible by students in pursuit of a general education.

The problem at best is a very difficult one, but we have enormously complicated its solution by acting as if undergraduate education in a university can be the same thing as undergraduate education in a four-year liberal arts college. We suffer, I suggest, from the fallacy buried in the assumption that the first two years of higher education should be the same in all institutions, be they independent colleges or universities. We also suffer from the even more profound fallacy that all students who enter the liberal arts college or the university have the same educational needs and motivations.

These two broadly held and fallacious assumptions are at the heart of the strain between instruction and research at our universities. Those who hold them insist on a generality of studies that serves only to drive out of the lecture halls many faculty who are committed to research. We have often assumed that where teaching and research do not mesh, the research faculty should be punished and the teaching faculty rewarded. Special inducements for teaching may well be necessary, and they may help reduce the problem. But the means are artificial.

The fact is that undergraduate instruction and admissions policies need modification in order to assure the internal coherence and integrity of the university through a closer coordination of the teaching and research functions. I shall not lay out a blueprint here, but some general observations are in order.

First, I think we must break the lock step that would keep all institutions and students working in the same patterns and at the same pace. We must be prepared to recognize that undergraduate instruction can and must be different in a university than it is in a college, for example, and that it can and must appeal to a special category of student. The trend to design different programs to fit different institutions and different students has already begun; we must accelerate it.

Second, we shall have to hold tight to the ideals of a liberal education but recognize that, in the face of rapidly improving secondary education and the multi-concerns of the modern university, the style of liberal education will have to be adapted to its environment. We might all agree that the threefold purpose of liberal education is to learn to know nature, society, and ourselves; to acquire certain skills, such as clear expression and a grasp of the scientific method and discipline; and finally, to embrace certain values, such as intellectual honesty, tolerance, and the capacity for wise judgment.

But the curriculum and the system for assuring a liberal as well as a professional education must surely take into consideration the missions of the university. This will mean, among other things, a reexamination of the idea that general education is something that is sandwiched between secondary-school and upper-class work. Rather than occupy two or more years of pre-professional study, liberal education may have to run on a track parallel with professional work. For the student who wants to specialize, therefore, liberal education will have to be provided either by the secondary school or by a special program that includes liberal along with professional studies—or a combination of both. After all, a liberal education is the objective of a lifetime. Why assume it should be crowded into the first two postsecondary years?

The improvement of liberal education in the university will also require attention to the way subject matter is presented. There can be a liberal and a professional way of treating any subject. In a university it becomes particularly important that the research-oriented professors have as broad a view of their subject as possible. Just as instruction will have to be adapted to interest the professor, so will the professor have to teach his subject in a liberal style to interest the student.

Third, the flexibility and independence of graduate-level work will have to characterize a larger proportion of undergraduate education, too. This is already beginning to happen in the upper-class years; it may have to be extended down into the first two years for those students who are ready for it—and there are many more than we think. Honors work and educational experimentation can also help lighten the heavy dough of our undergraduate course programs. Whatever solutions we provide, we will have to give our fullest attention to improving our programs for our best students if they are not to be lost in the crowd.

Finally, we must know a great deal more about the kind of preparation, maturity, and motivation that should determine the selection of students for university-level work. Those who need the sense of security that comes from being a member of a smaller, tighter community should not come to the university. For when they do, they keep looking for a kind of faculty-student relationship that can best be found in an independent liberal arts college, a fruitless search that adds to the problem of internal cohesion in the university.

The application of these criteria might drastically modify the number of undergraduates who would come to the university as opposed to the college. Such criteria would surely affect the whole tone and purpose of the university, and they would make possible the reintroduction of the undergraduate to the research professor. But most of all, they would tend to bring teaching and research together and so help make our university communities coherent again.

Let us examine next the relations between the transmission and application of knowledge—between instruction and public service. Too frequently, I am afraid, we view the intellectual development of the student, to paraphrase Alfred North Whitehead, as if he had neither a body nor a soul. But even when we don't, we consign his physical and spiritual requirements to the area of extracurricular activities—a term frequently conjured up to secure the intellectual purity of the classroom.

Still, the student needs some connection between his studies and his concerns, between what he reads and what he sees, between what he thinks and what he does. This is complicated, because university-level study should require long periods of solitary study and reflection.

But the underclassman is not yet a library or laboratory scholar and must not be treated as one. Otherwise he will seek outlets for his concerns without the benefit of the moderating influence of his studies upon his actions. The head of the student government can discover to his lasting benefit that his experiences in campus affairs and his studies of public administration have some relation to each other. The same is true of the sociology student just returned from the South.

We have not been very inventive about how to relate studies and experience or thought and action, and the result can be frustration, or apathy, or even revulsion on the part of good students. There is an excitement and an important feedback that comes from actually seeing and experiencing the relevance of intellectual exercises.

Unquestionably, the notion that knowledge can and should be pursued for its own sake is at the heart of our lack of interest in connecting studies and concerns. We pay the price in student disinterest and in the proliferation of activities which do not have the discipline of intellectual content. A closer coordination of the student's two lives would bring the university into better focus, and it would serve to aid the development of appropriate extracurricular activities, as well as add an important stimulus to intellectual growth. If there be doubters, I suggest they talk with a professor who has just seen his first book on publication day, or an anthropologist who has just returned from working with the Andean Indians, or an astrophysicist who has just seen his theories confirmed by recent descriptions of the moon's surface. The excitement of these men will be a reminder that the connection between thought and action, or between theory and results, which is so important to adults on the faculty, is even more important to students in the university.

In a larger sense, the ultimate use or application of knowledge must be brought under the restraints of research and instruction or the university is likely, in my view, to become unhinged. The pressing requirements of government and industry are, for the faculty member, full of the heady aroma of larger public purpose or prospective private gain. Both sensations are pleasant to an academic fraternity which for decades has been caricatured as impractical and which believes, with good reason, that it has been financially starved. In these circumstances, it is not surprising that faculty have taken to consulting with zest.

Again, we need criteria that will be useful in determining the directions and the merits of extra-university activity, and these criteria are to be found in our model of the three interconnected missions of the university. We must refer to the other two missions if we are to make valid decisions about the university's outside involvements. How can these strengthen the research and teaching functions?

Let me promptly remove from the discussion those matters which occupy the faculty in their capacities as private citizens. Everyone owes a part of his life to his society for public service, whether or not this service is directly connected with his profession. For those with a trained intelligence, such calls will not be lacking: they will increase as expert and disinterested service for the general welfare is in greater and greater demand.

But the outside activity which has a professional connection should, in general, have some feedback or use to the research interests of the professor and to the students who are dependent on him. Otherwise, the professor is just in business, or moonlighting, and his students are being shortchanged. Activities that are simply training projects, or are merely involved in implementing established knowledge and are not answering questions, should fall outside the boundaries of acceptable public activities for the university faculty.

The integrity of the university involves, then, a resistance to over-expansion of any of its three institutional functions, and the accompanying requirement that each institution will select its fields of specialization. Integrity involves, perhaps even more importantly, an insistence that all of the university's activities advance its capabilities to pursue each of its missions—that, as Whitehead has said, "all its various parts are coordinated and play into each other's hands."

This is a fine prescription, but it is idle to lay it down without talking about how it is to be achieved. Who is going to "manage" integrity? Who will select and control the complex and tightly interrelated tasks to be undertaken by the university? Who is to make the critical decisions that will prevent each phase of activity from growing out of balance and stifling the others? Who is to make the university and its missions a coherent whole?

It is clear, at the outset, that the answers will not be precise or unequivocal. The university is not an orderly structure that yields to authoritarian management as does the military division or the corporation. The university's function is to serve the private processes of faculty and students, on the one hand, and the large public interests of society on the other. In this sense, it has no balance sheet of its own, no single product that can be annually measured, no performance tables for judging success. Even when seniors do well on admission to graduate school, there is always the haunting suspicion that success may be due more to the skill of the admissions committee than to the performance of the students.

Three groups participate in university management—the students, the faculty, and the administration. Let us talk about the student first. The undergraduate is generally on the campus no more than four years, a fact that tends to put the leadership of student movements in other countries more often than not in the hands of graduate students, and sometimes in the hands of those who make careers of student activities. The most vigorous student activities in the developing nations are led by students who have been enrolled for ten years and work full time at the business. But in this country, it is difficult to be a student and not attend classes sometimes. Furthermore, the prospects of a career are so bright that most students don't wish to delay their departures. Hence, management of the university is generally only on the edge of student interest.

In any case, management is not just a matter of deciding what would be good to do. Most importantly, it involves what is timely and what is possible. It involves what is wise. And wisdom requires, among other things, an understanding of the spirit of a particular institution, the interests of its campus leaders, its financial prospects, and the priorities it gives to various academic ventures. There is no substitute for careful observation of people and events over time. This kind of experience is denied the young, and it is an almost fatal disability for constructive participation in most university decisions.

Finally, the student is a student. He is at the university to learn, not to manage; to reflect, not to decide; to observe, not to coerce. The process of learning, like the process of research, is in the end a most private affair, requiring for the most part detachment and not engagement. If we learn to involve the student more highly in the formal learning process, we may even further reduce his desire for management.

But there are two comments that must be made on the other side of the argument. Some students will become strongly interested in university affairs. The student body will always include some with talents as administrators or leaders. These young people gravitate naturally into student government or the campus newspaper, seeking outlets for their interests. Their participation in university institutional activities is important for them because the university machinery is an immediate outlet for their organizational proclivities. It is also good for the university, which, at least as much as any other organization, is most likely to be improved by the ideas and the enthusiasms of imaginative, energetic young people.

There are, in connection with all of this, powerful forces at work that are raising the political temperature of the student and increasing his interest in university affairs. He is the product of an age of earlier freedom and later responsibility. Left on his own as a teenager, he is coming to the university and finding that the faculty is as peripatetic as his parents. He encounters a vacuum at the point of his greatest need—wisdom and advice on how to become an adult. He also finds a community which frequently seems not much interested in his education. He may well be mistaken in many cases, but he does feel an impersonality about the campus and a concentration on matters that involve him only tangentially. For many the answer is access to the machinery of the university—they want to reorder its priorities in their favor.

It would be foolish to deny the elements of justice in this line of reasoning. It would be equally foolish to refuse to listen to those who wish to be heard. We welcome them as freshmen with speeches that tell them they are now adults, and so we must expect to treat them as adults.

There is another point to be made. Students do not like to be excluded, *in principle,* from the machinery of the university. Nor, indeed, does anyone else. A careful selection of places where student participation can be accepted because of known interest or known talent will most frequently be a stabilizing and integrating act rather than the contrary.

The disabilities of the students' short stay, inexperience, and scholarly preoccupations remain. But as long as students feel they have entered a place where there are no priorities, or where the priorities work against their real interests as students, the pressure for involvement will be strong and perhaps irresistible. Uncontrolled, this will ruin good scholars and good universities. Dealt with sympathetically, it will help bring about successful campus integration.

The faculty, as managers of the modern university, also offer certain limitations, arising from quite different circumstances. The community of masters was a noble and even feasible idea when there were only the four faculties of medicine, theology, law, and philosophy, and when the professor lectured several times a week and rarely saw students—as individuals—except in the corridors. The universities were in the big cities and the faculties were given appointments in the university but continued to participate in the main stream of city life. Outside the lectures there was precious little to administer in the university, so faculty decision-making was largely limited to appointments to the faculty itself. The nearest analogy would be to a modern departmental meeting, although the departmental meeting deals with academic affairs and logistical considerations in far more detail than did the whole university faculty of even a century ago.

But apart from size and complexity, the faculty as faculty has faced the additional difficulties we have noted in the enormous fractionalizing of the fields of knowledge, combined with an equally great increase in outside activities. The faculty has now become dispersed in several faculties, colleges, and departments; it has been divided into C. P. Snow's two worlds; and it has turned increasingly outward, away from the institution of the university, to the "guilds" that the scholars' special interests have led them to set up for themselves.

Partial views which are based upon increasingly specialized interests make it difficult for the faculty as faculty to have a point of view on broad institutional matters. Consequently, the faculty's administrative stance contains elements of senatorial courtesy—maximum permissiveness with respect to individual faculty desires, combined with maximum protection if anyone would interfere with this permissiveness. Such a posture is exactly right for the protection of the classroom, but it is quite inadequate for educational or institutional management.

So the university can never again run on the assumption that it commands or can command the full-time interest and attention of all its faculty. The nature of knowledge today is such that it requires minds and talents of quite a different order from those needed to make administrative decisions. And the faculty should be left as free as possible of administrative duties in order to do its work. As the interests of the disciplines and professions cut increasingly across institutional lines, faculty members must have access to the stimulation and fresh ideas that will certainly come from the interchange of outside meetings and conferences among specialists. The role of the university is to provide a framework and an environment where these ideas can be put to use—laboratories, libraries, classrooms, and studios—where creative work can be conceived, tested, explained, reformulated and tested again, and then sent out into the world.

But if faculty as a corporate body cannot be expected to manage the university, individual faculty members are indispensable to the management process. Indeed, I would put high on any university priority list the identification and support of those members of the faculty whose viewpoint is broad, who have that rare quality of seeing problems in operational terms, and whose faculty standing is solidly based on a specialized competence. They do not have to be drawn into full-time or even part-time administration. But they are the mainsprings of the university works, the heartbeat of its body, and the real initiators of reform and progress. Any university with a dozen such men as Mike Oates of Princeton and Max Black of Cornell can expect to grow and prosper; without them it will surely be bound in shallows and in miseries. Presidential leadership consists, in large part, of discovering these faculty leaders and then staying at their elbows, supporting their ideas, finding them money, guiding them when necessary, and encouraging them when the going seems rough.

Finally, there is the administrator, who is, in the end, charged with managing the integration of these many different and at times conflicting elements. The leadership of individual faculty members has brought new vigor to the university and will always be indispensable in accomplishing the particular tasks that interest them. And the faculty must always largely determine the shape and content of educational standards and educational policy.

But someone must be concerned with the institution as a whole, the activities it supports, the public face it presents, and the private concerns with which it is occupied. This job cannot be divided among disparate elements of the university. So it is the administrator—the president and others with managerial responsibility, cooperating with faculty and student leaders—who must be concerned both with the apparatus of the university and with the idea it represents. He must be able to involve himself directly in the central academic business of the university, to exert educational leadership, to be an agent for both stability and change. He must be capable of institutional justice and personal compassion. He must not fear power or be afraid to exercise it, because he must know that power cannot be the direct concern of either student or teacher. He must always be sensitive to the difference between the process of management and the process of education, and he must understand that the former must always serve the latter. Few large faculties have been able to provide this leadership for themselves. But without their general support, leadership cannot be effective.

It is this combination of institutional management and educational leadership that makes academic administration a unique and vital business. And it is this combination that is so necessary if any of the internal developments we have outlined are to have a chance to succeed.

The internal coherence of the university involves, then, attention to the missions of the university, their interdependence, and the optimum roles of student, teacher, and administrator in the management of this complicated task. It involves internal restraints in the pursuit of each mission, and the restraints that come from the necessity of considering the university missions as a coordinated whole. It involves clarity with respect to an educational philosophy that is appropriate to a university. It involves understanding of the respective roles and contributions of administration, faculty, and students to the internal management of the university.

In the center of this complicated community there are a group of students with strong administrative and educational instincts, a much larger group of faculty with strong institutional instincts, and a group of administrators sensitive to student values and aspirations and to faculty interests and attitudes. No university can function properly unless it has a balance of these groups who are preoccupied with its health and vitality. No university can develop in sensible ways unless a general consensus has been achieved at the heart of its institutional life among those concerned with its future. But it will be, I suggest, those who spend full time at the business of direction and management who must assure this consensus—who must see to it that educational purpose and institutional interests develop in harmony.

Even when the community has mastered the difficult task of internal self-government, the task of university direction, stability, and growth has not been stated in its full complexity. We have already said that the university is no longer a self-sufficient world: it has a central role in the drama of higher education in the world at large. The university must achieve not only an internal harmony, but a harmony that is in a state of constant adaptation to the outside world. It is to this matter of the evolving role of the university in the total structure of higher education that we must turn next.

15

Dean of the Princeton faculty for two decades until his recent retirement, J. Douglas Brown (1898–   ) received his B.A., M.A., and Ph.D. degrees from that university. A teacher in Princeton's economics department for most of his professional life, he has served on many New Jersey and Federal commissions and advisory committees, including groups involved in developing and revising the Federal Social Security program. In 1960–61 he served on a committee to advise the Secretary of Health, Education and Welfare on the revision of the National Defense Education Act.

The Squeeze on the Liberal University

J. DOUGLAS BROWN

In the climate of bigness and diversity which pervades America today there is danger that we may lose sight of those values in our society which size and complexity do not automatically enhance. In fact, there is reason to believe that bigness and diversity make it ever more difficult to reinforce in the minds and purposes of the multiplying numbers of persons and groups in our society the values which should motivate the whole.

This danger of attenuation of a sense of values in an

197

organization peculiarly responsible for enhancing such a sense is clearly evident in the evolution of the American university. A university bears a name which embodies its purpose of resolving diversity into a unity centered in enduring values. However, the name carries such a tradition of dignity and distinction that it has come to be applied to what are, in fact, complex state systems of higher education held together largely by the control of funds and the veto power which such control affords.

By assigning the name "university" to an aggregation of professors, students, administrative staff, and structures, the American people have come to believe that a marvelous combination of operations can result:

1) An almost limitless number of our youth can be developed into business and professional leaders in their communities.

2) The salaries of the great majority of these young people can be raised by an imposing lifetime total.

3) Courses can be given on any subject on which a textbook is available or for which a class can be gathered, either voluntarily or by requirement.

4) Knowledge can be subdivided into smaller and smaller packages related to any special use, so that, for example, the offering of seventy-two courses in educational psychology is an evidence of progress in assuring effective teaching.

5) Ph.D.'s can be produced by the thousands by some magic of mass production to service the insatiable demands of education itself and of industry and government.

6) Knowledge or know-how of almost any kind can be obtained by "research" and supplied on order for a price.

7) A "livery stable" of specialists can be made available, on call, to government, industry, and community agencies with no impairment of the university's normal activities.

8) Thousands of people, ranging from eighteen years of age to eighty, can be provided adult education in all flavors and package-sizes, and at all hours and locations, to satisfy the citizen-taxpayer or, at least, those willing to pay a tuition fee.

That the American people believe all these results to be possible is not surprising. It is but a reflection of our national assumptions that bigness and diversity are goals in themselves and that division of labor and specialization will assure success in any difficult endeavor. It is incumbent upon those who question these assumptions in their application to the age-old concept of the university to speak out. Perhaps it is already too late!

To recognize a university of the kind which has made the term meaningful over the centuries, it may now be necessary to call such institutions "liberal" universities. The adjective is useful not only to distinguish such universities from their vast and diversified counterparts, but to reassert the true function of the traditional university in the reinforcement of a sense of values in society. For want of a better term, and for purposes of discussion, it may be appropriate to call the newer aggregations of educational, research, and service instrumentalities "multi-versities," as President Kerr of the University of California has done.

In addition to a climate of bigness and diversity, America has inherited a drive toward pluralism. This is a source of great strength. It would be a serious error of arrogance to assert that America should have but one kind of institution of higher education. It would likewise be fatalistic and most discouraging for many if it were held that the "multi-versity" is on the wave of the future and that the "liberal" university is an obsolete hangover of the past. Each type of institution reflects the traditions and environment of the people and communities which give it support and leadership. But it is important to consider the differences in goals and assumptions of the two types of institution. To distinguish these goals and assumptions, the following comparisons are purposely stated in more positive terms than can be illustrated in particular institutions. While institutions at both ends of the spectrum exist, many others have attributes of both types.

To put the comparisons all too simply, the multi-versity appears to emphasize useful knowledge; the liberal university emphasizes humane values and the personal development of the individual student and scholar. The multi-versity assumes that values and dedication are a man's own business; the liberal university assumes that knowledge is but a means to attain wisdom and that the university should, through its way of life and example, enhance the values and dedication of those participating in that way of life. The multi-versity accepts an attenuated sense of personality largely limited to prestige and easy visibility; the liberal university strongly maintains its sense of personality in the continuity and relationships of its trustees, alumni, faculty, and student body. The multi-versity tends to consider its undergraduate colleges as but one part of its general assignment and not necessarily the most important; the liberal university continues to place its undergraduate colleges at the center of its interest, as an integrating factor in institutional personality and purpose.

Perhaps it would be fairer to outline the case for the survival of the liberal university in a great democracy and to permit the exponents of the more recent development, the multi-versity, to make their own case. It is difficult to present fairly an approach to education for which one lacks the enthusiasm gained from personal experience. One's philosophy of education is likely to be autobiographical. Also, one's interpretation of social forces reflects one's environment. Henry George developed his concept of the single tax on land while living in San Francisco at a time of great land speculation.

To the exponent of the liberal university, the obligation of a university transcends the development and distribution of knowledge, no matter how useful. As a perpetual and self-perpetuating institution—a corporate personality—it must stand for those basic civilizing concepts and values which free men from ignorance, superstition, prejudice, arrogance, hatred, tyranny, greed, insensitivity, and cynicism, and which strengthen in men their sense of dedication to the dignity of their fellowmen and their self-fulfillment in all things good and beautiful before God. A liberal university is not neutral in these matters; nor does it believe, corporately, that knowledge is an end in itself. It is concerned with producing responsible leaders in all worthwhile activities in its society and time, and with preserving its capacity to provide these and other leaders with the bases in knowledge, values, and wisdom to advance our way of life and enhance the intellectual, moral, and spiritual qualities of our people.

In sum, the liberal university is *not* neutral. It is not merely an enterprise manufacturing and dispensing knowledge. Knowledge *is* neutral, and those who believe that obligation stops when it is distributed over the lecture desk or through the printed page should recall the impotence of the German universities in counteracting the obscenities of Hitler. The extremes of prejudice and hate in our own country and in our own time do not speak well of the influence of our universities.

It may be countered that this exposition of the nature and functions of the liberal university is old-fashioned and out-of-date. It may be argued that the inculcation of a sense of values is the job of the church or of the family, and that universities and university faculties should not tamper with such personal concerns. Students and faculties alike, it is said, appear self-conscious when personal values are discussed.

But this is a narrow, unreal, and peculiarly recent notion about higher education. The communication of values goes on, whether overt or not, in an institution in which young men and women spend years in intense intellectual and emotional activity. The university cannot take responsibility for providing the environment for four years or seven years of the most impressionable period of a man's life and claim it is neutral in influencing the value system of that man for life. The church and family may preach. The university communicates by assumptions. These are the most effective means of developing values. It has always been so. The influence of higher education in the dedication of leaders in a wide spectrum of American life, public and private, is all too evident. Our precious tradition of this basic purpose of the university goes back to Great Britain far more than to modern Germany.

It is not easy to maintain the traditional role of the liberal university in a century of exploding knowledge. The multi-versity allows itself to ride with the forces toward increasing differentiation which are ever present in specialized scholarship and research. The harder task of assuring a counterforce toward the integration of fundamental truth receives far less emphasis. But the liberal university, which faces the same forces, must, if it is to fulfill its proper function, strive vigorously to bring order and relationship to expanding knowledge as a means to human understanding and fulfillment. By so doing, the liberal university serves to orient both scholarship and the scholar in a time of widening tangents of interest and increasingly difficult intercommunication.

The integrating function of the liberal university is of great importance not only to society but to the advancement of knowledge itself. With increasing specialization there comes an easy assumption of arrogance and of intolerance among the competing areas of learning. There result not merely the two worlds of science and the humanities, but scores of little worlds, of more manageable size but even further apart. Not only do areas of specialization lose valuable contact, but they also lose reasonable proportion. The counting of this or that may become a discrete end in itself in any line of research. Knowing more and more about less and less is not an empty quip. It can become a way of life of a scholar who has removed himself from the integrating influence of relationship with scholars in other disciplines, or even in his own, in a university which does not encourage the mutual reinforcement of learning.

There is much reason to believe that true creativity in scholarship, as well as in the arts, does not flourish in a climate of overspecialization. The steady accumulation of detailed findings, significant and insignificant, may be the result of isolated and unrelated efforts, but the powerful conceptions and hypotheses which underlie great advances in knowledge appear to arise in the minds of individuals who are stimulated by more than a microscopic view of their field of investigation. Creative ideas appear to result from some subtle process of association, deep in the mind of the scholar. The elements of thought which come together in creative combination may be derived from diverse experiences in time and area. They do not seem to be confined to a single discipline or even to a single major area of learning. In the creative mind, there may be the interaction of mathematics and music, of physics and philosophy, of biology and sociology, of psychology and literature. It should be the purpose of the university to enhance the climate which supports creativity even though the process of creative thinking remains a mystery.

There is need at this time for the liberal university in America to encourage integration as a counterforce to the pressure for differentiation in scholarship and research. An impressive proportion of the significant conceptual contributions in recent years has been contributed by scholars educated abroad. The supply of such scholars will soon run out unless we keep on tapping Europe, which needs them for its own progress. It seems unlikely that America will produce the creative scholars it so greatly needs if specialization is permitted to flourish at the expense of integration and the reinforcement of disciplines.

Large-scale methods of education play down the precious influence of teacher upon student, of various teachers upon the particular student, and of neighboring disciplines and general cultural environment on the individual striving to attain a degree. Most serious of all, highly differentiated programs of instruction emphasize the accumulation of knowledge to pass an examination set by specialists, rather than the total obligation of the student to become a learned and learning man. There is a subtle difference between the student who studies to acquire the bits and pieces of knowledge considered important by older specialists and the student who is challenged by the vast complexity and interdependence of knowledge and its function in human affairs. The one student may plod up the foothills with his eyes on the trail. The other may take occasional sights on the mountain peaks and thereby gain strength to proceed. It is the function of a liberal university to help men look upward and beyond their special tasks. By so doing, it will help provide creative and dedicated scholars who will retain humility while seeking mastery, and who will remember that knowledge is not an end in itself.

Whether the liberal university can survive in America depends upon the support of several key elements in our society. In our climate of bigness, diversity, and specialization it is not likely that such universities will receive widespread popular support. Their goals appear too visionary for many to accept. For others, there are overtones of emphasizing an elite stream of students and scholars rather than a wide cross section of generally useful citizens. America as a democracy needs leadership in a vast range of activities, but the institution which dedicates itself to producing them must almost apologize for such a presumption. Who are the people who must support the concept of the liberal university?

First, in their immediate responsibility for the future of their institutions, are the administrations and trustees of liberal universities. To sustain the nature and personality of such universities requires great self-restraint. The pressure for differentiation and atomization of schools, departments, and programs must be carefully controlled, and the counterforces for integration must be constantly encouraged, by heavy expenditures for high talent and facilities if necessary.

Second, an even harder task falls upon the faculties of liberal universities. They face the pressures toward greater and greater specialization in their daily activities. Recognition, especially for younger faculty members, comes more readily if one publishes highly erudite books and articles in an area known only to a few. The teaching of undergraduate nonspecialists appears to be less rewarding than that in advanced courses in a narrow field. Participation in interdisciplinary programs may delay scholarship or cause more specialized colleagues to discount one's progress in the "inner mysteries" of one's discipline. To assure the mutual reinforcement of scholarship and instruction, the faculty members of a liberal university must acquire mutual tolerance and respect, and sustain a belief in the need for mutual interaction, despite an unfavorable external climate.

Third, the alumni and friends of a liberal university must recognize their special obligation to sustain a vital concept in American higher education. Governments, state and federal, by vast appropriations, will support the multi-versity in both the education of large numbers of students and the prosecution of specialized research. But it requires the understanding gained by personal involvement in liberal education and in liberal learning, for social rather than personal use alone, to encourage men to support a liberal university by their wealth, wisdom, and work. The appeal of the liberal university is to men of vision, those very leaders it seeks to produce. Without their sustained support, it will gradually become another multi-versity, big, useful, and impersonal.

PART IV

Some
Criticisms

Protests by students and teachers against conditions in both the university and the world at large are hardly peculiar to the last few years. But throughout the nation the dissatisfactions of various elements in the university community have been demonstrated recently in unusually dramatic forms—forms which many critics regard as entirely inappropriate to the academic tradition of thought rather than action, rationality rather than emotionalism, and neutrality rather than partisanship in contemporary affairs. With the occupation and sacking of buildings, the imprisonment of administrators in their offices through sit-ins, and even the destruction of university property by bombs and arson, some fear that the very existence of the university as an institution may be in danger.

Apologists for such activity maintain that only by such means can their radical criticism of the university and the society to which it is so closely tied be expressed, and the changes they demand be effected. Unfortunately, many observers both within and outside the university are unable to see beyond the actions and rhetoric of campus demonstrators to an understanding of the issues which prompt such activity. The essays collected here present the resources with which to begin a reasoned inquiry into the sources of such campus discontent.

The authors represented in Part IV are not academic anarchists. They do not desire, as some avowedly do, the destruction of the university. They do, however, seek some fundamental changes in the institution so that it may become a more congenial place for the teaching and learning, which they hold are its primary functions, and so that it may work in what they consider the true service of society.

Here, as in many essays in Part III, the issue of the university's service to society figures frequently. There, we recall, Presidents Kerr and Perkins spoke of service largely as: accommodating the increasing number of people, young and old, eager to pursue advanced study; continuing the university's traditional contribution to the expansion of knowledge; and providing the intellectual and physical resources for the nation's continued technological development. The writers in Part IV also see the university in the service of society. They are not "ivory-tower intellectuals," urging that the university abstain from involvement in the contemporary world. But they see its function of service in a quite different light.

The university's greatest service, in the words of Kenneth B. Clark, would be ". . . in providing morally sensitive intellectual leadership for our society." In a world troubled by poverty, slums, racial injustice, and a controversial war such as the American involvement in Vietnam the morally sensitive intellectual leadership of the university would more likely express itself in criticism of the status quo than in contributions to the development of the society in its existing shape.

As we saw in Part II, it is somewhat fanciful to think of colleges and universities as entirely free of society's control. Although the academic community traditionally has been granted extraordinary liberty to explore and express controversial ideas without fear of direct social repression, the more subtle forces bearing on the university often are repressive. A scholar receiving generous support from a Defense Department contract, for example, is not likely to be extremely vocal in his criticism of America's military activity. The writers here would doubtless prefer that such a scholar forego his contract in order to maintain his integrity and freedom of expression. At a time when universities have become involved in so many areas of society, the dilemma of the individual scholar is multiplied many-fold in the institution as a whole.

Richard Lichtman's "The University: Mask for Privilege?" insists that the professed objectivity and neutrality of the university are more apparent than real. Its overt cooperation with society is clear in its receipt of large amounts of money from government and industry which it, in turn, serves. For Lichtman, however, the covert involvement is equally distressing. Education, he feels, is now organized not to challenge the student to change the world by giving him a vision of what it might become, but rather to help him understand, accept and adjust to the world as it is. In designing courses and selecting texts for, say, a sociology course, a professor might choose provocative readings stressing contemporary problems which could inspire in the student a critical awareness of and a desire to solve those problems. Or the professor might choose a highly specialized text that removed social theory from its immediate reality and could never bring the student to an understanding of the relevance of sociology to life. No less than government research, Lichtman asserts, such dispassionate teaching serves the status quo. By fostering complacency rather than concern it fails what Lichtman sees as the true mission of the university, ultimately that of cultivating ". . . the human spirit, which is the capacity of man to transcend his present context for the sake of a more comprehensive, articulate, and worthy vision of himself."

It is clear on attentive reading of these essays that implicit in the authors' criticisms of college education as it is currently conducted is an assertion of what education should be; fundamental to their apparent negativism is a highly affirmative sense of the university's potential for vital and proper service to the modern world. In "Intelligence, the University and Society," using terms that have not often appeared thus far in this collection, Kenneth B. Clark calls for the university to temper intelligence with empathy and to direct that intelligence in the service of love and kindness. Cataloguing some of the areas in which the university, lacking these qualities, has failed society, Professor Clark pleads for a renewal of that institution so that it may take up the position of moral leadership, which he sees as being lost by religion in the decline of the church.

As with Lichtman's and Clark's articles, in the background of Theodore Roszak's "The Complacencies of the Academy: 1967" lies the issue of the Vietnam war. Clearly the war, coupled with the civil rights movement and the crisis of the cities, has led to a pressing awareness of what Roszak describes as ". . . the protracted emergency in which our civilization finds itself." It has also led to an increasing recognition of the past indifference and, in some instances, positive complicity of the academic community as that emergency developed. Almost echoing Lichtman and Clark, Roszak calls for the university to accept anew its responsibility to society, and for students and teachers to reunite their scholarly activities with their lives as human beings and citizens in a dangerously troubled world.

Most of the criticisms in Part IV concern the failure of the university, and especially of teachers, to take a sufficiently direct role in meeting contemporary social problems. As much recent campus activity has indicated, many students, themselves involved in various forms of social action, also are troubled by the social detachment of the universities. But many matters, bearing more immediately on student life, also generate campus unrest. The final essay in this section, "The College as Rat Race" by Robert Paul Wolff, focuses on one of these problems: the intensely competitive atmosphere of student life and the tyranny of testing which, in large part, is the cause. With the increased pressure to gain admittance first to college, then to graduate school, education has become a "rat race." Too often creativity has been stifled, the joy of learning has been lost, and each step in the educational process becomes a means to an end rather than an end in itself. For Wolff, too, a discussion of the defects in the educational system implies a consideration of remedies and alternatives. Part V pursues still further alternatives for those critical of the shape of existing institutions of higher education.

*Richard Lichtman (1931–)
received his B.A. at the University of Pennsylvania and his
M.A. and Ph.D. from Yale
University. He taught four years
at the University of Kansas City,
became a fellow of the Center
for the Study of Democratic
Institutions, and now teaches
philosophy at the University of
California at Berkeley. His publications include a monograph,
"Toward Community: A Criticism of Contemporary Capitalism"; philosophical essays in
learned journals; and a series of
studies on the role of value judgments in the social sciences. A
version of this essay first appeared as "The Ideological Function of the University" in the*
International Socialist Journal.

16

The University: Mask for Privilege?

RICHARD LICHTMAN

Nothing can better illustrate the collapse of reason as an independent, critical agent in our society than a comparison of the remarks of two observers, separated by one hundred years, on the nature of a university education. In the middle of the nineteenth century one of its astutest critics noted:

> The proper function of a University in national education is tolerably well understood. At least there is a tolerably general agreement about what a University is not.

It is not a place of professional education. Universities are not intended to teach the knowledge required to fit men for some special mode of gaining their livelihood. Their object is not to make skillful lawyers, or physicians, or engineers, but capable and cultivated human beings. It is very right that there should be public facilities for the study of professions . . . But these things are no part of what every generation owes to the next, as that on which its civilization and worth will principally depend. They are needed only by a comparative few . . . and even those few do not require them until after their education . . . has been completed . . . Men are men before they are lawyers, or physicians, or merchants, or manufacturers; and if you will make them capable and sensible men, they will make themselves capable and sensible lawyers or physicians.

What professional men should carry away with them from a University, is not professional knowledge, but that which should direct the use of their professional knowledge, and bring the light of general culture to illuminate the technicalities of a special pursuit . . . And doubtless . . . the crown and consummation of a liberal education . . . [is that the pupil be taught] to methodize his knowledge; to look at every separate part of it in its relation to the other parts, and to the whole . . . observing how all knowledge is connected, how we ascend to one branch by means of another, how the higher modifies the lower and the lower helps us to understand the higher . . . combining the partial glimpses which he has obtained of the field of human knowledge at different points, into a general map . . . of the entire region.

This view has given way in our time to a very different conception:

The University . . . once was an integrated community . . . It had a single purpose . . . The conversation was in common.

This community chose to destroy itself. It became larger. It became heterogeneous. It came to talk in many tongues . . . With the rise of science over the past century, more and bigger laboratories have been required . . . The pressure of population, the explosion of books, the scientific revolution . . . all press for size beyond the limits of the face-to-face and mouth-to-ear community.

Knowledge has expanded and expanded, from theology and philosophy and law and medicine and accounting to the whole range of humanities, the social sciences and the sciences and the professions. More knowledge has resulted from and led to more research on a larger and larger scale. Research has led to service for government and industry and agriculture . . . all of this is natural. None of it can be reversed . . . Small intellectual communities can exist and serve a purpose, but they run against the logic of their times.

The campus has evolved consistently with society. It has been pulled outward to society and pulled to pieces internally. The campus consistent with society has served as a good introduction to society—to bigness, to specialization, to diffusion of interests.

The welfare-state university, or multi-university, developed particularly in the United States to provide something for nearly everybody—for farmers, for the minor and newer professions, for the general citizen who wanted to satisfy his curiosity . . . It made the welfare of society in nearly all its aspects a part of its concern . . . the University has served many masters in many ways.

The University and segments of industry are becoming more and more alike. As the University becomes tied to the world of work, the professor —at least in the natural and some of the social sciences—takes on the characteristics of an entrepreneur . . . The two worlds are merging physically . . . [The University is] a mechanism held together by administrative rules and powered by money.

The first of these comments is from John Stuart Mill; the second, from Clark Kerr, until recently President of the University of California.

I have quoted them at length because they illuminate one of the great transitions of the modern age—the decline of autonomous, rational criticism, and the rise of what Professor Herbert Marcuse entitled "one-dimensional man."

They represent the early and terminal stages in the development of centralized, bureaucratic economic power—extended now to such a point that it is able to absorb what was once proclaimed to be a transcendent center of analysis and judgment.

We need not romanticize Mill's age, nor pretend that the university students of whom he spoke acted in radical concert to revise the foundations of their time. They were, in their own way, as readily absorbed into the hierarchy of domestic civil service and foreign imperialism as students of our own society are absorbed into comparable institutions. Of crucial significance is that the very ideal of autonomy has been denied and that those who speak for higher education in this country come increasingly to derive their definition of purpose from the existing agencies of established power.

The pronouncements of Mill and Clark Kerr differ in several significant ways. The first stresses coherence, the second fragmentation; the first is exclusionary, the second is ready to incorporate any interest that society urges upon it; the first distinguishes between higher and lower knowledge, while the second distributes its emphasis in accordance with available financial support. Of greatest importance, perhaps, is that the older view regards itself as bound by intrinsic canons of culture, while the current conception accommodates and molds itself to prevailing trends.

The first view holds to an ideal of transcendence while the second is grossly immanent in its time. For contemporary doctrine, the ancient tension between what the world is and what it might become has all but vanished. The current perspective is an apologia, a celebration, an ideological consecration of this most lovely of all possible worlds—in short, a consenting academy.

This conclusion follows directly from Mr. Kerr's own analysis, for if the University performs all the functions that society imposes upon it, it will in due course most ably fulfill the predominant function every social system requires for its very existence—the justification of its established structure of power and privilege, the masking or idealization of its deficiencies, and the discrediting of dissent.

The history of all previous societies reveals to us a group of men whose primary function was to legitimate established authority. Our own time is only notable for the special urgency it imposes on the task. There are various domestic and international reasons for this development.

The first concerns the growing complexity of our technological order and its encompassing social organizations. The requirements of intelligence become more exact and the skills needed for managerial and bureaucratic roles more demanding. Accompanying these economic developments is the parallel transformation of the society from one concerned primarily with the manipulation of material things to one concerned with the manipulation of individuals. The role of physical labor declines and the role of intellectual skills and personal services is augmented in a growing white-collar stratum.

There is a change in emphasis in the industrial system from force to persuasion, a growth of public relations, managerial counseling, and mass advertising; in short, an extensive shift from production to consumption and from overt authority to covert ideological inducement.

Second, the development of a mass society tied less to specific locations and cultural traditions than to the common mass media for the formation of their life styles produces a populace eager to be formed and potentially dangerous to the status quo if it is not adequately standardized.

Again, the growing education level and sophistication of some sectors of the population make it necessary to mollify the possible dissent of those who might discover flaws in the social facade. But, paradoxically, the development of education facilitates this enterprise, for there are some deceptions which only a semi-educated man could be expected to believe or sacrifice his life for.

But the most important internal need for ideology grows from the slowly developing awareness of the discrepancy between what this social system has the power to provide its members and what it actually makes available to them. Technological resources are adequate to provide a very high level of material welfare to the entire population if the control over these facilities can be made to pass progressively from the hands of a self-authenticating business autocracy to the authority of the people as a whole.

Venerable arguments for the necessity of social injustice, class privilege, physical and cultural deprivation, and the dehumanization of labor are being corroded by the potentialities of abundance. Those who hold power in this system, then, are forced to construct elaborate theories to justify persisting misery. Here, the aid of the University can prove extremely valuable.

But there are two additional motives for illusion which derive from the international position of the United States today. Both stem from the fact of America's predominant economic power and expansiveness in the world, from its dominance over foreign economies on a global scale, and from the need generated by its productive system for subservient foreign nations to act as the suppliers of its resources and the outlets for its dislocations.

The two challenges come from the Soviet Union and China on the one hand, and from the underdeveloped third of the world on the other. The first are threats because they reject capitalistic values and compete with us in the world for economic power. The second set of nations is even more disquieting, however, for they are seeking their self-liberation at the precise moment at which the United States has emerged unmistakably as the world's dominant imperialist power. But we are not prepared to grant them control of their own industrial development, and our counter-effort is an attempt to destroy their movement toward economic autonomy through financial pressure when possible, and military intervention when necessary.

The national attempt at defense against these threats to the United States world hegemony produced the hysteria of the last twenty years of rabid anti-communism and cold-war containment—the euphemism for America's self-righteousness in domination. Intellectuals have played a significant role in producing the obfuscations of the time, and the educational system has been one of the leading contributors to the pathology of awareness.

Vigorous rebellion or revolution may fail to occur for two very different reasons: either because men are so equal to each other in their social relations that it is unnecessary, or because, while radically unequal, they perceive no way of altering their situation. But the development of technology in this country is making it progressively clearer to the impoverished in this country and to the underdeveloped countries that the suffering and injustice they are forced to undergo is not inevitable. Therefore, the more technology develops, and the more its benefits are expropriated by the privileged of the world, the greater becomes the need of the dominant class to cloak its injustice and to pretend that its actions are in the common interest or beyond the powers of men to change.

The growing division between what the world is and what it might become is the primary force behind the intensification of ancient ideological functions.

The consequence of these various internal and external pressures is that the United States is urgently compelled to disarm radical dissent and insure the performance of roles necessary to continued international hostility.

Those in power recognize the importance of domestic consensus to achieve these ends. The educational views of men like Mr. Kerr, which stress the need for molding reason to the pattern of contemporary power, appear conveniently to facilitate economic and military service and the soothing of discontent.

A University patterned after Mill's ideal could not possibly perform this task, but the contemporary University performs it masterfully. Approximately 75 per cent of the research budget of the University derives from Federal contracts, and, as Mr. Kerr notes: "Expenditures have been largely restricted to the physical and bio-medical sciences, and to engineering, with only 3 per cent for the social sciences and hardly any support for the humanities."

This distribution is defended on the grounds that it represents the national interest and the flow of money after "the most exciting new ideas." What we are being offered here is a new version of the invisible hand in which Gresham's Law is inverted to the effect that good money always drives out bad money and produces just that balance which promotes the public good.

The Federal funding of the University is only one of the media through which the pattern of society is impressed on higher education, but it exemplifies the defects transmitted through all the available media. The most crucial of these corruptions is the destruction of the internal community of the University and its replacement by a series of fragmented and isolated departmental structures without common speech, common imagination, or common purpose.

Mill's conception of a University as a place in which the student was taught to "methodize his knowledge; to look at every separate part of it in its relation to the other parts, and to the whole," is not only all but nonexistent in the current academic world, it is increasingly difficult for a growing number of educators to understand. Mr. James A. Perkins, President of Cornell, for example, has suggested that the conflict between research and scholarship might be reconciled by simply abandoning liberal education and beginning the process of specialization at matriculation. (*The University in Transition.* Princeton University Press: 1966.)

The causes of the diffusion of the University need be noted solely for the light they throw on the nature of the disintegration involved. The reason most intrinsic to the University is the fact that knowledge has been growing at a very rapid rate, making it continually more difficult for any one thinker to grasp the whole domain. But this in itself would not produce the fragmentation which occurs (since it is not the case that everything known must be taught by a University) except for the presence of other factors.

First, there is a tendency to refinement in specialized roles which seems to occur in all advanced technological societies. Next, there are the distinctly American elaborations of this theme. One derives from the anti-intellectualism of our life with its distrust of achievement for its own sake and consequent insistence that thought subserve specific ends and redeem itself through the practical results of concrete actions. To this must be added the sense of many intellectuals that if they cannot alter the shape of massive, unresponsive social power they can at least derive some satisfaction by serving it.

In this mood reason gives up the claim to direct social change. It settles instead for the immediate rewards of technical manipulation and becomes an efficient means to ends beyond its power or judgment.

The tendency is strengthened by a widespread assumption that in America the good life has already been achieved in a system of democratic, corporate pluralism. The quest of the ages having been completed, there is nothing more for reason to do but maintain the current structure and make the necessary minor corrections. This tendency is supported by the loose, casual patterning of American life, the laissez-faire climate of American political and economic history, and the general conviction that the pursuit of private, local ends will miraculously produce a public good.

It is not that public life is devoid of integration and rational planning. Industrial firms plan to the limits of their ability, and the foresight of some oligopolies and international cartels is undoubtedly extensive. But these plans are made and the activities coordinated for the sake of individual corporate ends, not for the sake of the polity as a whole. Nothing displays such technical intelligence and ingenuity as an automated factory and produces such irrational dislocation in the lives of men who are unemployed through this human achievement. The sense of the whole system is of rationality defeating its own humane requirements.

As Mr. Kerr has led us to expect, this pattern of sporadic rationality in conflict with its own potential achievement is found within the structure of the University. There, education is defined mechanically as the piling up of specific skills and bits of information, as a mound is constructed out of the piling up of individual grains of sand. The student is never required to state the relevance of one area of understanding for another, nor relate their distinctive methodologies and insights in coherent, synthetic connection. It is assumed that the summation of individually correct answers will produce something more than fragmented understanding.

The center of this disruptive environment is the individual department, where men competing for recognition establish small empires under a mutual security agreement that insures each the safety of his own domain. This safety is further enhanced against the forays of others by increasingly narrowing the limits of one's investigation until the subject is so esoteric that each individual can rightly claim to be the only living authority in the field.

Such a systematic fragmenting of knowledge cannot be corrected by the simple insertion into the curriculum of a few interdisciplinary courses. If the teachers of these courses have to win departmental approval, they are likely to come under the wrath of specialists who rightly see in the man of vision a threat to their insular success. Furthermore, as the current system prevails, the continued existence of comprehensive teachers is more and more problematical.

The immediate result is that the University is more and more populated by scholar-researchers who more closely resemble idiot-savants than men of wisdom; students find it more and more difficult to gain some comprehensive vision of themselves as world-historical beings.

In the social sciences it is very close to the truth to maintain that any problem which appears open to solution within a specific discipline is either misunderstood or of secondary importance. But the most important, over-all effect of this continued division of incommunicable skill is its ideological consequence—the tendency to stifle social consciousness and the need for radical social change.

A large social vision need not be radical, but a fragmented vision cannot be radical. The piecemeal, technical thinker can see a small advantage here and a corresponding defect there. His vision is additive; he sums up the merits and defects of a system and makes his judgment in the face of the total balance. What he lacks is dialectical understanding, the capacity to see how a specific social defect is rooted in a large structural pattern—for example, how the abuses revealed in the drug industry stem from the irresponsible power and social avarice of corporate liberalism as a system, and indicate the hopelessness of conventional attempts at regulation. Or the technical thinker sees a particular social benefit, such as the increase in average working class wages and gross national product, but he lacks any capacity to place this fact in the context of fixed maldistribution of income, or in the larger system of exploitative relations which America bears to the underdeveloped nations of the world.

That ideology is generally an inversion of reality is borne out by the current educational situation, for the University is in the process of intellectual dissolution at that precise moment of history in which the development of centralized, bureaucratic corporate power has been dominating progressively larger areas of national and international life and drawing the world's economy and destiny into an increasingly seamless whole.

The period of American domination over the world economy coincides with the period in which global concepts have been increasingly abandoned by large numbers of social scientists, whose range of interest has contracted; in specific areas of inquiry the problems they confront are of very limited relevance to the emerging world reality.

This confinement of understanding disrupts the foundations of intellectual life. The man of reason is being dismembered before our eyes. In his place appear pairs of adversaries—the teacher stands against the researching scholar, the man of thought against the man of action, the neutral analyst against the man of passionate commitment.

In the University the teacher retreats before the onslaught of the research technologists and knowledge diffusers. Every university maintains a house Negro or two—a professor whose advancement has been based predominantly upon his power as a teacher and who is dragged out on ceremonial occasions to silence the critic. But for every such anachronism there are one hundred practitioners of the conventions who have scrambled to respectability over a mass of journals and anthologies. The teacher who embodies a vision, whose life manifests in its own activity the content of his teaching art, is vanishing from sight.

What the current generation of students discovers immediately in those who profess to teach them is an almost impassable chasm between the nature of their intellectual pronouncements and the content of their lives. This is one of the grounds of the charge of irrelevance in education and one of the main reasons for student disaffection. Nor is it a defect that can be remedied without transforming the University, and that would in turn require the radical reconstruction of the society in which the University exists.

As William Arrowsmith has commented,

> At present the universities are as uncongenial to teaching as the Mojave Desert to a clutch of Druid priests. If you want to restore a Druid priest-

hood, you cannot do it by offering prizes for Druid-of-the-year. If you want Druids, you must grow forests. There is no other way of setting about it.

If it is in fact true that the University has become a service adjunct to prevailing social powers it should not be surprising that so much of its activity is taken up in the intense cultivation of disinterested intelligence. There is a clue to this process in one of the works of the German aesthetician Wilhelm Worringer. In his book, *Abstraction and Empathy* (International Universities Press: 1963), he identifies naturalism with a feeling of confidence in the external world, and particularly the organic, living world. The experience of naturalistic art is held to depend on the subject's identification with organic forms as exemplified in his own existence. Abstract art, on the contrary, is traced to a feeling of anguish and confusion in face of the complexity and instability of living beings; it is viewed as an attempt to flee this realm of dissolution for the sanctity of abstract order.

A great deal of contemporary research appears to be similarly motivated. If it is not immediately useful to established power it tends to withdraw and place between itself and the anxieties and responsibilities of the world what Bullough called "aesthetic distance" and what W. H. Auden referred to as "lecturing on Navigation while the ship is going down."

The University can accommodate itself to national power in one of two ways—overtly or covertly, through subservience or indifference, through the performance of assigned tasks, or the distraction and trivialization of potentially critical thought.

For subservience we can do no better than the introduction to Seymour Martin Lipset's *Political Man* (Doubleday: 1959). We discover there a number of astounding things: "that the United States [is] a nation in which leftist values predominate"; that "the values of liberty and equality become institutionalized within America to a greater extent than in other nations"; that "the values of socialism and Americanism are similar"; that, economic systems apart, Herbert Hoover,

Andrew Carnegie, and John D. Rockefeller "advocated the same set of social relations among men" as Marx, Engels, and Lenin; that democratic regimes are characterized by an underlying desire to avoid war.

The key to this innovative reconstruction of history is provided in the last chapter of the volume, wherein we are informed that

> . . . the fundamental political problems of the industrial revolution have been solved: the workers have achieved industrial and political citizenship; the conservatives have accepted the welfare state; and the democratic left has recognized that an increase in over-all state power carries with it more dangers to freedom than solutions for economic problems.

How good it must be to see the world as sociologists see it—devoid of economic exploitation, of Iran, Guatemala, the Dominican Republic, and Vietnam; devoid of poverty, injustice, and brutalized technology. History may yet record these sweet reflections less as a hymn to quietude than as the last muffled cry of the ostrich as its mouth fills up with sand.

The proper parallel to the subservience of the social sciences is the irrelevance of a great deal of contemporary philosophy. Nothing sums up the prevailing condition quite so well as the following remarks of C. D. Broad in the preface to his *Five Types of Ethical Theory* (Littlefield, Adams and Company: 1959):

> Fellows of Colleges, in Cambridge at any rate, have few temptations to heroic virtue or spectacular vice; and I could wish that the rest of mankind were as fortunately situated.
> Moreover, I find it difficult to excite myself very much over right and wrong in practice. I have no clear idea of what people have in mind when they say that they labour under a sense of sin; yet I do not doubt that in some cases this is a genuine experience . . . I recognize that these practical and emotional limitations may make me blind to certain important aspects of moral experience. Still, people who feel very strongly about any subject are liable to overestimate its importance in the scheme of things.

The fragmented intellect lives in comparative safety and quiet in the security of its own conceptual enclave. Here, it sets barriers against reason and the world. One social scientist tells us:

> . . . science achieves its unparalleled powers by the continuous break-down of its problem into smaller units and refinements of methods made possible by this division. On the other hand, so deeply entrenched is the humanistic supposition that "to see a man at all one must see him whole" that not even the continuous work on the dikes of their separate disciplines by academicians can keep social thought flowing in its prescribed channels without continuous leakage into and from others. (Don Martindale, *Functionalism in the Social Sciences.* American Academy of Political and Social Sciences: 1960.)

One can almost feel the shudder along the author's pen as he notes the "leakage" which tends to confuse the comfortable precision of his categories. Nor are we surprised when he proceeds to inform us that the social sciences must analyze their "problems dispassionately in a value-neutral manner," and that the aim of "turning these disciplines into genuine sciences"—that is, of breaking them down into smaller conceptual units—"is only possible through dredging operations to remove moral commitments that block the development of scientific objectivity." In these few lines, fragmentation, neutralism, the assimilation of the social to the physical sciences, and the confinement of thought to disinterested contemplation, the entire mythos of contemporary social science is concentrated and made apparent.

The connection among these factors is no mere accident. There are some perceptive comments on this matter in E. P. Thompson's *The Making of the English Working Class* (Pantheon: 1964). At one point the author comments on the contemporary discussion among historians on what has come to be known as "the standards of living controversy." He maintains:

> The objection to the reigning academic orthodoxy is not to empirical studies, per se, but to the fragmentation of our comprehension of the full historical process. First, the empiricist segregates certain events from

this process and examines them in isolation. Since the conditions which gave rise to these events are assumed, they appear not only as explicable in their own terms but as inevitable . . . But there is a second stage, where the empiricist may put these fragmentary studies back together from a multiplicity of interlocking inevitabilities, a piecemeal processional . . . we arrive at a post facto [sic] determinism. The dimension of human agency is lost.

We have come across the language of inevitability before. It was Mr. Kerr who informed us that the "community of scholars disappeared gradually and inevitably over the centuries . . . [that the University] must adapt sufficiently to its culture if it is to survive. All of this is natural. None of it can be reversed." One is inclined to reply that the inevitability of history could only have proceeded through the choice of human beings like Mr. Kerr and others who played a significant role in forming education in our time. In Mr. Kerr's analysis, however, human agency is made to dissolve, and a new rational man appears who is simply the vessel of necessity.

The crux of this conception is Mr. Kerr's judgment that the process is *natural*, a view which assimilates human history to the processes of nature and the physical sciences, in which the observer contemplates the behavior of material which possesses no responsibility for the direction of its process.

No reading of the future could have prescribed to American educators the choice they should have made for the American University —this choice was dependent upon the values, principles, and limited wisdom they brought to their understanding of history. What we are really being told in these fragments is that the American educator chose to capitulate to one of the tendencies of his time, that he agreed to relinquish his rational autonomy, and that, having made this specific decision, he is now incapable of regarding himself as anything more than the medium through which the course of the future blindly passes. But this logic unmasks the myth of neutrality, for the choice of passivity, the commitment to subservience, produced the observer's sense that he is the mere conductor of an irreversible process.

The same loss of rational autonomy and moral responsibility which underlies the division between thought and action is the source, too, of the dichotomies of fact and value, means and ends.

The prevailing credo of contemporary social inquiry limits reason to an analysis of those means which will lead most efficiently to given ends; reason is strictly precluded from passing judgment on the ends themselves. The value of the exercise is said to lie in the accumulation of stores of neutral knowledge, useful for whatever ends we intend to employ them.

The significance of this position is that it places reason and technological expertise at the disposal of prevailing power. The thinker who has abdicated responsibility for the purpose of his life by placing control over his actions in powers beyond his authority has made himself a hostage to the times. Having relinquished his claim to normative reason, he is without mooring in the world. The tides of current times, degenerate as they may be, will sweep the uncommitted in their course.

We are witness to the spectacle of men of small imagination, limited in comprehension to diminishing areas of inquiry, lacking the capacity to note the import of their activity for the more pervasive aspects of human enterprise, subservient to an establishment that does not hesitate to use them for the most inhuman and obnoxious ends—men of technical reason, as skilled at killing as at healing, progressively unconcerned with the distinction, and unaware that value resides anywhere but in technique itself. So, crippled reason pays obeisance to power and the faculty in man most apt to nurture life becomes the instrument of violence and death.

The consequence of fragmentation and of a division in the life of reason is the destruction of human autonomy. The University is thickly populated by cynical or silent men. In response to the compartmentalization of intelligence, pseudo-syntheses appear—unified visions of social man, built on the crudest model of physics or animal psychology. A widespread behaviorism appears in social thought, grounded in a methodology derived third-hand from a defunct philosophy. Quality, uniqueness, creativity, and the moral dimension of existence fall before a reductive insistence upon measurement, qualification, and restrictive processes of infinitely tedious and irrelevant observation. The view of man which emerges is ahistorical, atomistic, mechanical, disjunctive, and, again, ostensibly neutral.

For example, Robert Dahl, a behavioral political scientist, informs us in the course of an investigation of democracy in New Haven that he will interpret the terms "benefit" and "reward" as subjective appraisals—an unobjectionable procedure on its face but one supported by the astounding reason that by this device the author can maintain his neutrality, as though subjective theories of value were any more or less neutral than their objective counterparts. Or, as we are instructed by an advocate of scientific method in sociology:

> Scientific knowledge operates . . . as a sort of mental hygiene in the fields where it is applied . . . the advancement of the social sciences would probably deprive us in large measure of the luxury of indignation in which we now indulge ourselves as regards social events . . . Such indignation ministers to deep-seated, jungle-fed sentiments of justice, virtue, and a general feeling of the fitness of things, as compared with what a scientific diagnosis of the situation evokes. (George A. Lundberg, *Can Science Save Us?* Longmans, Green: 1947.)

Justice, then, according to this account, is merely a vestige of primitive existence, to be dispensed with by mature, scientific awareness. We ought not to be surprised, then, when the author develops the logical conclusion of his analysis in the following suggestion:

> If social scientists possessed an equally demonstrably relevant body of knowledge [as physical scientists] . . . that knowledge would be equally above the reach of political upheaval. The services of real social scientists would be as indispensable to Fascists as to Communists and Democrats, just as are the services of physicists and physicians.

This is merely the rationale of intellectual subservience carried to fruition. If the militarized, economic bureaucracy that defines established power in this country has no need for culture, if neutral technology is what it wants, the handmaiden of power but complaint as to ends, what shall we expect the "service-station" University to become but the internalized, refined, and rationalized conception of this barbarism?

If the humanities present man with an embodied vision of his full potentialities, they are of no use to power, and they will decline. Thought and action define each other; men of technical reason and great power brutalize the world, confirming by that fact those views which contract humanity to its prevailing business and which send men forth into the world again with more restricted versions of themselves. The dehumanization of man is reflected in the dehumanization of the study of man; its categories contract and dissolve.

We come at last to the scholarship of civility: devoid of passion, lacking love or outrage, irrelevant to the agency of man. "The advancement of learning at the expense of man," Nietzsche wrote, "is the most pernicious thing in the world."

Exactly what is the moral obligation of the University as a corporate body? It is no use telling us now, as we were told recently by Richard Hofstadter, that while individual members of the University may voice conviction, the University as a public institution is bound to strict neutrality. Mr. Kerr has demolished that argument for all time. It is no less neutral to oppose society than to support it, to refuse a place to military service than to credit it.

Neutrality is only conceivable with isolation. Nothing in the public realm can fail, at specific points, to aid or undermine established power. Man's existence is only possible through action, which requires the selection of choices and the foreclosure of others. One cannot, in all instances, avoid choice; the only hope is to choose responsively, in light of the largest understanding and the most humane commitment.

As the University is rooted in the world, it must, at given moments, choose a public course. The liberal contention that the University should refrain from criticism is an expression of "preferential neutralism," a transparently hypocritical device for the maintenance of continued service.

Of course, it is not the corporate function of the University to speak to every public issue, nor even to the vast majority of prevailing social concerns. The fundamental purpose of the University does not encompass any specific policy in regard to most contemporary matters. In its public pronouncement and corporate activity, the University should refrain from endorsing particular views in the overwhelming number of cases. But when the University's support is solicited by established agencies of power, it must decide if the services requested of it violate its defining purpose, and reject them if they do. And so, it is also obligated to protest when society has undertaken to violate, in regard either to the University itself or to humanity at large, values that the University is specifically charged to honor.

To discover the public function of a University one must begin with its internal imperative—the gathering of a community of scholars in devotion to disinterested knowledge. Such, at least, is the traditional wisdom. But it is not adequate to our time.

John Stuart Mill wrote for an age in which the distinction between pure and applied research was largely valid. The man of science could pursue his theory in the general expectation that it would not be employed to endanger mankind. Today the distinction between pure and applied science is disappearing with the growth of a state power so imperious and technologically competent that it can transform the most esoteric knowledge into techniques of terror.

Science has itself contributed to the creation of that state machinery which now makes the enterprise of science hazardous. It has done so because it has lacked responsibility for its growth. It is too late now to fall back on the platitudes of academic freedom; no biochemist can be sure that in pursuing the structure of an enzyme he is not perfecting a lethal form of warfare. This government will have to be disarmed before the clear and present danger now subverting thought can be dissolved. Until men of knowledge act to change the world, they cannot claim the unrestricted right to understand it.

But what is the obligation of those members of the University whose knowledge cannot be technologized? To answer this question we must answer another. What is the true nature of the University?

The University is the institutionalized embodiment of the life of the dialogue; that is, of communal inquiry. Dialogue is rooted in the fact that men are imperfect and perfectible. Comprehensive knowledge is not given to man in an instant. It is the elaboration of history. Nor is it given to any single man; it is the cooperative achievement of a human community. Dialogue cannot be perfected unless it is free, and the basis of rational freedom is the self-determination of imperfect reason by its own ideal. It is freeing because it liberates intelligence from matter that is extraneous or destructive of its inherent purpose—knowledge.

A mind in pursuit of knowledge is one in which the various facets of awareness are active, cumulative, and mutually relevant, wherein observation, inference, imagination, and evaluative judgment inform each other in a cumulative achievement. It is a process which depends upon creativity—the capacity to construct new alternatives. To this end the University cultivates the arts, whose function is not merely to act as a critical interpreter of experience, but to manifest to us, through concrete works, those ideal possibilities of existence of which we were previously unaware. Whatever the differences between art and discursive reason, they share a common enterprise: they cultivate the human spirit, which is the capacity of man to transcend his present context for the sake of a more comprehensive, articulate, and worthy vision of himself. That vision, in all its forms, is culture, which it is the obligation of the University to honor and protect.

The peculiar alienation of the intellectual leads him to pursue culture as an abstract end. He becomes blind to the simple fact that there is no knowledge independent of the "knowings" of individual men, nor any realm of art or science separate from the creations of actual, concrete human beings. What the University is meant to house and celebrate is not a detached domain of lifeless categories, but the spiritual existence of man, in which those categories live and take their meaning.

What is the obligation of the University in a world in which one nation is reducing the people of another to the most primitive functions of its existence; when the very rudiments of civilization are being extinguished and the orders of life upon which reason grows are being destroyed by systematic violence? In such circumstances it is the obligation of the University to rebel against the violation of man and align itself in public witness with humanity.

Today, the University is required to condemn the government of the United States for its barbaric crusade against the life and spirit of the people of Vietnam. A university that will not speak for man, whatever tasks it continues to perform, has ceased to be a human enterprise.

The University can deny its times because, like any human agency, it is not wholly absorbed in its social context. It has a special capacity to transcend its social constraints because it embodies a tradition of intellectual diversity and articulate criticism and because, of all human functions, thought is the most difficult to curtail. But while the University is uniquely promising, it is also uniquely threatened by the pressures of ideology to which we have already referred. The University is in constant tension between its ideal critical capacity and the powers of secular service that delimit its hope. Therefore, while the protest movement is centered in the University, the activity of protest is not central to the University.

It is possible to act to change the world because we are not totally immanent in it; but it is necessary for us to change the world because we do not very much transcend it. Here is the point of truth in the conception of the multi-versity. The sheer understanding that society is corrupt does not place one outside corruption. For we do not experience social existence at a distance, we ingest it. The act by which the University affirms its humanity and denies American barbarism does not constitute the cure of the University.

It may be, as Hegel has noted, that the hand that inflicts the wound is the hand that cures it. But it does so only through an anguished labor. One cannot throw off all he has been made in the density of the social world with a simple shrug of the understanding. Plato knew this truth two thousand years ago. We are still bound by it. The University has been molded by current powers and we have been formed and malformed in our turn. The alienation of society has become our apathy and fragmentation; its anti-intellectualism and glorification of technology, our play at neutralism in an inversion of ends and means; its crude devotion to wealth and power, our imbalance and intellectual prostitution.

To reconstitute one's self is for a man to remake the world in which he is defined. To know what we might become is not a simple act of the intellect; it requires that we engage in such committed action as can destroy the deforming boundaries of our lives. So, action and thought require each other, inform each other, and complete each other. The obligation imposed on the intellectual, as it is imposed on any one man, is not merely to speak against the world but to re-fashion it.

It is not a violation of the purpose of a university that some part of its activity serve society; but the University must determine through its own critical agency that the society it is to serve is a place in which the spirit of man may be nurtured and advanced.

The University is at this moment an ideological institution, a mask for systematic dominance and privilege. But as Marx noted: "The call for men to abandon their illusions about their condition is a call for men to abandon a condition which requires illusion." A free and human community of scholars can only flourish when the multitudinous communities of the exploited, the wretched, and the brutalized peoples of the earth have broken the bonds of their subservience and established themselves as men of full stature. To participate in the projection and the making of that world is the responsibility of the intellectual.

*Kenneth B. Clark (1914–)
is a noted civil rights leader,
educator and psychologist. His
studies of the effects of racial
discrimination were cited in the
Supreme Court's 1954 school
desegregation ruling. Born in the
Panama Canal Zone and reared
in Harlem, he holds a B.A. from
Howard University and a Ph.D.
from Columbia. Now a professor at the College of the City of
New York, he is author of* Prejudice and Your Child *and* Dark
Ghetto. *In 1966 he was elected
to the New York State Board of
Regents, the first Negro on the
state's educational governing
board in its 184-year history.*

17

Intelligence, the University and Society

KENNETH B. CLARK

Man is an organism that seeks and demands explanations. He has sought to understand the mysteries of his environment. He has asked questions, and searched for answers, about his origin and the meaning of his existence. He has been profoundly concerned and anxious about his ability to survive in the face of his comparative physical weaknesses and the multiple dangers of his environment. Man asks these questions and seeks their answers because he is an intelligent being who is not limited to mere behavioral interactions with his environment. He is a conscious, reflective, evaluative, anxious being who is required to be as responsive to the realities of his ideational and created environments as to his physical and biological environments. The fact of human intelligence demands this. Human intelligence also provides the key to the answers to the questions it is capable of raising. Man believes that he has survived as a species and will continue to survive in spite of his skeletal weakness because he has the intelligence necessary to probe, to seek to understand and to control the environmental forces that threaten him.

So far, his experience supports this intellectual circularity and chauvinism.

The critical question of this period of human history—the answer to which, paradoxically, must also be obtained through the critical use of man's mind—is whether human intelligence as traditionally defined offers any reliable assurance of human survival. This question may seem hopelessly abstract, even trite. But nothing could be more concrete. Is pure intelligence enough to protect man from self-inflicted destruction?

Paradox and irony are inherent in this question:

—The choice is between a world of leisure, of productive and creative humanity, or a world destroyed through human intelligence. Man's understanding and his mastery of matter and energy justify his claims to godlike superiority; provide him with the basis for enriching and deepening human experience; and, at the same time, provide him with the instruments for ultimate destruction.

—Science and technology, among the constructive benefits of human intelligence, cannot, at present, be divorced from possible destruction or inhuman uses. Some have sought to resolve this dilemma by suggesting that certain scientific discoveries be destroyed or blocked before fulfillment. Yet the power of thought cannot be artificially or arbitrarily controlled without atrophy. We cannot have the benefits of the unfettered mind without freedom and risk. To control intelligence in the attempt to insure only benevolent consequences would be a Pyrrhic victory sentencing the human race to ignorance, stagnation and decadence, and probably would be impossible.

—Free human intelligence and its richest consequences—science, technology, art, literature, philosophy and religion—are essential to human progress and survival. But in their pure form, they are not enough. They do not in themselves reduce the capricious dangers and hazards to life. They bring with them now the novel and awesome possibility of self-inflicted annihilation.

Now our gods are the gods of Intelligence, Science and Technology. These gods have their powerful priests and apostles. Their true believers are uncritically abject, obsequious and worshipful in the faith that these omnipotent and omniscient gods will protect and save them and enrich their lives. But there remains the gnawing suspicion that these contemporary gods are fickle and treacherous. They promise and they taunt. They fulfill and they tantalize. They offer the extension and the deepening of life and they threaten imminent extinction. They play with man as they dare him to question their power. They know that man dares not doubt, dares not question and dares not now reject them because to do so would be to throw him back to a state of futility, helplessness, insecurity and despair even more stultifying than that faced by his most primitive ancestors. Man now emerges as the victorious prisoner of his own intelligence. He cowers in each victory. As he rockets to the moon, he plans the futility of protection from nuclear devastation on earth.

This paradox of human intelligence can only be resolved through the use of courageous and creative human intelligence. A reasonable starting postulate could be that the present threats to survival do not result from too much intelligence, or too much science or even from too much technology. Like his ancestors who faced crises of survival, contemporary man is also threatened by ignorance. The ignorance of modern man, however, is not that which can be cured by the exercise of pure intelligence. His critical ignorance lies in an inadequate functional sense of social morality.

Social morality is illusive and difficult to define. It involves not only man's intelligence but his feelings and his total being.

Social morality depends upon man's capacity to give and to receive love, to be kind and to be empathic. Love in its most concrete sense is a primary emotion essential to the preservation of the species. It is a positive and adaptive emotion, which involves an affinity and desire for closeness with another human being. It is essential for survival. Kindness may be viewed as the generalized expression of love, concern and sensitivity in interpersonal relations. A kind person seeks to be helpful. Empathy is the ability to feel into and to identify with the needs of another human being. An empathic person shares another's concerns, joys, anguish, despair, frustrations, hopes and aspirations as if they were his own. Empathy, unlike love, is not concrete and primary but rather requires the capacity for abstract thought. Empathy is not possible for a limited, defective, egocentric or animalistic human organism. Without empathy, social morality, social responsibility, justice, and human society itself would not be possible. Empathy involves the convergence of human intelligence, love and kindness.

There are those who are described and who describe themselves as tough-minded realists who contend that love, kindness and empathy are mere disguises for more powerful and primitive egocentric and animalistic impulses in man. They contend that there is no stable basis for social morality and that all morality is a thin pretensive veneer quick to disappear under stress, deprivation or adversity. This debate between the advocates of man's moral capacity and obligations and those who contend that only egocentric power imperatives are important has dominated man's struggle to define the dimensions of his humanity from the awakening of human consciousness up to the present Vietnam protests.

Those who argue that man is incapable of a dependable functional form of social morality have given up and written the epitaph of the human species. This is so because the chief threat to human survival is to be found in the exercise of pure, amoral human intelligence in the service of man's irrational, primitive, egocentric, animalistic impulses harnessed to his blind quest for power and status.

Probably the only protection for contemporary man is to discover how to use his intelligence in the service of love and kindness. The training of human intelligence must include the simultaneous development of the empathic capacity. Only in this way can intelligence be made an instrument of social morality and responsibility—and thereby increase the chances of survival.

The need to produce human beings with trained morally sensitive intelligence is essentially a challenge to educators and educational institutions. Traditionally, the realm of social morality was left to religion and the churches as guardians or custodians. But their failure to fulfill this responsibility and their yielding to the seductive lures of the men of wealth and pomp and power are documented by the history of the last two thousand years and have now resulted in the irrelevant "God Is Dead" theological rhetoric. The more pragmatic men of power have had no time or inclination to deal with the fundamental problems of social morality. For them simplistic Machiavellianism must remain the guiding principle of their decisions—power *is* morality, morality is power. This oversimplification increases the chances of nuclear devastation. We must therefore hope that educators and educational institutions have the capacity, the commitment and the time to instill moral sensitivity as an integral part of the complex pattern of functional human intelligence. Some way must be found in the training of human beings to give them the assurance to love, the security to be kind, and the integrity required for a functional empathy.

This task will not be any easier for our colleges and universities than it has been for our churches, for our universities are a part of a society dominated by power. They too seek the protection, safety and status that come with identification with those who have power. The avoidance of this socially and morally responsible role takes many forms—some subtle and some flagrant. Among the more subtle forms of escape are the postures and assertions of moral relativism, of academic detachment, of philosophical purity and scientific objectivity.

According to the proponents of moral relativism, right and wrong, good and bad, justice and injustice are relative values which are not subject to empirical, objective or consistent definition. They assert that moral values are determined by the society or culture within which the individual is socialized, and that the prevailing social norms will determine what a person believes and how he behaves toward his fellowman. Initially this view arose from the important work of the cultural anthropologists and reflected the growing liberalism and tolerance of human differences characteristic of certain aspects of twentieth-century American social science. But the fashionable oversimplification of moral relativism and its confusion with moral nihilism masked the basic fact that man is unique as a value-seeking and moral organism. Nor can the horrors of infanticide, genocide and Hitlerian Nazism be comprehended or dealt with within moral relativism's limited and naïve conceptual framework. Literalistic moral relativism must be seen as indifference, as insensitivity, and as moral and intellectual confusion. To the extent that colleges and universities promulgate this point of view without powerful countervailing probes, they provide an adequate escape from any moral commitment for themselves and they leave their students without moral guidelines essential for the responsible use of intelligence.

The same must be said for the postures of academic detachment and scientific objectivity when they are defined as precluding the making of moral judgments and the rejection of the responsibility to remedy that which is wrong or unjust in our society. It is argued that detachment and objectivity are required for the discovery of truth. But of what value is a soulless truth? Does not truth require meaning? And does not meaning require a context of values? Is there any meaningful or relevant truth without commitment?

How is it possible to study a slum objectively? What manner of human being can remain detached as he watches the dehumanization of other human beings? Why would one want to study a sick child except to make that child well?

Intellectual detachment and scientific objectivity can be most insidious and dangerous forms of moral irresponsibility. Indifference, equivocation and expediency avoid the risks engendered by the use of human intelligence for the attainment of social justice and human progress. When our colleges and universities become havens from value, when our teachers become defenders of such transparent escapes, they abdicate their responsibilities for moral leadership and they contribute to, if not help to create, the profound tragedy of the moral erosion and emptiness of those who have the intellectual gifts that might make human advancement and survival possible.

The persistent protests of a small number of our college students extensively reported in the newspapers beginning with the first sit-ins of Negro college students, followed by the Berkeley rebellion, and the Vietnam protests can be seen as symptomatic of the deep undercurrent of moral uneasiness of sensitive young people. They are demanding of their colleges and the universities some demonstration of humanity. They are demanding honesty. They are demanding evidence of concern with justice. They are demanding that colleges and universities be socially and morally relevant. They are few, and they are anguished and confused; but they are concerned—and they assume the risks of the concerned.

So far our colleges and universities and the men who control and run them have not yet answered these young people affirmatively. Perhaps they do not understand them. It is probably that the years of moral denial and studied blindness to flagrant problems of social injustice that were deemed essential to the efficient financing and administration of a large and complex educational institution have made it difficult and impractical to listen to pleas for dialogue and for resolution of fundamental moral issues. Our colleges and universities have a long history of default on important moral issues. They have frequently tried to make a virtue of isolation from the problems of the marketplace and from the anguished yearnings of the deprived and powerless people of our society. They have thrown in their lot with the powerful in government, business and industry. Their concern with purity of research is reconciled with relative ease as they accept larger and larger grants and subsidies from the Defense Department, from the C.I.A., and from big business for work on practical problems— problems of power. It is only when the issue is directly or indirectly one of social justice or fundamental social change that our colleges and universities raise questions concerning the propriety of institutional involvement or the role of a professor, and ask whether involvement is consistent with the pure and detached quest for truth.

An attempt at a somewhat balanced appraisal of the role of American universities requires one to mention some exceptions to these severe charges. Probably the chief exception would be found in the research and teaching in the medical and public health schools of our universities, which are directly tied to human need and human welfare. Their findings must be directly or indirectly relevant. They cannot be pompously trivial. But even they are more concerned with individual cure than with the prevention of the conditions of poverty and degradation that lead to disease.

There are many specific and relevant areas in which American colleges and universities have defaulted in providing morally sensitive intellectual leadership for our society:

—They have watched silently, and facilitated, the process whereby education from the primary grades on has become ruthlessly competitive and anxiety-producing—in which the possibility of empathy, concern for one's classmate and the use of superior intelligence as a social trust are precluded, as our children are required to learn by their experiences in the classroom, by the demands of their teachers and the insistence of their parents, that education is competition and that intelligence is a device to obtain superior status and economic advantage over others.

—Under the guise of efficiency, the demands of mass education and the pressure of limited facilities in colleges, they have facilitated the reduction of the educational process to the level of content retention required for the necessary score on the College Boards and the Graduate Record Examinations at the price of reflective and critical thought.

—They have permitted our elementary and secondary schools to become contaminated by and organized in terms of the educationally irrelevant factors of race and economic status.

—They have watched without sustained protests the erosion of the quality of education provided for minority group children and other lower-status children—erosion to the point of criminal inefficiency and dehumanization.

—They have watched in silence the creeping blight of our cities and the spawning of Negro ghettos, concerned only when the pathologies associated with the ghetto come too close to the walls of the university. Only then do they seek to protect themselves, sometimes through a ruthless and callous dispossessing of the unwanted lower-status people.

—They have abdicated any sustained, forthright moral leadership in America's attempt to resolve the anguish of its pervasive racial problem. Leadership in the civil rights struggle has come from civil rights organizations, from the federal courts, and more recently from the executive and legislative branches of the federal and some state governments; and from the Catholic, Protestant and Jewish churches and synagogues. Despite the commitment of some of their faculty, American colleges and universities have, as institutions, remained detached and nonrelevant to this major domestic issue of our times. Indeed colleges and universities are major bastions of a subtle and persistent form of white supremacy.

In summary, the major charge that must now be made against American colleges and universities is that they have not fulfilled their responsibility and obligation to develop and train human beings with a morally relevant and socially responsible intelligence. They have operated as if it were possible for a detached, amoral intelligence to be adaptive. They have not provided their students with the moral guidelines essential for the effective, creative and adaptive use of superior intelligence. They have not provided their faculties with the stimulation or protection for a socially responsible use of their own critical intelligence. And above all they have not provided the moral leadership for society—they have not alerted the public to the urgency of finding moral and democratic solutions to critical domestic and international problems.

Given these real and chronic deficiencies, how can one hope that American colleges and universities can become morally relevant in time to make any difference in the destiny of man? One can hope because one must. The deficiencies in our educational system are remediable. The first step in any attempt at remedying a problem is the courage to recognize it as a problem—followed by the commitment to change.

A realistic basis for hope is found in the fact that man has the capacity for empathy. He struggles for values. He insists and argues and demands and dies and kills in his tortuous and often pathetic quests for moral stabilities. Another basis for hope is that empathy, like intelligence, can be made more functional and effective through education. If it is trained and directed it can become meaningful for the individual and adaptive for the society. If it is untrained it becomes unpredictable, random, misdirected, or it atrophies. The acceptance of the responsibility to reinforce man's empathic capacity as an integral part of the responsibility to train intellect is now the clear challenge of relevance confronting contemporary educational institutions.

American higher education need not continue to subordinate itself to the goals of efficiency, expediency, power, status and success. Young people can be trained in our schools, colleges and universities to value critical and independent thought above affability; to value individuality and creativity above conformity and packaged opinions; to value evidence of concern, commitment and social sensitivity above personal acceptance and mere social success. Once they understand the stakes and the nature of the challenge, it will be possible for our colleges and universities to produce totally educated persons.

A truly educated person is trained to mesh his intelligence with his feelings in a disciplined whole. He cannot deny or subordinate either his brain or his heart because each is essential to the effective functioning of the other. Our colleges must provide the opportunities for students to test their courage to stand alone—to accept the risks of alienation and aloneness that come with the anguish and the torture of the search for moral commitment and disciplined, intelligent action. Colleges must be the place where human beings are prepared to bolster intelligence with compassion, courage and increasing wisdom. American colleges and universities will demonstrate that they are relevant to the crucial issues of our times, that they are morally adaptive, and therefore that they can contribute to the survival of the human race, when they fully and functionally accept as their responsibility the need to train individuals of moral intelligence who demonstrate by the totality of their lives that they understand that an injustice perpetrated upon any human being robs them of some of their humanity and demands of them personal, constructive and intelligent action for justice. Wisdom and moral sensitivity tempering human intelligence are not now ethical abstractions. They are survival imperatives. Relevant colleges and universities can and must make them real.

Though the controversial issue of American involvement in Vietnam stands in the background of this 1967 essay, its attack on educators and their schools has much broader applicability. Theodore Roszak (1933–) served during 1964–65 as editor of the British pacifist weekly, Peace News. *Recipient of the doctorate in history from Princeton University, he has taught at Stanford and at California State College at Hayward, where he is associate professor of history and chairman of its History of Western Culture program. An expanded version of this essay appeared as the introduction to* The Dissenting Academy, *edited by him.*

18

The Complacencies of the Academy: 1967

THEODORE ROSZAK

Pascal thinks that men pursue their business and their sciences with such single-mindedness in order to escape the most important questions which every moment of loneliness and true leisure would urge upon them—questions concerning the Why, Whence, and Whither of life. But curiously enough, not even the most obvious question occurs to our scholars: what benefit their labor, their haste, and their painful ecstasies can possibly have? . . . But if, as men of science, you go about science in the same manner in which brokers go about the tasks which life's daily necessities impose upon them, then what is to become of a culture condemned to await the hour of its birth and its salvation amidst this excited, breathless, aimless, fidgeting infatuation with science and learning? [1]

FRIEDRICH NIETZSCHE

The "Men of Science" who were on the receiving end of Nietzsche's typically abrasive contempt when he issued the above challenge nearly a century ago were his own colleagues in the German universities. But he might have been speaking with undiminished force to the present generation of American scholars and scientists. And would the account they could give of themselves be any less pathetic than the account German science and scholarship has had to tender in our time? No doubt there are fine distinctions that can be made between the concentration camp and the strategic hamlet, the gas oven and the thermonuclear missile. But with how much pride can any of us undertake the exercise in moral pedantry it would require to draw these distinctions?

It is by no means an historical coincidence that both American and German academics should prove vulnerable to the barb of Nietzsche's insight. For much of the character of higher learning in America was established in the post-Civil War period by a generation of scholars and scientists who had received their advanced training in the German academies. For men like Josiah Royce, G. Stanley Hall, Henry Baxter Adams, the German university with its lecture method, its seminars, its laboratories, and its rigorous Teutonic conception of *Wissenschaft* was what higher education was all about—or certainly ought to be all about. Universities such as Heidelberg, Leipzig, Göttingen and Berlin became the academic New Jerusalem; their American disciples brought home their style and standards like exotic treasures and redesigned higher education in America to serve as a suitable setting for them.

To be sure, the zeal of that generation of academics—the creators

---

[1] Quoted in *The Abuse of Learning: The Failure of the University* by Frederic Lilge (New York: 1948), pp. 92–93.

of the "graduate school," of aristocratic scholarly communities like Johns Hopkins and Clark, of the American learned societies—helped to save the American university from becoming a very philistine place indeed. For the academic world which they confronted in the latter nineteenth century was rapidly being submerged in that peculiarly American vulgarization of higher learning known as "service." "Service," as it was, and still is, interpreted by the administrative, financial, and political forces that govern American higher education, meant the indiscriminate adaptation of the university to the interests of the private or public groups that supported it. It meant, for example, offering "professional study" and even degrees in boy-scouting, fire insurance, home economics, and hotel management. (Such courses were available in schools of the caliber of Cornell, Chicago, and Wisconsin.) It meant, in brief, conferring the prestige of higher learning on whatever kinds of technical information and vocational training, whatever modes of socialization and entertainment, the community wanted from the campus.

The conflict between service and scholarship in American higher education was not destined to be resolved wholly in favor of either side —at least not at the vast majority of the more important state and private universities. Instead, the conflict has gradually worked itself into an impasse. And, in our typically "pragmatic" way, the impasse has been given a name and has become a substitute for a solution. The name is "the multiversity"—the school which teaches, in Robert Hutchins' words, "anything we can get anybody to pay for." Including, let it be said, valid subjects. For if the "service station" concept of higher education has survived, and indeed prospered, over the past three generations, the principled academic has at least managed to carve out and fortify a niche for himself in the busy labyrinth of the contemporary campus. As Laurence R. Veysey shows in his excellent description of the clash of educational ideals in *The Emergence of the American University* (Chicago, 1965), such was the compromise that scholarly research and liberal culture finally settled for in the major state and private universities. In the graduate schools, in the colleges of arts and letters, in their portion of the general education requirements, the academics have achieved a kind of disgruntled coexistence with the home economists, the educationists, the engineers, the business administrators, and the vast contingent of those who train and entertain in the guise of teaching.

This historic competition between vulgar and elitist notions of higher education continues to structure much of the discussion that goes on in the multiversities about the ideals of education, as well as a great amount of faculty politics. The proponents of the multiversity still parade under the banner of "democracy"; the scholars still champion the virtues of disinterested intellect. But the truth is that their dialogue has become merely a peevish one, a debate between half-men who have lost touch with the essential meaning both of "democracy" and "intellect" and who are equally guilty of a cultural failure that is beyond the power of both to comprehend.

For what have these two academic traditions led to finally? On the one hand, the ideal of service has led to a collaboration between the universities, the corporations, and the government so indiscriminate that the American military establishment has no more difficulty in procuring academics to carry out any project—bar none—than its counterparts in totalitarian societies. Ranking physicists and engineers specialize in thermonuclear weaponry, and leading schools like MIT and the University of California at Berkeley derive a major part of their budgets from "service" of this kind. Biologists at the University of Pennsylvania have worked under secret contracts to develop chemical-biological weaponry.[2] As part of the Army's Project Camelot, social scientists have pooled their expertise in order to help our military plan counterinsurgency activities in Latin America.[3] In order to provide the USIA with cold-war propaganda of a scholarly cut, the University of Southern California has set up, with the generous support

[2] This project was finally discontinued in May, 1967, by a decision of the university's Board of Trustees, in response to several months of student and faculty protest, climaxing in sit-ins in President Harnwell's office. See *The New York Times*, May 7, 1967, p. 2.

[3] On Project Camelot, see Senator Fulbright's remarks in *The Congressional Record—Senate*, August 25, 1965, pp. 20905–06. See also the *Weekly Magazine*, a supplement of the *Daily Californian* (University of California at Berkeley), of November 25 and December 7, 1965, and February 24, 1966.

of a radical right-wing industrialist, a Research Institute on Communist Strategy and Propaganda.[4]

And so on. And so on. A full listing of such activities—including the prestigious employment academics have sought at military think-tanks like the RAND Corporation—could go on for dozens of pages. But the picture is clear enough: in the name of service, universities and university men have willingly collaborated in all the corruptions into which our government's exaggerated sense of omnipotence has led us. The concept of service, the willingness to do whatever society will pay for, has culminated in the virtually complete abandonment of moral discrimination—the indispensable element of wisdom. Until at last, the multiversity, morally speaking, resembles nothing so much as the highly adaptable brothel in Jean Genêt's *The Balcony*.

Meanwhile, what have Nietzsche's "excited, breathless, aimless, fidgeting" scholars come to in contemporary America? The answer is equally melancholy. For up until the recent flurry of campus protest against the war in Vietnam, the American academic scene has produced a virtually unbroken record of social irrelevance and moral complacency. Given the fact that American universities have drawn so heavily on the German scholarly tradition, one might have expected that the disaster in which that tradition participated would have led to a hard scrutiny of its influence in this country. If the homeland of *Wissenschaft* and *Lehrfreiheit* could experience such a reversion to barbarism with so little resistance from its universities, is it not clear that even such astute students, as well as influential planners, of higher education as Abraham Flexner were tragically wrong in contending (as they did right up to the brink of the Nazi revolution) that the German professors "in theory and in practise come nearest to giving higher education its due position"? [5]

[4] See Gladwin Hill's report in *The New York Times* for September 15, 1963, p. 118.

[5] For an examination of the role of the academics in Germany's cultural disaster, see Frederic Lilge's *The Abuse of Learning: The Failure of the University* (New York, 1948) p. 99. Lilge characterizes the grand tradition of scholarly "objectivity" and social neutrality as having afforded the German academics "the happiness of permanent employment and of concealing from themselves the futility of their efforts and their lives."

Certainly the opportunities for a strong show of intellect and conscience have not been lacking in America. The "balance of terror"—which comes down to an exquisitely rationalized social commitment to the strategy of genocide—has entrenched itself in the psychology and morality, as well as the economy, of our society. The threadbare ideals and rhetoric of an anachronistic nationalism continue to dominate our politics. The ominous imbalance of wealth between the world's rich and poor nations continues to increase. The control of democratic institutions over decision-making elites continues to weaken. But about all of these forces that threaten the spiritual, and indeed the physical, survival of civilization, the scholarly community has little to say.

Nor do American academics lack occasions for educating the general public. At least once a year, each of the learned societies that control the careers and standards of professional academics holds regional and national conferences. Very rarely, of course, do these conferences gain any public visibility, but this is not because the press is unwilling to provide coverage. On the contrary, a paper like *The New York Times* goes out of its way to find anything of public relevance that is discussed at these meetings. Thus, at the 1965 meeting of the American Historical Association, the *Times* reported fully on a paper dealing with the problem of violence in the civil rights struggle and on one concerning the relations of Pope Pius XII with anti-Nazi conspirators. At the 1965 meeting of the American Political Science Association, a *Times* reporter, clearly at the end of his resources, went about the corridors pressing political scientists for their cautious and pedestrian opinions on the Johnson administration. Following the 1965 conference of the American Sociological Association, the *Times* finally appeared to lose patience and, taking up some critical remarks made by the Association's president, went on to chastise the sociologists for offering so little that had any relevance to the problems of our times. Complaining strongly (for the *Times*) about the "mores of the academic world where demonstrations of abstract technical expertise—preferably of a mathematical nature—merit special status," the editorial went on to ask if the function of sociology is "to get particular individuals academic promotions, profitable grants of doubtful use, or is it to make pioneering contributions to the understanding of the nature and operation of a complex society undergoing rapid change?" [6] Otherwise there was nothing in 1965, as in previous years, that the academics had to say that was of interest to their fellow citizens. The Modern Language Association is reported to have discussed some new teaching techniques and methods of teacher training; the American Economic Association wondered, in very technical terms, whether the Vietnam war would distort our "manpower allocation" or lead to inflation. (The *Times* commented that most of the people at the latter meeting seemed to be much more interested in job-hunting.) The American Psychological Association included papers on psychological testing for Peace Corps applicants, the relationship of conformity to time-and-motion efficiency in industry, and a discussion by a Professor Birdwhistell on the way men and women use the word "no."

It was not until the 1966 conferences that two of the professional groups (the American Anthropological Association and the Eastern Division of the American Philosophical Association) saw fit to address themselves critically to the war in Vietnam. The anthropologists— mainly at the instigation of a small band of younger academics—managed to pass a resolution condemning the use of napalm against civilian populations in Vietnam, despite their chairman's strenuous contention that the resolution was "political" and out of keeping with the purposes of their association—which were "to advance the science of anthropology and to further the professional interests of anthropologists." He was reminded from the floor by one of his colleagues that "genocide is not in the professional interest of anthropologists." [7] Voting in favor of an antiwar resolution at their conference, the philosophers concluded—but it should have gone without saying—that "the traditions of our vocation make it appropriate that we express our concern on issues of great moral urgency." [8] But the concern of the philosophers and the anthropologists was not shared in any collective capacity

---

[6] "Sociology For What," *The New York Times,* September 21, 1965, p. 4.
[7] *The New York Times,* November 20, 1966, p. 13.
[8] *The New York Times,* December 30, 1966, p. 15.

by the other professions. Despite the pressure the war was putting upon male students, despite the fact that a Presidential commission was scheduled to make crucial recommendations on the draft only one month after the conferences convened, none of the professions even troubled to debate a resolution on conscription. None raised any question of the propriety of using grade records as a basis for Selective Service classification. The failure to do this was not surprising. The conferences, being august assemblies of professional scholars, place teaching and students in their proper perspective; out of sight and out of mind.

Clearly the conferences of learned societies are meant to serve other functions than that of communicating with the society-at-large. Their structure and tone derive from much the same purposes that shape the trade conventions of, say, the Association of Plumbing Contractors or the Association of Hotel Managers, where new and specialized knowledge is passed about, old friends get together, and valuable commercial contracts are made. Still it is odd, to say the least, that the conferences of learned societies in the humanities and social sciences should transpire so routinely and unobtrusively in our society. There is, after all, not a single one of the professions of higher learning that is not ultimately connected with that aggregation of ideals which distinguishes civilized life from barbarism. Indeed, few of us who teach in the universities would consider a student adequately educated who had not been asked to ponder the examples of Socrates and Abelard, Galileo and Spinoza, Voltaire and Pasteur, among all the other figures who fought to dignify the life of the mind and to assert the preeminence of the moral virtues. But what do the examples of these great forebears mean to academics themselves? What does it imply when those who are peculiarly charged with the cultivation and defense of intellectual and humane values come together year after year, ostensibly to make a collective assertion of their identity as teachers and scholars, but in reality with little more socially significant purpose in mind than can be found at a convention of hotel managers? Do they believe that civilized values in our day require no special cultivation or defense and that there are other and better things to do than to use these assemblies as forums for vigorous public discussion of public issues? Or do they believe that no matter what may be wrong with America, it is not at all the teacher's responsibility to address himself to its correction?

Let us examine a contrasting situation. The matters discussed and voted upon at the annual convention of the AFL-CIO are apt to be front-page news. No Presidential administration would dare let such a convention meet without entering thickly into its politics and attempting to influence its resolutions on public questions. But has any administration ever troubled itself to send representatives to meetings of the American Historical Association or the Modern Language Association with a view to "winning over" the conference? The prospect is absurd.

One may object that the AFL-CIO is after all a voting bloc of immense size and is courted as such by political leaders. The learned societies, being so inconsequential in their voting strength, receive no political attention. But this objection will not do. Obviously, the learned societies are in no position to compete as a "bloc vote" with other forces in our society. Nor would that be an appropriate form of competition for them. But they *are* societies of opinion-makers—or at least potentially so. They are composed of learned and articulate men whose words and deeds affect millions of students and could be of considerable influence with the voting public. Their opinions, if not their votes, should carry weight in Washington. The embarrassment of the Johnson administration at Robert Lowell's refusal in 1965 to accept a White House award is an example of how sensitive official society is to the thoughtful dissent of one intellectual. The press coverage given to the testimony of academics such as Henry Steele Commager at the hearings on Vietnam of the Senate Foreign Relations Committee is another example of potential influence. If the Johnson administration does not trouble itself for the opinions of academics—except of those who support its policies—it is simply because the opinions are not there in the first place. Academic societies are politically irrelevant and are treated as such—what academic societies do and say is, in the end, "academic."

This public irrelevance, this narrow professionalism of scholarship in the humanities and social sciences, makes it difficult to take seriously much of the conventional campus competition between "academics" and "nonacademics," between "technicians" and "humanists." For is not the scholar's lack of moral responsiveness really equivalent to the technician's lack of moral discrimination? Is the scholar who indulges in fastidious but morally undirected research into Shakespearean sonnets or nineteenth-century European diplomatic history any less of a mere technician than the typical electronics engineer? For what is it that significantly distinguishes the humanist from the technician, if it is not the willingness to ask: What is this knowledge *for*? Where does it lead?

Since such questions of purpose, direction, and value are no more fashionable among scholars today than among technicians, it is no wonder that the servants of learning and the servants of the warfare state have by and large been able to arrange a subtle and pervasive *entente* on the campuses. Ultimately, the antagonism between them runs no deeper than the bickering that existed between the Whigs and Tories of eighteenth-century England—rivals who always managed to collaborate in maintaining a regime of privilege beneficial to both. The name of the federal government's largest single, general commitment to the support of higher education is, after all, the National *Defense* Education Act. Though primarily a technician's gravy train, not many scholars would really care to see it derailed, for fear of losing such lucrative by-products as the $23 million which the Defense Department budgeted in 1965 for research in the social and behavioral sciences or the NDEA appropriations that go to the departments of foreign languages, which amount to $12 million for 1967 alone.

The world-as-it-is has become increasingly generous to its academics. It is only natural, perhaps, that academics are more willing than ever to prepare students to take their places passively in the world-as-it-is. The baccalaureate and doctorate provide admission into the ranks of an elite professional class distributed through the corporations, the military, and the government bureaucracies. The "humanities" serve the Great Society by providing the university graduate with a finer taste in music, literature, art, films: that is, a little cultural icing for the economic cake. Both humanist and technician can take pride in their joint product: let us say, an Aerospace computer programmer. Off the job, he is a man of easy culture. He listens appreciatively to his local "good music" station; his library is filled with paperback editions of Plato, Tolstoy, Shakespeare; his walls are graced with Modigliani and Braque prints. He remembers his Humanities IA and his English Lit. 44B, and they decorate his life. On the job, he complacently and ingeniously perfects the balance of terror.

To be sure, the issue of social responsibility is beginning to receive attention on the campuses, but serious discussion is taking place mainly among the students, graduate students, and junior faculty. Those on the commanding heights of the learned professions are doing little more than cautiously prowling about the margins of a question that is at least twenty years overdue for urgent consideration—and contenting themselves, finally, with that strange kind of pride academics seem to be able to take in "recognizing" a problem but not in solving it.

Thus, at the 1965 conference of the American Sociological Association, Pitirim Sorokin, in his presidential address, announced that it is time "to get beyond the phase of fact-finding to the creative, generalizing period that is now due." Or we have the example of Morris Bishop, president in 1965 of the MLA, lamenting the fact that there simply isn't any longer enough literature to provide work for all the scholars now on the scene. (But his solution is to suggest some further study of the literature of zoology or aviation!) Or we have Kenneth Boulding telling the 1965 meeting of the American Economic Association in no uncertain terms that ". . . the whole economics profession, indeed, is an example of that monumental misallocation of intellectual resources which is one of the most striking phenomena of our times." Boulding's complaint was that the economists have been "obsessed with macro-economics, with piddling refinements in mathematical models, and with the monumentally unsuccessful exercise in welfare economics which has preoccupied a whole generation with a dead end, to the almost total neglect of some of the major problems of our day." Did his remarks make any difference? Judging by the contents of those issues of the *American Economic Journal* published subsequent to his remarks; not in the least. For the image of economics we find there is still that of a chaotic mass of neat little conundrums for technicians to "kick around." But perhaps Boulding's criticism is being seriously "talked up" around the profession and will come to something . . . eventually.

Despite all the protest and unrest on the campuses, then, one must still say of the academics what C. Wright Mills said of them almost a decade ago in *The Causes of World War III:*

> They live and work in a benumbing society without living and working in protest and in tension with its moral and cultural insensibilities. They use the liberal rhetoric to cover the conservative default. They do not make available the knowledge and the sensibility required by publics, if publics are to hold responsible those who make decisions "in the name of the nation." They do not set forth reasons for human anger and give to it suitable targets.[9]

There are many more today who would associate themselves with that accusation. But the accusation remains in force; the cultural default Mills attacked persists. And the reason for its persistence still requires close study. For despite the fact that more academics now than perhaps ever before in American history are beginning to respond to the tug of social conscience, the problem we are confronted with is not simply a matter of overcoming a certain timidity or sluggishness on the part of individual scholars. The problem has an *institutional* dimension; it has to do with the total configuration of relationships in which the individual academic finds himself: his training, his habits of work, his patterns of friendship and allegiance. That is to say, it has to do with the fact that the academic man exists mainly within the environment of his own profession.

In a recent critique of higher education, Paul Goodman chided the universities for failing to be "communities of scholars" and the academics for yielding control of the schools to administrators of an organization-man mentality. The situation Goodman describes smacks of

---

[9] C. Wright Mills, *The Causes of World War III* (New York, 1958), p. 145.

usurpation and despotism. But it is not experienced as such by most academics. What the administrators have taken over—actually with the full consent of most faculty members—is simply the running of the particular campuses on which the professions are practiced. The campus is *not* understood to be the "community" to which a scholar belongs. Rather he belongs to a particular department and profession. It is in the department that a scholar makes his career; it is before a professional audience that every "serious" scholar performs and is judged.

In reality, the profession of History, say, is simply the sum total of all the history departments at all the colleges and universities in the country. The profession has no national organization of any significance—beyond, perhaps, the editorial board of its leading journal. Nonetheless, its informal networks of information, evaluation, and employment exist, and their standards count in the career of every historian who wants to succeed. In the mind of "academic man" there is a vision rather like Jacob's ladder: a great *cursus honorum,* which runs from an instructorship at Punxatawney State Teacher's Normal up to the dizzying heights of a full professorship at Harvard, Columbia, Berkeley. A knowledgeable academic can probably peg the relative standing on that ladder of every one of his colleagues.

Thus for most academics the locus of their allegiance is the department—and beyond the department, the profession. Everything in between, which includes the coordination and running of the campuses on which departments are encamped, is very largely left to the administrator. For, given the prevailing standards of the learned professions, what the administrators are concerned with—mainly local and "interdepartmental" affairs—has relatively little influence on the career of the academic.

This is, of course, the reason why academics—especially ambitious academics at the "best" schools—have so much trouble with the bothersome business of education. Students belong to the particular campus on which they are studying. Educating them provides no professional visibility, and therefore designing an educational environment for them is left primarily to the administrators. This problem shows up especially in the handling of general education. General education, being broad and integrative, does not run readily through the narrow channels of the standard professional disciplines. Nor can one make a career in the important schools as a "generalist." So what careerist in his right mind would want to teach courses in general education? When the Columbia University faculty abandoned the sophomore year of its Contemporary Civilization survey, it explained its decision by observing that "the members of the staff do not regard the course as a challenge to their professional skill. . . ."

As with education, so too with the obligation of the campus to its community: unless community problems can create professionally acceptable research, they are merely local issues. Academics may become seriously concerned with such problems, but the faculty departments, which are primarily professional entities, usually pay very little attention to what a man does in the way of education or community activity. When the English department at, say, the University of California, comes to make its decisions about hiring and firing, promotions and tenure, the voting members will be much more concerned about the impression their appointments will create in the English department at Harvard than in the local student body or the local community. This is what the "community of scholars" means as most academics understand that term.

From the moment that a student decides upon an academic career and undertakes graduate work, he becomes part of this "community." He must play the game by its rules or else abandon the board. His graduate studies, his dissertation, his ability to find a position at a "name" school—all of these are tokens in the game on which his teachers have gambled a certain amount of their professional prestige. If he is to find a job (indeed, in many cases, if he is even to be made aware that a prospective job exists), if he is to achieve tenure and promotions, if he is to survive and prosper, and especially if he is to acquire any amount of glory, then he must be obedient to the expectations of the professional powers that control these rewards. And he, in turn, will finish by enforcing the same expectations on the apprentices he ushers into the guild.

How, one wonders, have the professions managed to establish their authority so persuasively in the American university? David Riesman offers one illuminating answer. He reminds us that the academic life can very rapidly de-class those who enter it, drawing them out of family, regional, and ethnic backgrounds. This is bound to be the case with the student who comes from lower-class origins, from a minority group, or from a rural community. For those who are thus dislocated, the profession becomes "the scholar's country"—replete with its own jealous "nationalism." As Reisman remarks, "The fervency of this nationalism reflects the sacrifices the scholar has made to become a scholar, what he has had to surrender of earlier social-class origins and ambitions." The profession becomes, then, an anchorage, a place to belong. But if academic life de-classes, it can also re-class—into something that feels like and often even pays like the great American upper-middle class, from which many of the scholar's students (at the "better" schools at least) are apt to come.

The de-classing capacity of academic life (what Riesman calls its "universalizing quality") is, I think, a desirable feature. It is, potentially, a liberating experience. But the re-classing that usually follows is apt to be disastrous. It is at this point that the academic is integrated into the higher levels of the national society, with all that this means in the way of conformity to parochial loyalties. The universities, governed so ponderously by government and corporate wealth, finance and enforce the integration, and as we have already seen, few academics, whether scholars or technicians, exert themselves to avoid the tempting rewards. The American upper-middle class is a comfortable place to find oneself —especially when one adds just the right admixture of jet-set elegance for the highly successful academic: research grants with foreign travel, visiting lectureships, prestigious conferences, and perhaps even invitations to help out in Washington. It is a marvelous institution that can offer a young man who may have started with nothing but brains such an opportunity to rise so high in the Great Society.

Undoubtedly the social forces that structure the academic professions are powerful. But the fact that a temptation is offered does not excuse the acceptance of it. Nor does the fact that a social pressure is very strong mean that those it acts upon are totally without the freedom to

resist it. It would be pathetic, indeed, if those who have given themselves to the life of the mind were to plead that they were powerless to
reform their own professional environment, powerless even to save their
own souls by the brave attempt to achieve reform. But the plea becomes
outrageous when the forces to which men surrender exert their greatest
power, not by terror or repression, but by offering the bribes of prestige
and comfort.

Now what are the alternatives to this situation? Isn't this the way things
have to be, if the professions are to do their job—which is to accumulate knowledge? If one wishes to deny the authority of the status quo—
as we do here—then it is clearly necessary to formulate a different conception of what relevant scholarship is and of what knowledge is for.
One way to do this is by calling the attention of scholars and intellectuals to one aspect of their own heritage of democratic education.

In the eighteenth century, the greatest on-going "conference" of a
"learned society" was that of the *philosophes* who produced the famous French *Encyclopédie*. Year by year the great volumes of the *Encyclopédie* made their appearance, each one a coming-together of the
finest minds of French society to produce both a convenient distillation
of current knowledge and the keenest critical opinion of the day.
Conceivably the project might have gone on and on, down through the
alphabet and into revisions of earlier volumes, but it was inevitably
quashed and driven underground. Shortly before the enterprise was
suppressed by the French authorities in 1759, the Attorney-General of
France had this to say about eight volumes of the *Encyclopédie*:

> Society, Religion and the State present themselves today at the tribunal
> of justice in order to submit their complaints. Impiety walks with head
> held high . . . Humanity shudders, the citizenry is alarmed . . . It is
> with grief that we are forced to say it: can one conceal from oneself that
> there is a project formed, a Society organized, to propagate materialism,
> to destroy Religion, to inspire a spirit of independence, and to nourish
> the corruption of morals? [10]

[10] Arthur M. Wilson, *Diderot: The Testing Years* (New York, 1957), p. 333.

From the perspective of the past two centuries, we know quite well what the outraged M. de Fleury was railing against. In behalf of political and religious authoritarianism, he was berating what Peter Gay has called "the sovereign rights of criticism": free speech, free thought, free inquiry for the sake of public reform. He was, in fact, attacking the *philosophes* for inventing what we now recognize as "citizenship—citizenship not simply as a legal status but as a *moral calling*. Today, however, the *philosophes* are usually depreciated by the academic specialists as "popularizers" rather than as "real" philosophers or scholars. This typically misses the crucial point: that the practice of citizenship must necessarily be a "popular" activity. It must have to do with influencing and educating people, with shaping knowledge into a basis for action. For the *philosophe*, one of the necessary characteristics of real knowledge, of real philosophy, was that it should make a *difference*. To be an intellectually vital man of letters during the French Enlightenment, therefore, implied an active sense of citizenship. And, of course, citizenly initiative then, as now, involved the aggressive questioning of authority, privilege, and tradition.

In other words, the *philosophes* insisted that intellectuality implied responsibility. This responsibility, they emphasized, was not simply to read, study, inquire, solve problems, and accumulate knowledge. For to do that is not to discharge a public responsibility; it is to pursue a pleasure. As every academic knows, learning and problem-solving are fun. And for having fun one should not expect special distinction. Fun is something everybody ought to have the chance to have—and the only sensible position to take about fun is that it should not infringe upon the well-being of others. Beyond that, one must be pluralistic. For some it is fun to study Shakespeare's sonnets; for others to examine the stars; for others to bake apple pies or compose music or play baseball . . . It is nothing but arrogance to pretend that research in medieval iconography is intrinsically "better" and more "responsible" than ceramics or cabinet-making. None of these activities has anything to do with intellectuality—not within the tradition of the *philosophes* we are following here—for none of them has to do with citizenship. Rather the intellectual was one who intervened in society for the defense of civilized values wherever they were threatened; one who clarified reality so that his fellow citizens could reason toward the solution of their problems.

It is evident that the ideal of "service" is involved here, but not as it is understood within the multiversity: The service of the *philosophe* did not mean indiscriminately assisting society in every project it might undertake, but rather criticizing, clarifying, dissenting, resisting, deriding, exposing—in brief, educating in the broadest sense of the word, as a member of the "party of humanity." It is precisely this tradition of "humanitarian meddling" (to borrow another phrase from Peter Gay) that has been lost in the long debate between "service" and "scholarship." It is as if the *philosophes* were able to synthesize the two ideals that have since been separated and deformed in our universities into mindless collaboration on the one hand and irrelevant research on the other. What we propose here is to recreate this synthesis and to establish it as the commanding ideal of the learned professions.

It is legitimate enough to observe that the *philosophes* were not, in our usual sense of the word, "academics." That is to say, none of them were primarily university men. They preferred to think of themselves as "men of letters," and they are frequently referred to today by the more generic and free-wheeling term "intellectuals." But this is only to observe that the French universities of the eighteenth century were also inhospitable to the most advanced and critical thought of the day. The important intellectual history of the time, one that was to influence the democratic revolution and experiment in America profoundly, had to be made very largely outside the narrow and oppressive environment of its academic establishment.

It is also true that for all of its original impact on American democracy, the tradition I speak of has never found much of a home in our universities. Only now and again at some one school or department or in the life of an individual academic—a Richard T. Ely, a Thorstein Veblen, a John Dewey, a C. Wright Mills—can it be said to have flourished. Thomas Jefferson's plans for the University of Virginia typically followed the *philosophe*'s by envisioning a school that exercised an independent criticism of those forces of "Church and State" which opposed education because of its capacity to "unmask their usurpation, and monopolies of honors, wealth, and power" and which "fear every change, as endangering the comforts they now hold." But Jefferson's influence on education was limited. Eventually his notions of nonsectarian institutions of higher learning and instruction in practical knowledge were developed in the nineteenth century by the great state universities, but his ideal of the university as a center of dissenting criticism never particularly appealed to the forces of church, state, or corporate wealth which were to dominate the funding of higher education.

It was only at exceptional schools like Oberlin and Antioch that the ideal of intellectual dissent was honored. By the end of the century, when the modern academic establishment had fully "arrived," the closest any of the major universities cared to come to exercising the "sovereign rights of criticism" was by way of providing advice to the regulatory agencies that were attempting to cope with industrial America. The University of Wisconsin probably went farthest in making this form of service into an academic doctrine—especially during the presidency of Charles Van Hise. But even at Wisconsin, the administration clamped down once the First World War began: expert criticism, yes; radical dissent, no.

It was precisely to make sure that the America university would not restrict its politically engaged faculty that the demand for "academic freedom" came to be formulated during this period. Championed by the newly founded American Association of University Professors, the ideal was intended to liberate the scholar *and* to direct his primary allegiance toward the general public. The General Report of the Committee on Academic Freedom and Academic Tenure, published in December, 1915, defined the liberty and responsibility of the academic faculty in no uncertain terms:

> The responsibility of the university teacher is primarily to the public itself, and to the judgment of his own profession; . . . in the essentials of his professional activity his duty is to the wider public to which the institution itself is morally amenable . . . the university should be an intellectual experiment station, where new ideas may germinate and

where their fruit, though still distasteful to the community as a whole, may be allowed to ripen until finally, per chance, it may become a part of the accepted intellectual food of the nation or the world. . . . One of the university's most characteristic functions in a democratic society is to help make public opinion more self-critical and more circumspect, to check the more hasty and unconsidered impulses of popular feeling, to train the democracy to the habit of looking before and after. It is precisely this function of the university which is most injured by any restriction upon academic freedom; . . .

It was the widespread and often ruthless repressiveness of university administrations that followed upon America's entry into the First World War which was to put the AAUP to its first real test—a test the Association was to fail. After a period of pathetic soul-searching, the Association agreed that dissent may legitimately be silenced on the campuses in the face of national emergency. The AAUP's 1915 code of academic freedom was a milestone in the progress of American higher education toward this ideal and its responsibilities, while the report of its Committee on Academic Freedom in Wartime proved to be a tombstone:

When . . . a democracy finds itself forced into war in defense of its rights, . . . it will, if it has any practical wisdom, temporarily adapt its methods of political action and of governmental procedure to the necessities of the grave and perilous business immediately at hand.

If academics were still to enter prominently into the political life of the New Deal period, the 1918 statement nevertheless prefigured the willingness to compromise, retreat, and conform that has characterized the universities during and after the Second World War. Once so much had been conceded to "practical wisdom," the government—or a Senator McCarthy—would have little trouble providing the "grave and perilous business" that justified the loyalty oath, the security check, and all the overt and subtle techniques of regimentation which have descended upon us in the past two decades. As a result, the ideal of academic freedom has been saved the need of strenuous defense by way of diminishing exercise. Robert Hutchins neatly sums up the reason why:

. . . thought implies criticism, and criticism of a social, political, economic system to which one is looking for admiration and support is impossible unless the public, through a long course of education and demonstration, has become convinced that thought, including criticism, is the purpose of the university, that this is what it exists for, and that independent thought and criticism are indispensable to the improvement, and perhaps even the survival of any society.[11]

Now if one gives any attention to the learned journals, the monographs, the dissertations that flow from our schools in such abundance, one sees how far the academics are from undertaking the "long course of education and demonstration" that Hutchins mentions. How is this to be changed? It would, of course, be little more than philistine to suggest that all scholarly research should be abandoned unless it relates immediately to social criticism. Many perfectly valid fields of knowledge cannot be directly related to the problems of the day. Just as there are others—like economics, political science, sociology—which have very little business being anywhere but in the thick of public controversy. There is, however, a way in which mature wisdom in all the fields of the humanities and social sciences can be related to the needs of the time, and that is by way of reevaluating the personal character of the scholar.

The pursuit and communication of knowledge—whether it be concerned with the sociology of the Pentagon or the aesthetics of Chaucer —is, or ought to be, a noble enterprise. The rhetoric that academics are in the habit of expending on this point is, indeed, almost dizzying. I suspect every one of us carries around a fat selection of favorite clichés about the "beauty," the "moral worth," and the "dignity" of the "search for truth": for example, Carl Becker's statement that "the value of history is, indeed, not scientific, but moral; . . . it prepares us to live more humanely in the present, and to meet rather than to foretell, the future." Very well, then: if the quest for knowledge is indeed a noble enterprise and so ennobles those who undertake it, what is the

[11] Robert Hutchins, "An Appraisal of Higher Education," in William Brickman and Stanley Lehrer, eds., *A Century of Higher Education* (New York, 1962), p. 203.

measure of a man's nobility? It it not, in very large measure, his sensitivity to what is ignoble—to all that is base, false, ugly, barbaric? Is it not his willingness to speak out bravely against those forces that debase our lives and threaten the survival of civilized life?

Let us suppose, then, that an instructor in American history takes an active part in organizing a thoughtful, well-conceived campaign against capital punishment in his state. He musters the students to the cause and succeeds in engaging public officials and people generally in a searching debate of crime and punishment. Has he not made a more genuine *intellectual* contribution than if he had written a definitive study on the decline of cotton factorage in the American South for the period of 1865–1894?

Or, again, suppose that a psychology instructor, feeling that the politics of his community has gone slack, undertakes to run for Congress, with an eye to stimulating serious public discussion of pressing local problems. His campaign is responsible from start to finish, and he forces his opposing candidates to take clear-cut stands they would otherwise have avoided like the plague. How shall we assess the man's *intellectual* behavior? Is it more or less valuable than an exhaustive study of olfaction in the unrestrained rat?

Suppose an English instructor devotes a large amount of his time to organizing "freedom schools" in the slums and conducting a creative writing workshop there. Should we, for purposes of promotion and tenure, count his *intellectual* efforts as highly as if he had produced a critical study of Golding's translation of Ovid's *Metamorphoses*?

Suppose an anthropology instructor busies himself organizing a teach-in on the Vietnam war. Perhaps he even travels to Vietnam for the Inter-Universities Committee and then writes a solid analysis of the effects of the war on the rural population for the *Atlantic Monthly* or *The New Republic*. Is his work worth more or less—*intellectually* speaking—than a study of unity and diversity in the celebration of cattle curing rites in a north Indian village?

No doubt many academics will say that since these men are involved in "action" as distinct from "thought," why do they deserve any academic consideration at all? Isn't the academic's function to "think" rather than "act"? This is the question that frequently arose in discussions among the members of the now-defunct Council for Correspondence, which made probably the most significant single effort in the postwar period to organize academics into a political force. The reply to it is, I think, to ask how much sense it makes to regard "thinking" and "doing" as separate, if not incompatible, activities. Analysis and discussion, where they are politically relevant, become political *acts*— and it is this that we have specified as the peculiar social responsibility of intellectuals. To think, to speak, to teach, to write: all these *are* forms of doing. They ought properly to be seen as integral components of action and as an indispensable part of the political process. Without doing any more, an academic may help make the life of his society richer and nobler. But what if he wants to go further? If a man's thought should carry over into more overt forms of action, such as those we mentioned above, are we to regard it as somehow automatically debased? Surely not. For in a healthly personality "thought" and "action" merge gracefully along a single spectrum, and there is no natural barrier that prevents a man from undertaking some task of public leadership or organization in order to realize in fact what his understanding tells him must be done. Indeed, action—say, in the dramatic form of civil disobedience—may be the only way of forcing an intellectual dialogue upon reluctant and secretive authorities. In such situations, the unwillingness to act, to "make trouble," may imply that one is less than serious about the intellectual position he holds.

One can imagine all sorts of other questions being raised about our hypothetical instructors. But the truth is that only at the barest handful of schools in America today would their citizenly conduct be given any weight whatever in making "professional" decisions about them. No matter how intellectually sound or morally courageous that conduct might be, no matter of what benefit it might be to students or community, it would normally be discounted out-of-hand in evaluating the man. And that is the measure of how far removed the modern academic conception of intellect is from that of the *philosophes*.

Why should this continue to remain true when almost every aspect of American life has become a matter of open concern? Is it because we feel that anybody can "be political"—and so it isn't much of an achievement to do these things? But there are wise and foolish, profound and superficial ways to "be political," just as there are wise and foolish, profound and superficial exercises in scholarship. A. Warren Harding might indeed be a fool. But a Thomas Jefferson, a Norman Thomas, an A. J. Muste, or to bring the point closer to our own time, an H. Stuart Hughes running for the Senate in Massachusetts—are men who have made intellect central to their politics. To be deeply and wisely political is a rare and commendable achievement—and one that often takes a great deal more courage than "pure research."

Should citizenly conduct be discounted because one fears that politically engaged academics won't be able to train graduate students in scholarly techniques and may fail in their duty of discovering knowledge? One is reminded here of the embittered objection a University of California professor raised in late 1965 against the student activists on campus. They were, he charged, seeking to "politicize" the university. Indeed they were. And why not? If one accepts that it is the function of intellectuality to make knowledge work in the defense of civilized values, then we may be dealing here with men who are indeed more capable than most of "training" intellectuals. They may be able to do precisely what our present forms of graduate instruction never do: namely, to force a man to reflect on the function and purpose of his professional commitment.

What we contend here is that the training of teachers and scholars and the pursuit of research—as these activities are presently handled—result in a great deal of mindless specialization and irrelevant pedantry that ought not to be credited with intellectual respectability. There is probably not a single field of the social sciences and humanities that does not already boast a larger body of "knowledge" than can be "popularized"—and so assimilated into the cultural mainstream of our society—within the next fifty to one hundred years. Is it more "knowledge" of this surplus kind, expertly gleaned by precise techniques, that we exclusively require? Or, in the protracted emergency in which our civilization finds itself, shouldn't priority be given to a scholar's ability to link his special knowledge or moral insight to our social needs? In assessing a scholar's intellectual quality, shouldn't we be prepared to ask what the man's thought or the example of his actions has been worth in the defense of civilized values? If these are not the only questions to be raised in evaluating an academic, they ought at least to be among the first.

What we ask here of individual academics ought to be demanded of the professions generally. Suppose the professions were to be evaluated by putting to them the following question: In what intellectual areas have the leading institutions of our society—and especially the government—learned to tread lightly for fear of arousing collective critical resistance by the academic community? The answer would not be an encouraging one. Where the humanities and social sciences are concerned (and often enough the natural sciences, too), the government knows that it can, whenever it needs to, get away with any kind of slapdash propaganda. It confronts, in these areas, no organized critical authority—beyond that, perhaps, of the more conscientious journalists. Among the academics, it will find only scattered dissenters, many of whom may only be able to reach minority audiences; and the dissenters are easily offset by the influence of the academic "experts" who implement or defend government policies and are often enough figures of great prestige in our otherwise apolitical learned professions.

It does not take much imagination to see how vastly enriched our society's politics would be by citizenly "service" from the professions. We do not have an intellectually respectable politics in America, very largely because the single largest intellectual interest group in our society—the learned professions—has opted out of politics, except where it defends the status quo. It has felt no professional obligation to relate the life and work of its members to the problems of justice and survival which dominate our times. It does not insist that intellect embrace a dimension of citizenship. But if the major institutions of our society were made aware that the things they do and the things they say were being carefully scrutinized by a public of knowledgeable and conscientious academics, if the opinions of professional thinkers and teachers became a constant and recognized part of public controversy, that controversy, at the very least, could be elevated to the level of a rational dialogue, instead of remaining the province of shabby slogans, cynical propaganda, and engineered consensus. One may grant that the rights and wrongs of great public issues do not always yield to simple and unequivocal solutions. But rational solutions become impossible where, as in contemporary America, policy-making remains a mystery of state sealed off from a lethargic public by vested interest and esoteric expertise.

So long as our politics retain this character, there is very little that academics—whether they are humanists or scientists, specialists or generalists, scholars or technicians—have any right to be proud of. They may indeed be cultivating a luxuriant garden of knowledge and theory, and cultivating it with fastidious skill and taste. But the obscene shadows of misguided power and thermonuclear extinction brood over that garden and all the world surrounding it. And any conception of intellect that leads men to ignore that fact is ultimately futile and cowardly.

Currently a member of the department of philosophy at Columbia, Robert Paul Wolff (1933–   ) also has taught at Harvard, the University of Chicago, and Wellesley College. He has received three academic degrees, including the doctorate, from Harvard. Among his philosophical publications are Kant's Theory of Mental Activity *and (with Herbert Marcuse)* A Critique of Pure Tolerance.

19

The College as Rat Race

ROBERT PAUL WOLFF

In 1950, 2,214,000 students were enrolled in American colleges and universities. By 1960 the total had grown to 3,570,000 and projections for 1970 range as high as 7 million. This increase is not merely a consequence of the growth of the American population. Of 1000 boys and girls in the fifth grade in 1942, only 205 entered college in 1950. But of 1000 fifth graders in 1954, 336 entered college in 1962. By the time the present grade school children have reached college age the proportion may exceed one half.

The consequent rise in college applications has of course been distributed unevenly among America's colleges. Although there are still many

271

accredited institutions which begin the year with room in their freshman classes, the elite schools—the Ivy League, the seven sisters, the
best state universities—are faced with many times the number of students they can accommodate. The result has been a fundamental re-
orientation in the attitude of colleges toward the selection of students.
Instead of setting admissions *requirements* they have to develop an
admissions *policy* by which to choose from among the excess of well-
qualified applicants.

The applicants fall readily into three groups: the clear admits, the
clear rejects, and (characteristically) a large middle group of possible
admits. In this third segment are to be found the students with
strengths and weaknesses which must be weighed against one another
and translated into a one-dimensional scale of preference. Should the
college admit a boy with strong but not spectacular grades and little
evidence of independence, or the boy (from a different kind of school
and background) whose relatively weak but not disastrous grades are
balanced by signs of creativity and ambition? Should the admissions
committee deliberately strive for a heterogeneous freshman class or
judge each case purely on its merits without reference to the character
of the other applicants already admitted?

The situation is aggravated by a number of interactions between
colleges and high schools. Students, aware of the increasing difficulty
of obtaining admission to their chosen schools, begin to make multiple
applications in order to protect themselves. The result is an inflation
of applications to the best colleges, forcing them to estimate the percentage of admittees who will actually show up in September.

Simultaneously the "college advisers" in high schools and preparatory schools, alerted to the problems in the colleges, begin to discourage
students from applying to schools to which they have little chance of
being admitted. This entirely laudatory move merely aggravates the
problems for the colleges, for it reduces the number of "clear rejects"
in the file of applications, leaving a still more unwieldly group of
"possible admits" from which to select a freshman class. The colleges
also experience considerable anguish at the thought of gifted students
being discouraged by uninformed college advisers.

Meanwhile the colleges have been making their task still more difficult by their attempts to adopt objective, non-parochial criteria of admission. It is true that athletic ability, the right prep school tie, or an alumnus father will improve a student's chance to get into many schools. But as applications mount and colleges strive to improve their student bodies these factors play a decreasing role in admission decisions. By and large the men who run the admissions offices of the top schools are dedicated to the principles of fairness and equality of opportunity which generally serve Americans as ideal standards. Their quite admirable dedication merely intensifies the problem of selecting an entering class from the mass of applicants.

APTITUDE TESTING

At this point a different and originally separate factor in American education comes into play: the increasing use of aptitude and achievement testing. The Educational Testing Service first administered the Scholastic Aptitude Test, or SAT, in 1926, almost forty years ago. In that year only 8040 students took the examination. In 1961–62 this figure had increased one hundredfold to 819,339. Virtually every applicant to a good college or university now takes the SAT, and large numbers take achievement tests in particular subjects as well.

The SAT is an objective examination of the multiple-choice type. The faults of such tests are too well known to require rehashing. What is less appreciated by laymen (although this is clearly understood by admissions officers) is that, strictly speaking, the Educational Testing Service does not *claim* to be measuring intellectual capacities such as intelligence, creativity, receptivity to new ideas, or the ability to see conceptual relationships. It only claims to measure the probability that a student will do well in college. It is, one might say, an extrinsic, or black box, prediction. Students who do well on the test tend to do well in college. This may be because the test measures capacities which are later drawn upon by college work. Or it may be because the test measures exam-taking ability, which also serves the student in college. In any event it is a statistical fact that the probability of a good college record is higher for the student with a high SAT score.

The test is far from accurate, however, even in terms of its own criteria. According to the 1961–62 annual reports of ETS, the divergence of any given score from the "true" score (i.e., an average over a long period of time of a student's scores on similar tests) is on the order of thirty points two thirds of the time. That is to say, "if a student's 'true' score is 500, the chances are two out of three that the score he will actually make on the SAT will be between 470 and 530." Out of every six students, one will probably score more than thirty points above his "true" score, and another probably more than thirty points below.

If multiple-choice tests are suspect in themselves, and if their accuracy as predictions of college success is far from adequate, why are they used so extensively by admissions officers? There appear to be three reasons:

First, and by far the most important, is the admissions officer's need for some way of comparing the cases in his burgeoning file of "possible admits." Fairness and the bureaucratic strictures of committee work require him to produce reasons for favoring one candidate over another. When the dossiers are mixed bags of strengths and weaknesses, it is in practice impossible to defend one's ordering of five hundred or a thousand cases without reference to some objective criterion. The SAT serves as just such a measure.

Closely related to this is the desire of admissions officers to reduce the percentage of admits who later flunk out. The SAT claims to predict college success: deans are haunted by the possibility that a good and potentially successful student will be turned down in favor of one who eventually fails to complete the college course. Since deans (and professors) by and large conceive of success in education as a matter of grades, credits, and degrees, such a case appears to them to be an educational failure. A low percentage of dropouts is considered a sign of a good admissions program.

Finally, as the average SAT scores of incoming freshman classes rise at the elite schools, ambitious colleges begin to treat the scores as a sign and measure of their own place in the educational system. A rise of fifty points in the freshman average is used by recruiters as an additional inducement for prospective students and their parents.

What began as a means of handling a swollen tide of applications becomes in the end a measure of educational status.

Here, as with the pressure of admissions itself, there is feedback to the secondary school level. Parents quickly become informed (and misinformed) about the importance of "college boards." Pressure is put on high schools to coach the college-bound seniors in the mysteries of multiple-choice tests. Despite ETS's insistence that careful research reveals the futility of such preparations, classes sprout in SAT-taking. Soon high school *juniors* are submitting to "Preliminary SATs" whose purely tentative results are then used to guide the students in their college choices. As figures pile up, tables are constructed showing the statistical relationship between junior and senior SATs. (ETS report, 1961–62, pp. 34–35.) Indeed, ETS tells us that it is "possible to make similar estimates of senior-year SAT scores from the scores on the School and College Ability Test (SCAT) taken even earlier. There are tables which provide these estimates based on SCAT scores as far back as the eighth grade." (ETS report, 1961–62, p. 35.)

DAMAGING PRESSURES

The ever earlier testing is merely the most striking element in the frenzied business of college preparations. Students are exhorted by parents and teachers to raise their grades. The colleges, which have never based their decisions solely on academic achievement, begin to emphasize "extracurricular activities," and as the news filters back to the high schools, teenagers are hastily enrolled in dance classes, music lessons, outing clubs, and intramural sports. The colleges counter with a search for signs of individuality and originality; desperately teenagers are pushed into beekeeping and piccolo playing. And so it goes, on and on—colleges searching for ways to sort the applicants and predict their college careers, students desperately twisting themselves into what they hope will be appealing shapes, anxious to be singled out from the crowd of fellow students.

What has been the effect of the endless testing and evaluating on our high school boys and girls? First of all, the ever present imperative to "do well" in an objective and measurable way is intensified, to the detriment of real education, or even of non-"educational" growth experiences. Americans have come to treat education as a process of homogeneous, crisis-free absorption of information and development of skills. The irregular, the irrational, the unconforming, the random, is seen as a *failure* of education. The only difference between the traditional and progressive attitudes is that the first blames these aberrations on the student while the second blames them on the school. That they are undesirable is never questioned.

But as so many perceptive observers of adolescents have pointed out, growth from childhood to maturity is *necessarily* ungainly. It is the trying on of ideals and life styles, the committing of new-found emotional energies. As Erik Erikson has shown us through his study of Luther, the "identity crisis" of late adolescence or early adulthood is positively *creative,* and certainly not an embarrassing misfortune to be excused and quickly suppressed.

Unfortunately the college race has just this repressive effect on many of the most intelligent and sensitive—hence vulnerable—youngsters. Experiment and commitment require a willingness to accept the possibility of failure. They demand an incautious, even imprudent singleness of purpose. The wise counseling and anxious hectoring of the collegemongers is death to experiment.

In his junior year in high school John, an A student, becomes fascinated by boats. He spends hours at the docks, quizzing sailors about their tasks, cadging rides on tugboats, dreaming of distant places. For a year he is completely wrapped up in the sea. Then, abruptly, the passion leaves him and he puts behind him as childish the dream of becoming a sailor. He has tentatively tried on a role, given himself up to it, and found that it does not answer his needs. The year has been immensely valuable to him as a stage in his growing up. But it has been a disastrous year at school. Absorbed in sea charts and sailing manuals, he has had scant time for history, French, math, and physics. In his record there is no indication of the milestone which this year has marked in his life; only the low grades, dropping his cumulative average below the "top college" level. Discouraged by the unaccountable slump of a promising student, John's college adviser directs him to a solid local state college. The competition is so stiff for admission to the elite schools that there seems no point in his trying to overcome the handicap of that junior year.

John has been hurt by the system, for the education available to him at the top schools really is superior to that offered by the local college. But at least he has had his junior year, and he will be a better man for it. Far worse off are the other young men and women who have been cajoled or harassed away from creative adolescent commitments by their parents and teachers. In the name of a "good education" in the future, these well-meaning adults stifle the good education of the present. The energies which should be used by boys and girls for growth are instead diverted to useless and deadening "college preparation."

Aware of the tragedies of secondary education, many colleges have begun to make room in their admissions policies for a controlled measure of irrationality. Each year a school will accept a certain number of applicants who defy all their objective criteria but simply "smell right." Admirable as such risk-taking is, it has no effect on the high school student, for he cannot be sure that he will be one of the mavericks who is saved by an intuitive dean. If the internal dynamic of his growth carries him outside the limits of secondary school acceptability he must be prepared to forfeit the race to college.

The successful college applicant has thus frequently mortgaged himself to the future, sacrificing a genuine education in high school in order to obtain a superior education in college. What does he find when he finally enrolls at the school of his choice? No simple description can be given, any more than for the high school, but again trends are visible which are deeply disturbing. Until a very few years ago the entering freshman at any of a number of top colleges would have been confronted with a mixed program of broad survey courses designed to make him "liberally" or "generally" educated, more specialized courses from among which he could select a sample, and in his last year or two a departmental "major" requiring him to concentrate on a single discipline. In addition he would have the opportunity to do independent research, usually as a means to a degree with honors. The premises of this sort of undergraduate program were basically two: first, that the typical freshman had not yet had a chance to roam at will in the realm of ideas, acquainting himself with the excitements and potentialities of the intellectual life (I remember my astonishment when, as a freshman, I discovered that there was a field of knowledge—sociology—which I had not even known to *exist*! It was like discovering a new color, or better, a whole new sense); and second, that several years should be given over to relatively uncontrolled experimentation before a young man or woman was required to make a decision about a career.

RACE FOR EDUCATION

In the past decade, however, both of these premises have been yielding to pressures from below and from above. The General Education movement is under severe attack at Columbia, Chicago, and Harvard, the three schools which have done most to foster it. The causes are complex, involving problems of personnel and administration as well as of educational principle. One reason is that good high schools have instituted "advanced placement" college-level courses using many of the same books which appear on the General Education reading lists. Consequently more and more students have had the material by the time they reach college. Now just what it means to have "had" Dostoevsky or Freud or Marx is, of course, problematical. It may mean that the student had read works by the author, brooded over the ideas, and grown through his struggle to understand them. It may also mean that he has been intellectually immunized by being inoculated with small, weakened dosages of the author. At any rate the well-prepared student can pick the right answer out of five choices an adequate number of times, and so he is assumed to be generally educated.

In response to the improved preparation of the freshman (which manifests itself in better language, math, and English composition training as well as in advanced placement courses), the colleges decide to "enrich" the undergraduate curriculum. The job is turned over to the departments or—at universities—to the graduate faculties, whose general view of undergraduate education is that it is a watered-down version of graduate education. Everywhere the same solution is hit upon: give the bright, able, well-prepared undergraduates a first-rate training in some graduate department. Administratively, this amounts to listing graduate courses in the undergraduate catalogue and requiring the concentrator to take baby generals and write baby dissertations. At a school like Harvard, for example, a senior honors thesis in history may be a 150-page research monograph, and the honors general in English demand a professional mastery of large segments of the literature of the last millennium.

At the same time pressures of military service, postgraduate professional training, and the cancerous growth of specialized knowledge place a premium on choosing a career early. The sciences have long insisted that they cannot give adequate graduate training to the college graduate who has not already tucked some of the requisite material into his mind, and medical schools of course set "premed" requirements. But now the same song is sung by economists (who fancy themselves really mathematicians), psychologists, philosophers, and historians. As the undergraduate population swells, the admissions squeeze reappears at the best medical, law, and graduate schools. Once more the education of the present—for which the student gave up so much in high school—is sacrificed to the demands of the future. Eager to relax and reap the fruits of his race to college, the student must climb onto the treadmill to graduate school.

But here the race for education ends. Upon entering graduate school, the student—now an adult—is told that his education lies *behind* him. From this point on his intellectual and spiritual maturity is taken for granted. Graduate schools do not educate the whole man; they train the specialist. So it seems that somewhere, somehow, the successful student has lost an education. Always it was before him, over the next exam, beyond the next degree. Now suddenly it is behind him, and that unique moment of potentiality in the growth of the soul is gone.

What has gone wrong? The answer is simple: each present was sacrificed to the future, until the presents were all past, and the future an empty present. It is a familiar enough story in our society. We call it prudence, or deferral of gratification, depending on our tastes in moral discourse.

AVAILABLE ALTERNATIVES

What can be done? Alas, the answer is not so simple. It won't help to administer the system with more intelligence, awareness, compassion, and imagination. These qualities are already in surprising abundance among the educators of our country. The solution, if there is one, must cut to the root of the problem. It must reverse the order of priority and at every stage subordinate the education of the future to that of the present. A good high school experience must count for more than admission to a great college. An exciting college education must in turn take precedence over preprofessional preparation for postgraduate training. How can this be done?

First of all, there is no point in demanding that college admission procedures be made *fairer*. The harm they inflict on high school students does not flow from their imperfections. It flows from their very existence. So long as the education in our colleges varies widely in quality, and admission to college is based on an evaluation of pre-college performance, parents and teachers will push students into a competition for admission. Nor should we issue pious warnings to high school students about the dangers of listening to their elders. They do not yet have the inner resources to withstand the threats and seductions of the adult world. Indeed, their spiritual growth demands identification with precisely those individuals who are encouraging them to compete. The adolescent student is faced with an impossible dilemma. If he accepts the values of his elders he loses his chance for real growth and instead climbs on the treadmill. But if he shies away from the grade race, where else is he to find the adult figures through identification with whom he can realize himself? As Paul Goodman has pointed out, the only alternative is to retreat into a sterile, adolescent world of beats or gangs.

The solution to the problem, if it exists, must be institutional: the temptations of the admissions race must be destroyed. So far as I can see, there are two ways in which this might be done, neither of which will meet with instant acclaim. Either the value of admission to one college rather than another must be eliminated; or admission to college must be made an irrational process on which the student can have no influence. The first could be achieved by a nationwide forced homogenization of institutions of higher learning, the second by assigning high school graduates to colleges at random. Both alternatives have analogues within the educational world. The academic high schools of a large city system like New York are kept approximately equal by budget allotments and the policy of teacher assignment. Most students then go to the school in their district. And many colleges assign their students to dormitories at random, for the very sound reason that competition for rooms would lead to discrimination, jealousy, cliques, and all the unpleasantness associated with fraternities or private clubs. My personal preference is for a process of random admission. It is by far the easier of the two to administer, and could be instituted immediately.

The objections are obvious. They will already have sprung to the mind of every person who reads this essay, particularly if he is a teacher at a good college. But before the proposal is rejected out of hand as absurd and impractical, let me urge one consideration in its favor. If I am right that our present educational system stifles the intellectual growth of millions of young men and women, then surely we should be willing to pay a very great price to set them free. It is absurd to build the schools, stock them and staff them, and then hustle our children through them in a frenzy of college-oriented competition. In education, imprudence is a virtue.

PART V

Some Alternatives

In these turbulent days on campus, few things are certain. One prediction, however, can be made with some certainty: the shape of higher education in America will continue to change, and at an even quicker pace than in the past. There can be no ignoring the pressures exerted by society, on the one hand, and the criticisms of university life heard increasingly both in the student center and the faculty club, on the other. Accommodations will have to be made to satisfy some of the demands society places on the university and also to make it more hospitable to the teaching and learning which is its principal reason for being.

Less certain than the imminence of change is the form that change will take. The university might simply continue to grow, adding thousands upon thousands to its already swollen enrollment, while maintaining its present institutional form. But it is just such unimaginative behavior that has led to much of the present unrest. On the other hand, administrators, guided perhaps by student and faculty sentiments, might embark on bold new ventures to reshape the structure and programs of our colleges and universities so that growth in size will not necessarily imply a lessening of effectiveness.

It is assumed here that the second, more constructive, path will be followed. The essays in Part V consider some of the alternatives available to contemporary colleges and universities. And as with nearly every essay in this book, these proposals grow out of assumptions, sometimes stated, sometimes not, regarding the aims of education and, ultimately, the goals of man in the modern world.

The first three essays in this section consider, from various points of view, the perplexing problem of reconciling the desire of students and teachers for some measure of social and intellectual community with the burgeoning enrollments and the proliferation of knowledge.

"The University," by Jacques Maritain, presents not so much a concrete proposal for the immediate remodelling of the university as a vision of the structure an ideal university might possess. Maritain works from premises that some may find difficult to accept: that certain subjects should have precedence over others; that there is a hierarchy of values in life and, thus, in education; and that the reality of God is very much alive. It is interesting, nevertheless, that many of the suggestions made by Maritain are echoed by other contributors to this section: that the gargantuan university embracing many unrelated disciplines be divided into several small units, each concentrating on a few related areas of knowledge; that the teaching function of the university be recognized as being distinct from and prior to its research function; and that interdisciplinary endeavors to relate areas of knowledge to each other be encouraged.

In many ways, the "cluster colleges" proposed by Clark Kerr in "Toward the More Perfect University" resemble Maritain's teaching institutes. Significantly different, however, is Kerr's concern for bringing together within a single residential unit students and faculty of various interests. He would hope that a productive cross-fertilization of ideas would issue from their proximity to each other and that the limitations on numbers within any single cluster college would result in a greater academic flexibility and sense of community than has been possible in the large university. In passing, Kerr suggests a number of specific steps that might be taken, even within existing structures, to provide more congenial conditions for undergraduate education. In such innovations as pass-fail grading, honors programs, more opportunities for independent study, and "problem-oriented" courses in the social sciences may lie at least temporary solutions to the unhappiness of many students with the nature of their education.

Behind many of Kerr's suggestions is the feeling that a new flexibility and individual concern must replace the present rigidity and impersonality of many undergraduate programs. He assumes that such goals can be achieved within the context of the existing university. Paul Goodman is not so hopeful. His "A Simple Proposal" advocates not a reforming of the university but, instead, the secession from the university of small, spontaneously gathered groups of students and teachers to form their own academic communities apart from the recognized centers of learning. As Goodman points out, his community could draw on numerous historical precedents; it might look also to the "free universities" that have recently arisen adjacent to many established institutions of higher learning. Worthy of special attention in Goodman's proposal is his intention of bringing such active, nonacademic professionals as practicing artists, politicians, and scientists into the academic community. The "irrelevance" so many students feel in their studies might thus be overcome as they saw in the examples of the so-called "veterans" how academic knowledge could be translated into "relevant" social action after graduation.

Many students seem to use the charge of irrelevance to attack any course that does not have an immediately obvious application to their lives. Such students are often simply unwilling to make the imaginative effort to probe for the meaning and, indeed, the excitement that superficially unappealing material may hold. For many others, however, formal college courses are, in fact, hopelessly remote from their true interests and aptitudes. From both groups comes that large number of students who "drop out"— some formally, by withdrawing from the university; others informally, by attending only perfunctorily to their courses while their real enthusiasm and energy are directed towards some more attractive activity such as campus politics, athletics, or partying.

Colleges have a responsibility to kindle the imaginations of the first group. They have an equal responsibility to urge those who truly do not belong there to seek their higher education elsewhere. The essays by John Gardner and John Keats, "College and the Alternatives" and "Some Reasonable Alternatives," ask the reader to consider that for some students the proper alternative to attendance at college is pursuit of further learning far beyond any academic institution's walls.

Especially with the increasingly widespread availability of free, conveniently located, public colleges and universities, Americans are coming to assume that all students, upon completion of high school, should proceed to work on a formal college degree. Such narrow and rigid thinking, however, ignores individual differences. It ignores the fact that there are many paths to happiness and individual fulfillment, not all of which are academic. Excellence, as Gardner stresses, appears in many forms; and our nation, if it is to achieve excellence as a whole, must encourage and cultivate that quality in whatever form it appears. The potentially excellent auto mechanic, coerced into a collegiate pre-law program, is likely to become neither an excellent lawyer nor an excellent mechanic. Both Gardner and Keats discuss some of the alternatives to formal, academic education. Both high school graduates and their parents need to understand that there is nothing sacred about four consecutive years of college immediately following high school.

It is fitting that this volume should close with an essay by a student, for it is the student, after all, who must remain at the center of the consideration of colleges and universities in which we have been engaged. In "A Case for Humane Intelligence" Michael O'Neil demonstrates a sensitive awareness of the political realities that must provide the context for any comprehensive discussion of higher education. His awareness is complemented by a bracing faith in the ability of man, America, and the university in particular to help provide the solutions to some of these contemporary problems. Proposals like his for reforms in the structure of the university are being heard with increasing frequency from students and teachers across the country. The proposals put forth somewhat tentatively in this section today may well be translated into the realities of higher education tomorrow.

*Himself a convert to Cathol-
icism, Jacques Maritain
(1882–   ) became one of
the leading Catholic theologians
of the twentieth century.
Although he has lectured in
American universities and served
as French Ambassador to the
Vatican, Maritain has lived
primarily in his native France.
Inspired in his thinking by the
philosophy of St. Thomas
Aquinas, he has written extensively on art, literature, and
politics as well as religion.
Maritain's 1943 lectures at
Yale, upon which this essay is
based, explored the applicability
of medieval thought to all
levels of modern education.
Here he considers advanced work
in the university.*

20

The University

JACQUES MARITAIN

THE ARCHITECTURE OF AN IDEAL UNIVERSITY

The third and advanced stage in education concerns the young man and woman. These have already entered the adult universe of thought and are preparing themselves at close range for the tasks of manhood and womanhood. They enjoy the first hopes and experiences of their coming of age, and of self-determination due to reason and free will already shaped. The life and concerns of the mature world are now theirs. Marriage will come shortly for most of them. Perhaps in some ideal future society all youth—I mean those who possess the required gifts and eagerness—will have the possibility of being only concerned with advanced training until their twenty-fifth or twenty-sixth year. Yet, as a matter of fact, many now are obliged to work full time in order to earn their living. If, according to the European habit, we reserve the name university for higher learning in advanced and graduate studies, we might say that the aim of the university is to achieve the formation and equipment of the youth in regard to the strength and maturity of judgment and the intellectual virtues. As Cardinal Newman puts it, a university "is a place of *teaching* universal *knowledge*." He adds: "Whatever was the original reason of its adoption, which is unknown, I am only putting on its popular, its recognized sense, when I say that a University should teach universal knowledge." [1]

Yet, paradoxically enough, university teaching coincides with a definite specialization of studies. Each particular science and art demands a highly specialized training. And in our age, when such teaching does not deal, as in the Middle Ages, with the formation of an intellectual leadership essentially consisting of clerics, nor, as in the following centuries, with the formation of the potential members of the ruling classes, but deals, according to a more democratic pattern, with the formation of a much larger and more diversified mass of outstanding citizens of all ranks in the nation, it is suitable that actually all the arts and sciences, even those which concern the management of common life and the application of the human mind to matters of practical utility, should be embraced by the typical modern university. The latter would thus have its field of specialization multiplied still more, as well as the number and diversity of its courses, a very small part of which each particular student can attend. The university should nevertheless still keep its essential character of universality,[2] and teach universal

---

[1] Cardinal John Henry Newman, *On the Scope and Nature of University Education*, Preface and Discourse I.

[2] "For those whose formal education is prolonged beyond the school age, the University course or its equivalent is the great period of generalization. The spirit

knowledge, universal not only because all the parts of human knowledge would be represented in its architecture of teaching but also because this very architecture would have been planned according to the qualitative and internal hierarchy of human knowledge, and because from the bottom to the top, the arts and sciences would have been grouped and organized according to their growing value in spiritual universality.

Thus a first order of subjects would be concerned with the realm of useful arts and applied sciences in the broadest sense of these words, and with advanced studies in technical training, engineering, administrative sciences, arts and crafts, agriculture, mining, applied chemistry, statistics, commerce, finance, and so on.[3]

A second order would be the realm of those practical sciences—practical either because they belong to the domain of art or because they belong to the domain of ethics—which, though covering thoroughly specialized fields, nevertheless relate to man himself and human life: medicine and psychiatry, for instance, and, on the other hand, law, economics and politics, education, etc.

---

of generalization should dominate a University. . . . At the University the student should start from general ideas and study their applications to concrete cases. A well-planned University course is a study of the wide sweep of generality. I do not mean that it should be abstract in the sense of divorce from concrete fact, but that concrete fact should be studied as illustrating the scope of general ideas." A. N. Whitehead, *The Aims of Education and Other Essays* (The Macmillan Co., New York, 1929), p. 41.

[3] With regard to this first order of subjects, as well as to the second, it is to be emphasized that the reason for teaching such subjects in the university and the viewpoint from which they should be ordered and organized as part of the university curriculum must remain solely the *universality of knowledge*. It is as parts of the manifold body of human knowledge and for the sake of (practical) truth that they have to be taught and organized. Everything would be warped if the aim, incentive, and dominating concern of the teaching were directed toward success in the experiences of life and in money-making. The students may take such motives into consideration when they choose to enter a given course of study. But the curriculum itself must be directed only toward a sound and comprehensive organization of universal knowledge, to be taught according to the internal and objective structure of the parts thereof.

A third order would be the realm of the speculative sciences and fine arts, in other words it would be concerned with the liberal arts proper and with that disinterested knowledge of nature and man and of the achievements of culture which liberates the mind by truth or beauty. At this point we find the immense chorus of the free workings of the spirit, mathematics, physics, chemistry, astronomy, geology, biology, anthropology, psychology, prehistory, archeology, history, ancient and modern literature and languages, philology, music, fine arts, and so on. That is the very core of the life of the university and the very treasure of the civilized heritage. And this third order is to culminate in a fourth one, which is the highest animating center in the architecture of teaching, and which deals with those sciences that are also wisdom because they are universal by virtue of their very object and of their very essence: the philosophy of nature, metaphysics and the theory of knowledge, ethical philosophy, social and political philosophy, the philosophy of culture and of history, theology and the history of religions.

In such an ideal university, I see the diverse parts of the vast body of teaching divided into Institutes, each one possessing its own complex organization and being organically linked to the others, rather than into separate Departments or Faculties. The Institutes of the first order would compose a teaching City concerned with the technical means of human life, or with the practical domination and utilization of matter. Those of the second order would compose a City concerned with the means which deal with human life itself for its maintenance and improvement. The Institutes of the third order would compose a teaching City of pure knowledge concerned with the intellectual ends of human life which are reached by encompassing in the mind the manifold universe of nature and man and the achievements of human creative power. The Institutes of the fourth order would compose a teaching City of the higher and intrinsically universal knowledge concerned with those intellectual ends of human life which are reached by grasping the trans-sensible realm of Being, Spirit, and Divine Reality, and the ethical realm of the aims, conditions, and rational ordering of human freedom and conduct.

THE CONSUMMATION OF LIBERAL EDUCATION

Obviously it is not enough that the universality of knowledge and the superior unity of intrinsically universal sciences be embodied in the general architecture of such teaching Cities. It is also necessary that in some measure they actually inspire the intellectual development of that living subject, the student, and become for him an integral part of him, whatever the special requirements of his course may be. Here we are confronted with the main duty and the main difficulty of university teaching.

The universe of thought we are contemplating in this last stage of formal education is in process of definite differentiation and formulation. Judgment and the intellectual virtues are no longer in the stage of preparation but in the stage of actual acquisition. And it is then, as I pointed out, that specialization necessarily occurs. The intellectual virtues acquired by one student are not those acquired by another, be it a question of techniques, useful arts, and applied sciences, or of practical sciences dealing with human life or of speculative sciences. The knowledge which has to develop during university years is knowledge in a state of a *perfected and rational grasping* of a particular subject matter. Truth, which is the mental atmosphere and the inspiring force needed more than ever, is henceforth an objectively circumscribed truth, speculative or practical, at which each of the diverse sciences and arts aims.

How is it possible to assure at this stage the universal inspiration and mental comprehensiveness of which I just spoke? An organic coöperation will be necessary between the diverse Institutes of the university; there will be required of each student, whatever his special training may be, a measure of general training in those subjects which constitute the very core of university life and with which our third and fourth orders of teaching are concerned. As a matter of fact, the use of technical means cannot be really profitable, nor the practical sciences be well directed without general enlightenment about nature and man. Medicine, public sanitation, psychiatry are extrinsically—

law, sociology, economics and politics, pedagogy are intrinsically—subordinated to ethics and natural law, and the very truth of every knowledge bearing on human conduct implies sound judgment about the ends of human life, that is to say the actual knowledge of ethical and political philosophy, which in its turn presupposes metaphysics. These requirements proceed from the very objects on which knowledge shapes itself. Even the scientist, as well as the historian, the scholar and humanist, the artist, cannot dispense with some philosophical inspiration; they need philosophical instruction, at least in order to be aware of the exact value and legitimate extent of their own activities among others of the spirit.

As a result, each university student should be required to attend a certain number of courses in the teaching Cities of pure knowledge and universal knowledge. Part of these courses, for instance in science, history, ancient and modern literatures, or fine arts, would be a matter of free choice, according to the personal inclination of the student, and to the need for complement or contrast in his special training. Other courses should be required for all, namely general philosophy, ethical and political philosophy, the history of civilization.

But, as Professor Nef rightly observes, such a measure would remain insufficient if it were not completed by an organic structure embodying that sense of unity and universality which should pervade university life. Special committees, composed of professors belonging to various Institutes, should ensure regular coöperation between these Institutes, guide the work of the student and help him scrutinize the connections of his own particular subject with other and more universal fields of higher learning: for instance, the connections of physics, biology, psychology, or medicine with the history of the sciences, the history of civilization, the philosophy of nature, and the theory of knowledge; or the connections of economics, social science, law, education, or of literature and art, with the history of civilization, ethical and political philosophy, and the great metaphysical and theological problems. Thus would be facilitated "study and research in which several disciplines, now separated, would be combined both by students working for higher degrees and by mature scholars in their creative labors." [4] And the knowledge of each one would be deepened and vitalized by the reëxamination of the value, purpose and logical structure proper to the various disciplines vitally brought together in this way.

For the reasons which I stated above apropos of the humanities, courses in theology, however important in themselves, would be a matter of free choice. Of course the question of theological teaching crops up with regard to the university as well as with regard to college education, and the considerations we previously laid down in this connection are here of special moment. Those who believe that God revealed to mankind His intimate secrets hold theology, or the rational development and penetration of the revealed data, to be in itself real knowledge in the strict sense of the term, though it is rooted in faith and grasps its object by means of concepts which are infinitely transcended and exceeded by it. In order to make philosophy autonomous, Descartes deemed it necessary to consider faith mere obedience, and to refuse to see any character of real knowledge in theology. Thus he threw out the baby with the bath. I am convinced that one of the main tasks of our age is to recognize both the distinction and the organic relationship between theology, rooted in faith, and philosophy, rooted in reason, and now secure of its sought-for autonomy. For it is not likely, is it, that if God spoke, it was to say nothing to human

---

[4] John U. Nef, *The Universities Look for Unity*, p. 36. The author wisely says that, in order to succeed in this progressive work of recasting, "unification could begin modestly, where the need for it appeared, between two or three subjects, considered in so far as possible in relation to philosophy and particularly to ethics" *idem*, p. 37. In connection with these remarks, the initiative taken by the Committee on Social Thought of the University of Chicago is to be pointed out. In order to have the Master's and Doctor's degrees prepared under its guidance, this interdepartmental committee combines in various ways courses of study such as social thought, historical fields (ancient Near Eastern civilizations, Far Eastern civilizations, medieval civilization, Renaissance civilization, eighteenth-century civilization, American civilization) and analytical and theoretical fields (anthropology and sociology, politics, economics, jurisprudence and ethics, education, psychology, and human development.)

intelligence? From this point of view, Newman was right in stating that if a university professes it to be its scientific duty to exclude theology from its curriculum, "such an Institution cannot be what it professes, if there be a God."

As for the many who do not share in these feelings about theology, they would nevertheless derive great advantage from theological instruction. They would gain horizons of highly rationalized problems thus opened up to them, and better understand the roots of our culture and civilization.

In nondenominational universities, this theological teaching would be divided into Institutes of diverse religious affiliation, according to the student population of the university. Such teaching should remain thoroughly distinct from the one given in religious seminaries, and be adapted to the intellectual needs of laymen; its aim should not be to form a priest, a minister, or a rabbi, but to enlighten students of secular matters about the great doctrines and perspectives of theological wisdom. The history of religions should form an important part of the curriculum.

I spoke a while ago of the large category of young men and women who after the college years (supposedly made accessible to all) must dedicate their entire day to earning a living. Those among them who are gifted and eager for intellectual work are thus made unable, whatever may be their personal desires, to become regular university students. For such a sad anomaly scholarships and grants can make up to a certain extent—they should be multiplied as far as possible. Yet the only way in which this anomaly can be compensated for in a general manner consists of extension courses and evening courses. The generosity and eagerness with which such teaching is given by so many professors and received by so many students, after a hard day of work, is one of the finest achievements of American education. There appears here a new function in university life, and it is probable that this function is called upon to assume ever greater importance, in proportion as economic progress will generally reduce working time and thus enable those who want to do so to use more easily the facilities of evening courses.

THE INSTITUTES OF ADVANCED RESEARCH

We may furthermore observe that the work of universities must find its complement in the work of Institutes of Advanced Research. It is no doubt normal that any instruction given in the university will result in some original work and the advancement of knowledge, especially in science. Yet this is in a way an overflow of the teaching scholarship. In the nature of things, the object of universities is the teaching of youth, and not producing books and articles and endless contributions, or making some scientific, philosophical, or artistic discovery. Man's education by means of courses, seminars, and laboratory training, on the one hand, and the advancement of knowledge through original enquiry, which implies both concentration and the "beautiful risks" of which Plato spoke, are two quite different things—we professors know this all too well. Specially organized and endowed Institutes of Research delving into the sciences of nature and of man have outstanding importance for the progress of civilization: they and the universities should help one another, but they should remain, for their mutual advantage, clearly distinct.

THE SCHOOLS IN SPIRITUAL LIFE

Another complement, relating to quite a different purpose, might also be considered.

In China and India, wise men living in solitude and contemplation gather together disciples who come to listen to them either for a certain number of years or at certain seasons of the year. The Hindu *ashrams* or schools of wisdom are well known. In Europe, some years ago, the need for such places of spiritual enlightenment was so great that schools of wisdom were created here and there, even by men who perhaps, like Spengler, hardly deserved the name of wise men. Here in America, the initiative taken by the Quakers with their school at Pendle Hill is to be considered with special interest. For centuries the

Catholic Church has had its own means of instructing those who aspire to spiritual perfection.[5] My point is that special initiatives have always been taken and must be taken according to the special needs of each time.

I do not feel qualified to discuss the matter from any outlook other than that of my own religious affiliation. Speaking therefore from the Catholic point of view, I should like to say that what seems to me to be especially required by our time is the creation of centers of spiritual enlightenment, or schools of wisdom, in which those interested in spiritual life would be able to lead a common life during some weeks, to be trained in the ways of spiritual life and contemplation, and to learn that science of evangelical perfection which is the highest part of theology. The immense treasure of the writings and doctrines of the great spiritual authors and the saints, which compose the mystical tradition of Christendom, from the Desert Fathers to St. John of the Cross and the mystics of modern times, would thus be made available to them. They would become acquainted both with the theological knowledge concerned and with the history, personality, and teachings of those heroes of faith and love whose call, according to Henri Bergson, passes through mankind as a powerful "aspiration" toward God. I conceive of these schools as houses of hospitality and enlightenment for human souls, which would be grounded on the integrity of a given religious faith and way of life, but which would be open not only to those sharing in this faith but also to all whose desire to spend some days of spiritual refreshment there and to learn what they are ignorant of. People who assure the continuity of life and teaching in these schools of wisdom would stay there permanently. The others would be guests, meeting each other at regular periods. As concerns youth especially, the university students, and the other boys and girls who enjoy a period of vacation and would like to use part of it in this manner, might spend some days or some weeks in such places of peace. I guess that the number of students in these schools would not be small.

[5] This is the aim of its religious orders, its confraternities of laymen connected with them, its spiritual retreats, and its innumerable activities of spiritual guidance.

During the nine years of Clark Kerr's presidency of the University of California, he saw enrollment grow from 45,000 to 87,000 students on nine campuses scattered over 500 miles. He also saw some of the earliest signs of student revolt in America, the Berkeley Free Speech Movement of 1964. Keenly aware of the necessity of adjusting the university to modern conditions, Kerr has become a prophet of the controversial institution he has described as the "multiversity." This essay was written at the request of Robert M. Hutchins, president of the Center for the Study of Democratic Institutions.

21

Toward the More Perfect University

CLARK KERR

"Toward the More Perfect University" is the title most thoughtfully and kindly provided me by President Hutchins. I have no reasonably clear idea of what he thought this title would call forth in my mind. He may have thought it would evoke *no* clear idea—in the sense of a vision of the "perfect university" unrelated to time and place, of an institution without spatial or temporal constraints. If so, he was right. There is not now, never has been, and never will be *the* "perfect university."

There is, or should be, however, always the search. My remarks will relate to one current aspect of this search by the modern American university.

The search is intrinsically a difficult one. Most definitions of perfection involve inherent contraditions, inconsistent elements. "We the People of the United States" once sought to "form a more perfect Union, establish Justice, insure domestic tranquility, provide for the common defense, promote the general welfare, and secure the blessings of liberty to ourselves and our Posterity . . ." We have spent a century and nine decades disturbing domestic tranquility in efforts to promote the general welfare, curbing liberty in order to establish justice, and so forth. So, also, it is with the university. There are inevitable contradictions inherent in the nature of the institution itself. This gives it many of its problems but also much of its dynamism. The search for the Holy Grail is the important thing; and it might be too bad if we ever really thought we had found it. As Robert Louis Stevenson said of El Dorado, "To travel hopefully is a better thing than to arrive." It might almost be said that the perfect university is an imperfect one urgently seeking perfection.

We should, consequently, set a reasonable goal for the contemporary university which will help to draw it closer toward such perfection as it may attain. James Perkins has recently suggested the goal of "internal coherence" so that each activity could "strengthen the others." If this were to be the firm goal relentlessly sought for Cornell, then much of Cornell as we now know it would quickly disappear. Do fraternities strengthen Southeast Asian studies? Does rowing on the lake strengthen the agricultural experiment station? Does the medical center in New York City strengthen industrial relations at Ithaca? If they are held to do so, then this criterion is so broadly applied as to provide little definition. Now there are those who really do think that much of the modern American university should disappear. But I do not agree that this is necessary or even desirable.

It seems to me that a more reasonable goal would be to require that activities carried on within a university should be able to coexist effectively with each other, each drawing strength from, and hopefully also adding strength to, their common university environment; and that each activity should be worthwhile and suitable in and of itself and be of university level quality. In this connection, I realize full well that the phrase "university level quality" is subject to a variety of definitions. This more modest goal will be difficult enough to achieve, for it will require major changes in content, in form, in attitude.

It is often said that the modern American university is in crisis. I do not believe this to be true in any general sense. A segment of the university is in crisis, and an important segment, but most of it is not. Most of it is moving along with unparalleled vitality and productivity, and in harmony. This is part of the trouble. It is partly in crisis, but mostly contented, and because it is mostly contented it is only half-hearted about doing something about the part in crisis.

The modern American university draws primarily on three strains of history. First, on the British tradition of high quality training for a select group of undergraduates; second, on the German tradition of research for society and specialized training for graduate students; and, third, on the American genius for service to many, if not most, elements of the surrounding community. Out of these three strains of history have come the three major functions of our contemporary universities. The second and third functions—research and graduate training, and service—have proved quite compatible. The first, undergraduate instruction, is finding it harder to coexist in its entirety with the other two.

The reasons for the growing conflict between some aspects of undergraduate education and the other major current functions are clear. Research, graduate training, and service are carried forward through specialization, and they increasingly relate also to the outside community, to government, to industry, to the professions, to agriculture. The specialist draws funds and problems from the outside and supplies ideas and skilled personnel to the outside. Undergraduate instruction, on the contrary, is inherently more internally oriented—toward the student—and some of these students are interested more in generalization than in specialization.

There is also a problem of scale. Research, graduate training, and service are best carried out in a very large institution, large enough to accommodate an increasing number of specialties and to provide large libraries and laboratories. But, though they take place in a large institution, the relationships they foster are personal. The professor works closely with relatively few graduate students and research assistants, or as consultant or adviser to a few clients. Undergraduate instruction, on the other hand, can be, and in the large institution often is, carried out on a mass basis—the large impersonal lecture. The small-scale relationship with the graduate student within the large-scale institution works better than the large-scale relationship with the undergraduate in the same large-scale institution.

The demands of those functions which can be carried on in a specialized and still personalized way within the large institution have so overwhelmed undergraduate instruction that it has ended, too often, by being handled in a specialized but depersonalized fashion. Universities have grown larger and larger. More and more faculty time and more and more facilities have been devoted to research, graduate training, and service. Specialization has been the key both to publication and to opportunities for consultation by the individual faculty member, and consequently to distinction for the institution.

The organizational structure has responded by creating the department with its own curriculum and the research institute with its own usually narrow segment of knowledge. The undergraduates have been offered specialized courses often imposed in a sequence developed for those majoring in the subject. And universities have come to be measured more by the distinction of their faculties and the quality of their graduate instruction, and less by the distinction of their undergraduate work, which has been much harder to rate on a comparative basis.

There has always been an inherent conflict between undergraduate instruction and the other functions of the university—a conflict caused by the differing degrees of specialization needed by each function, by the scale of the total institution within which each function is best performed, and by the comparative emphasis of the functions on external and internal orientation. But this latent conflict has become fully apparent only since World War II. Over the past twenty years, faculty members have increasingly been drawn into more and more specialized research with the new opportunities available to them, and into service, as external demand for their specialized knowledge has greatly increased. Concurrently, the undergraduates have entered the university better prepared than ever before, more of them have been oriented toward serious academic study, and more of them also have had broad social concerns. The gap has widened between what was offered from behind the lectern and what was demanded by those who sat in front of it.

This gap—between the new mission of many professors and the new desires of some students—might have gone largely unnoticed except for another development. Student styles changed. Apathy turned to activism. More students wanted more control over their institutional environment. Vocationalism also was replaced, in the case of a substantial number, by an even more intense interest in the world as a whole and their role within it. More students wanted to gain from their education a personal and social philosophy as well as, or even instead of, a vocational skill. Faculty members and undergraduate students, who should be in close contact, too often were moving rapidly in divergent directions. And a system of undergraduate education which had been, in part, undesirable became in some situations also less viable. Thus the crisis.

The crisis in the American university is much narrower than undergraduate instruction in general. There is no crisis in the professional schools. There, students have clear vocational aims, the curriculum is designed to further these aims, and the school is usually small enough so that the student is known as an individual. Nor is there a crisis, by and large, in the sciences. There, also, the student usually knows what he wants to do and what he wants to do leads down the path of specialization. Also, the laboratory is a more personal environment than the classroom.

The crisis is largely in the humanities and the social sciences. They have adapted themselves to teaching on a large scale. On a campus I know, one professor has sixty-three teaching assistants under his direct supervision. Large departments in particular tend not to view themselves as having any identifiable group of undergraduate students under their auspices. The students in the humanities and the social sciences are also more likely to have broad concerns about values or public policy which are not satisfied by specialized, segmented courses. Then, too, the political activists are mostly found in these areas of study.

This crisis in the humanities and social sciences at the undergraduate level carries over to a degree into the graduate level and thus into the ranks of the teaching assistants—for somewhat the same reasons, but for an added one as well. Selection and financing of graduate students are generally not as adequate in the humanities and social sciences as in the scientific and professional areas and standards for performance are not so clear-cut; thus, too many graduate students stay around for too many years and in the end achieve only disappointment. Moreover, some faculty members, particularly in the humanities, have felt neglected as the largesse of recent years passed them by, and as honors and acclaim went to the work of others.

Thus the crisis of the university is a limited crisis—limited to areas comprising perhaps one-quarter or one-third of a typical university viewed in terms of numbers of students, but considerably less than that in terms of total faculty time and far less than that in terms of money spent. And within this one-quarter or one-third of a university, there are great variations from student to student, from faculty member to faculty member, and from department to department. Among students, for example, the vocationally oriented major in economics is little different from his counterpart in business administration; and generally the student pursuing his major with vocational aims is much like the student in the sciences. But the crisis, though a limited one, is real. It is the dominant, although by no means the only, internal crisis in the modern university. It needs to be resolved.

Three potential approaches might lead to a resolution of the crisis in undergraduate education. Which solution best meets the problem and is most compatible with the other functions of the university?

The first is to withdraw from the crisis area; do away with the lower division or even with all undergraduate instruction. This solution over-reaches the problem. The problem does not involve all of lower division or all of undergraduate instruction. Much undergraduate instruction, even at the lower division level, is highly effective. University efforts at this level help set standards for the high schools, the junior colleges, and other institutions. They force the university to be concerned with the long span, rather than only the upper limits, of the educational process—and this works to the advantage of the university and the process. Undergraduates bring a spirit of freshness and enthusiasm to a campus. They provide an opportunity for graduate students to gain experience as apprentice teachers. Many undergraduates also benefit from spending a reasonably extended time in the same institution.

The second approach is to make improvements and adjustments within the existing university structure. Much can be done. Much has been done. Much is being done—perhaps more than ever before. The specific remedies are almost endless—freshman seminars, honors programs, credit for field study and other extra-university activities, more selective admission policies, spreading of liberal or general education throughout four years instead of the usual two and perhaps even into the graduate level, better advising procedures, devotion of more faculty time to undergraduate students in general and to lower division students in particular, more careful evaluation of teaching performance, introduction of pass-fail grading to encourage broadening of the student's study program, courses specifically designed for the non-major, more opportunities for independent study, introduction of "problem-oriented" as well as survey courses, consultation with students in the formulation of educational policy, better selection and supervision of teaching assistants, easing of methods for students to drop and resume their studies, improved and earlier orientation programs, and more effective machinery for the encouragement and approval of new and experimental programs.

All these devices have value. Some of them have great value. Their general impact will be to give the student a greater variety of choice and more individual attention. Their introduction marks an important change in attitude—from rigidity to experimentation, from uniformity to variety in the treatment of students, and particularly from a view of the undergraduate students as a grudgingly acknowledged responsibility to a view that these students are a potentially exciting asset to an institution of higher education.

As more and more universities make more and more use of these improvements within the existing structure, undergraduate instruction will become increasingly rewarding to teacher and student alike. The university itself will become a better balanced institution, less preoccupied with its non-instructional responsibilities which so frequently are externally oriented; more concerned with its internal cohesion and coherence. It will be more nearly what it once was—a community of scholars. All reasonable support should be given to these endeavors.

But some questions remain. Will these endeavors solve the crisis completely? Is the existing structure of the university an adequate one within which to administer these endeavors effectively? It seems doubtful to me that we can give a clear affirmative to either of these questions.

Will these endeavors solve the crisis completely? There is now a sizable group of students, particularly in the social sciences and the humanities, who want a really broad and coordinated program for their general education; and who often also want to work within an environment which provides some sense of community, where they can be known as individuals, where they can have an impact on their surroundings. These devices for reform can give them more choices but not a coordinated program; more individual attention but not a sense of community. Thus, for this group, there will still be a crisis, although one of lesser proportions. It should be understood, of course, that a university need not and cannot respond to the interests of every group.

Is the existing structure adequate for administering these endeavors effectively? For some of them it is, but for others it clearly is not. The department is the main administrative agency of the university. It generally handles its undergraduate majors quite well and its graduate students even better. But it is not well equipped by interest or by knowledge to advise or to supervise or to design a curriculum for the non-major; or to provide broadly oriented freshman seminars, or problem-oriented courses, or some new and experimental programs. And the traditional university structure usually contains no other administrative mechanism for handling these endeavors.

The third approach, then, leads to structural changes in the university as a further means for solving the crisis. Structures often seem immune to change, for they are not only the homes of the vested interests but also the judgments drawn from long experience by many people. Nevertheless, structures can and do change as new needs become evident.

We have in the past century created the department, the institute, the service bureau, to handle graduate instruction and undergraduate majors, research, and service. It should be equally possible to create structures that fit the needs of undergraduates not fully served by programs for departmental majors. If so, the department could concentrate on its majors and give them a more personal home. I should like to urge that we now give increasing attention to structures designed to fit the needs and interests of the non-specialized or broadly-interested undergraduates. This group includes some of our ablest students. Society needs the talents of generalists as well as specialists, and attention to their needs can bring a broader intellectual focus to the university as well.

The new Irvine campus of the University of California represents a significant attempt to revise the internal structure, while retaining the traditional framework, of the modern American university to serve better the particular needs of undergraduates. At Irvine, subject-matter is organized less by the standard departments and more by broad divisions and inter-disciplinary groupings. This structure, the culmination of eight years of planning and development of this new campus, is designed to counter the current tendency to over-fractionalization of knowledge, discourage premature specialization by undergraduates, and promote the broad-ranging approaches that are proving to be so beneficial to the solution of many current questions. Students at Irvine are allowed great leeway in organizing their own academic programs within this structure, with careful attention given to individualized advising. There are, in fact, few general university requirements for students. Requirements instead are set forth in the approved program for each individual student. Pass-fail options have been permitted from the beginning to encourage exploration of unfamiliar subject fields. Independent study is encouraged, with course credit available by examination in many instances. The historical separation between teaching and research is minimized. Thus, there are fewer structural barriers to student choice across the entire undergraduate curriculum.

This approach, however, is not the most promising structural change to solve the undergraduate crisis on older campuses. There, the traditional departmental structure is long and firmly established, and the conversion to divisional structure or to new types of departments could only be accomplished by extensive and often costly reorganization of the entire institution.

A more feasible and thus a more promising structure for present undergraduate needs is the cluster college, the relatively small and broadly oriented undergraduate college within a university. Organizationally, these units can be added to established campuses with a minimum of disruption of ongoing programs. Or they can be developed in sequence on new or rapidly growing campuses in conjunction with central libraries and other core facilities. The cluster college concept is being used in slightly different forms, for example, on the University of California's new campuses at San Diego and Santa Cruz.

President Hutchins was a proponent of a somewhat similar idea at Chicago before World War II. When I was chancellor of the University of California at Berkeley some years ago, I had a study made of the performance of students who had transferred there from other colleges and universities throughout the United States. I was impressed then, and I still am, that the students with the best records after transfer to Berkeley had come from the undergraduate college at the University of Chicago. Mr. Hutchins was said to be 500 years behind the times, harking back to Oxford and Cambridge of old, or 2000 years or more behind the times, looking back to the Academy and the Lyceum. If he had been fifty years behind the times, he would have been judged "sound," or if 500 or 2000 years ahead of the times, he would have been out of harm's way. I prefer to think that he was fifty years ahead of the times—not in the sense of a general solution to a general problem, but rather of a partial solution to a partial problem. The modern university must and will pursue specialization, but it can and should preserve some elements descended from earlier models. The Great Books cannot teach biochemistry. They can help teach broad understanding of broad problems.

The cluster college to be effective should be reasonably small in size, have a broadly oriented curriculum, and possess its own separate administrative identity. Reasonable size permits a sense of community. The broad curriculum will serve the student with general interests. The separate administrative identity will make possible a specialized style; more important, it will provide a more intimate group that can treat each student and faculty member as a unique individual. Within such a structure, personalized programs of independent study, field study for credit, dropping in and dropping out can effectively be developed. Students and faculty can consult on educational policy. Teaching assistants can be made a more integral part of the teaching staff. Many of today's piecemeal remedies can become more meaningful within such a structure. The cluster college can bring into the undergraduate level some of the personalized features that already mark graduate study, research, and service even in a large institution, and that help provide these functions with more effective relationships despite the scale of the total endeavors. Size need not mean depersonalization at the undergraduate level any more than at the graduate level.

The great success of the many excellent liberal arts colleges throughout the United States in attracting and training superbly the best of the undergraduates encourages imitation, and possibly even some efforts at improvement on their outstanding performance. The cluster college can operate under fewer restraints than the isolated liberal arts college. It need not cover the same range of subject material, for it can rely on its associated colleges and specialized departments in the central university for some of the total coverage. Thus, it can experiment more with diversity—in style, in emphasis, in method. Each of the colleges in a cluster can be more different from its associated cluster colleges than the single liberal arts college can be from other lone colleges. In 1958 when we at the University of California began planning colleges within our new campuses at San Diego and Santa Cruz, we considered it not only possible but desirable that each cluster college have its own quite distinctive personality and pattern. And each of these two campuses will relate the colleges to each other and to their general campus in quite different ways.

One or more cluster colleges within a university campus can offer to students and faculty members central library, laboratory, and cultural facilities inaccessible to the isolated institution, albeit with some loss of identity for the college in the cluster as against the single institution.

The nature of the faculty of a cluster college within a university will not be the same as in an isolated college or university. The faculty will contain more specialists than will the separate college and more generalists than will the traditional university department; and particularly may enlist more specialists with a deep concern for generalization than either the liberal arts college or the university department can command. To serve the research interests of this faculty, there can, of course, be the usual specialized institutes. But there are also unusual opportunities for institutes with broad orientation toward public policy and toward philosophical and esthetic issues. Then the university might really help shape the minds that influence the age, quite beyond the bits and pieces of new knowledge it now chiefly supplies. It is disquieting to note how many of the broad-ranging commentaries on the world at large that are read by students and faculty alike are written outside of the university. One remembers how science in England first developed largely outside the universities, which only very gradually accepted it as one of their intellectual concerns. The new age we now face might well benefit from efforts to comprehend it more broadly than through the separate fields of knowledge alone. The cluster college with this broad orientation might not only help undergraduate instruction to coexist with the other functions of the modern university but might also actually strengthen the university and its other functions. The cluster colleges within universities might also find a role to play in extension work by carrying their broader orientation to qualified adults, as the more specialized departments and professional schools now do in their areas of competence.

The cluster college within the university may well have some beneficial side-effects in addition to service to undergraduates. It can give faculty members who wish contact across the two or three or four cultures a better opportunity for dialogue. It can also help decentralize administration, particularly of student affairs, within the large campus. Too often now, undergraduate students belong to the Dean of Students rather than to any identifiable academic unit; or they just get lost (some of them, of course, like it that way). A modern university cannot be small but it can seem small to its individual participants. One of its challenges is to seem smaller even, indeed, as it gets bigger.

The cluster college may even possibly add to public understanding of and public benefit from the involvement of those persons identified with the university who participate in public affairs and political action. Too often, now, this involvement takes the form of simplistic slogans and even occasionally that of violent or potentially violent actions. Neither the slogans nor the actions are at a very high intellectual level. Yet the university, of all institutions, should encourage the application of reason and facts and persuasion to the solution of problems. The cluster college can provide a forum for the careful and informed discussion of broad issues of public policy far superior to that offered by the streets, the sidewalk, or the plaza. As a result, the impact exerted on policy by persons identified with the university can also be potentially more effective in the long run. Mind should influence mind, rather than passion pit itself against passion. The university should have ways of serving as a model for high-level public debate, as has the Oxford Union, and the program of the cluster college may provide one such way.

Oxford and Cambridge in England, and the Claremont Colleges and the University of the Pacific in California, have shown the possibilities of clusters of colleges within a larger system. The cluster college has been until recently almost entirely limited to private institutions in England and the United States. As enrollment emphasis shifts to the publicly supported institutions, these private college and university innovations have great value as successful examples to encourage public acceptance.

Not all universities, of course, need to have or perhaps should have cluster colleges, for although this solution may be desirable, it is by no means imperative. The established campus, in particular, may find it difficult to add colleges to itself—even physically, although residence halls can be remodeled or special facilities added to them. The present era, however, presents unusual opportunities. New campuses are being built. Old ones are being expanded. Michigan State and Michigan, for example, are undertaking some of their expansion in the form of undergraduate colleges, and the Santa Barbara campus of the University of California is doing likewise.

Growth holds within itself special capacities for new and, hopefully, better solutions. But new solutions, such as cluster colleges, hold within themselves some inherent problems too; and the new approaches will need to be viewed critically. Firm decisions about their precise form must be held open until we have more experience with them, and judgment of their full value must be kept subject to constant re-examination.

The university is becoming subject to a new set of judgments. For many decades now, since the impacts of the German university and the land-grant movement were felt throughout large American universities, they have been judged mostly by their research output, the quality of their graduate work, and the effectiveness of their service. Only in the older, private universities has the quality of undergraduate instruction been an important continuing criterion—this partly through the strong influence of the alumni. Now there is a greater interest among the public generally and within legislatures in particular in the quality of undergraduate teaching. The public universities will respond to the stimulus of this interest as the private universities have to their alumni. Beyond these external tests of performance lie the new intensity of undergraduate concern for the most effective educational environment and the reviving conscience about and interest in undergraduate teaching on the part of the faculty member. Moreover, there are now better means of rating undergraduate instruction—national test scores for entry into graduate schools, lists of scholarship winners, and the like. And nobody will wish to be last.

This limited crisis is not the first nor will it be the last to confront the American university, whose history occasionally seems to match the plot of the Perils of Pauline. Like Pauline, the university always escapes the immediate peril. I am certain that it will escape this one also. But there is always the next installment. We can face the future with full confidence, and even absolute assurance, that some new peril will come along to make life in the university more exciting. It may also make the university, in the process, more nearly perfect.

*One of the leading spokesmen
of the New Left, Paul Goodman
(1911–   ) is a prolific
writer of poetry, drama, and
fiction as well as literary
and social criticism. Holder
of a Ph.D. from the
University of Chicago, he
has been an especially acid
critic of American education.
A popular lecturer, Goodman
has held a number of
teaching positions, including
one at Black Mountain College
in North Carolina. The
college was founded in 1933
when a group of professors
and students broke away from
Rollins College because of
their dissatisfaction with
that school.*

A Simple Proposal

PAUL GOODMAN

I

For the near future the
prospect of significant reform
in the great majority of
schools and especially in the
most populous ones, is dim.
In the nature of the case the
very changes that are needed
are the ones that administrations must resist, for they curtail administration's reason for
being and jeopardize its security. Decentralizing control,
splitting up rather than expanding, dispensing with credits, grading, and admissions,
de-emphasizing buildings and

grounds, being selective about contracting research—all these make pale the hectic flush. It would seem to be self-evident that the only purpose of educational administration is to expedite education, but this thought is entirely naïve and out-of-date. Worse, however, the reforms toward freedom, commitment, criticism, and inevitable social conflict, endanger the Image and indeed nullify the historical role of administration which has been not to protect its community but to pacify it. So let us propose to go outside the present collegiate framework. The simplest remedy is the historical one, for bands of scholars to secede and set up where they can teach and learn on their own simple conditions. Such a movement is difficult but not impractical. In my opinion, if it could succeed in a dozen cases—proving that there is a viable social alternative to what we have—the entire system would experience a profound and salutary jolt.

Secession is inevitably occurring in any case. But for want of thought it is occurring wrong. Briefly, as our present social system approaches a cultural crisis of meaninglessness, dissatisfied young people cannot/ will not conform to it and they quit the schools. They group and try to find a culture or create it out of nothing. Even little academies are formed, led by tutors in their twenties and early thirties, e.g., Emerson, Blake, Pasternak. This is classical; but what is wrong is that they include few senior scholars who know something, and few veterans who undertake to teach professions in an objective and systematic way. This is because the seniors are a generation older and got their grasp when the situation was bad but not quite so desperate; therefore they are not now so completely at a loss. The young regard them—I have experienced it—with a mixture of superstitious respect and personal unbelief. The respect—sometimes envious, resentful, and hostile—is that these men have "made it," meaning that they have learned something, done something, or that they simply belong in the world in any reasonable and justified way whatever. The unbelief, because such a thing is for themselves impossible. The young have social, creative, intellectual experiences, and even a resurgence of religious impulses, but finally it is only big Society and big Culture that give meaning. The young know this not vaguely but acutely, and feel excluded, and of course magnify their difficulties to be overwhelming.

What is lacking as a bridge, of course, is just the objective culture and the professions that provide public identity and the ability to operate confidently, whether succeeding or failing, in society. But if this goes on a while longer, our culture and professions will be irrelevant; there will not even be "carriers" of them, except occasional dilettantes and dodos. By and large the present universities do not and cannot educate.

II

A young fellow who cannot/will not learn in school may consult his benevolent senior scholars, and he might get the following responses:

At the worst, he will be referred to Guidance. For his case is a psychological one and needs help of that kind. The case surely is psychological or rapidly becomes so, for a youth can hardly remain in a conflict of pressure to perform, including his own pressure on himself, and dumb conviction that it is meaningless to perform, without soon suffering anxiety, depression, and various kinds of flight. But such an academic response by the senior merely pushes off the problem onto an administrator who is even less qualified to help, despite his battery of tests.

On the other hand, the senior scholar may rather quickly identify with the youth's woes and gripes. He does not see any reasons why the young man should not quit, strike out on his own with the teeming projects of his brain that the school is stifling, and eventually educate himself. This response lets the young fellow down, because if he practically had such projects, he would be engaged on them. I think it betrays a lack of imagination. The senior has "made it," and from this vantage point he sees, what is obvious, that the schools are worthless for the gifted and original who do not happen to have the knack to take *anything* and profit by it. But the young man has not "made it" and is suffering. And it is too hard to educate oneself. The few who have the determination and synthetic power to do so are not the ones who cannot/will not learn even in a modern university.

A middle response—the one that I myself tend to give—is to stick with it by becoming aware of the situation just as it is, taking stupid rules whence they come, refraining anger, not being too co-operative and, above all, refusing to perform in any positive way that is base or dishonest. This formula, I argue, is usually possible because the teachers are not malevolent, and of course the subjects are great subjects. Also, I explain how I came to smoke a pipe: when I used to explode in a certain class at Chicago and make a nuisance of myself, McKeon, who was my mentor in such matters, showed me his pipe, the stem full of deep tooth-marks, and advised me to get me a pipe. Also, college has this undoubted advantage: although the young man won't get much from a college education, he will at least know that there is not much to be gotten, he will have run the obstacle course; he won't have to reproach himself stupidly later. All this advice is honest on my part and no doubt supportive.

Yet it is craven advice. I would not give it in politics, where I would rather say, Protest, don't vote, prudently disregard the laws that are harmful. I would not advise an adult to keep a useless and depressing job. This advice belongs to a veteran who occasionally does the best he can and therefore can stoically endure or merrily endure (depending on his character) the usual frustrations. But for a young person it is spirit-breaking and probably even unhealthy—mononucleosis seems to be the current psychosomatic effect of student blues.

The realistic response has to be: "You exaggerate, but you're essentially right. But then what? If you quit school as you are, any job you get will be worse, because you're not ready to make it better. You don't know anything." This is not supportive at all. The student doesn't know anything and the senior scholar doesn't know where he can learn anything. They look at one another.

III

Secession has been, I have said, the historical remedy for disaffected communities of scholars. But of course there are never real historical parallels. For instance, the classical strikes and migrations during the thirteenth century occurred because of direct clashes with church and state on doctrine, behavior, politics, by banded scholars defending their freedom and privileges; and at the same time, the universities had both a moral authority and an economic importance in their towns that made strike and migration a powerful weapon. In our own time, we have a unique system of co-ordinative management and democracy-by-consent designed precisely to prevent direct clashes; there is plenty of freedom and the whittling away of privileges is slow and subtle; and dissenters have no authority or economic power whatever. But more hopefully, our democracy and affluence, and the present expansion and turmoil of the colleges in any case, are unusually open to experiment, including even a simple experiment.

In the English-speaking world, the most important academic precedent for setting up shop in the face of the Establishment is the dissenting Academies that sprang up after the Act of Uniformity in 1662. More than 2,000 rectors and vicars resigned, including teachers at Oxford and Cambridge. "One of the first resources of the ejected ministers was to take to teaching, partly in order to eke out a living but mainly that they might not see their sons and the sons of the likeminded deprived of university education." (H. McLachlan, *English Education Under the Test Acts.*) They started with tiny schools of one to four tutors and five to six to thirty students; and during more than a century they were outlaws, either because they were not allowed to teach at the university level outside of the two universities, or because they did not subscribe to the Articles. Nevertheless, the secession survived, new texts were written and exchanged, students went from one little school to another, and during the eighteenth century these academies gave the best education in England and were probably the chief influence on the early American colleges. Some of them, subsidized by church bodies, were simply dissenting seminaries, but others became centers of rationalism and even politically revolutionary thought, influencing both the American and French revolutions and the reform movement in England, developing modern science and letters, and producing major changes in educational theory and practice. Their dissent happened to be the tide of the future. Their tutors and senior students, "unlike men studying for holy orders in the universities, were sent out to preach to congregations far and near"—and these included radical students from Joseph Priestley's Warrington. It is said that Marat was a tutor at Warrington. And to tie our story together, let us recall that it was Priestley's son-in-law, Dr. Cooper, who was barred as an atheist from Jefferson's great faculty by the House of Burgesses.

In America, we have already noticed the secession in the Dartmouth College Case. Another interesting secession is described by Professor Metzger in *The Development of Academic Freedom in the United States*. "In 1833 an antislavery society was formed at Lane Theological Seminary in Cincinnati by students and a number of the faculty. The board of trustees banned the society, stating that 'education must be completed before the young are fitted to engage in the collisions of active life.' . . . But the young in this case happened to be rather old —30 of the seminarians were over the age of twenty-six. 'Free discussion, being a duty,' they announced, 'is consequently a right. It is *our* right. It *was* before we entered Lane; privileges we might and did relinquish; advantages we might and did receive. But this *right* the institution could neither give nor take away.' After firing this broadside, the students removed in a body to Oberlin, where they won the concession that their faculty (which included a professor who had been dismissed from Lane) would supervise them without interference from the trustees." The case, Professor Metzger points out, was "unfortunately atypical. A mass boycott of this kind, reminiscent of the medieval universities, was never to be repeated."

More relevant to contemporary conditions was the founding of the New School for Social Research in 1919. This is best viewed as a secession of teachers, for some of its chief spirits—e.g., Beard, Veblen, Robinson—could not conform to the Stanfords and Columbias, and others were attracted who were restive in such places. Later the school was, not accidentally, spectacularly augmented by the refugees from Hitler, the "university in exile." Over the course of the years, to be sure, the New School has itself succumbed to expansion, buildings and grounds, etc., in the normal process of decay of the prophetic to the bureaucratic.

The secession that is most relevant for our purposes, since the nearest in time, is the founding of Black Mountain College by the teachers fired from Rollins because of the "academic freedom" case of John Rice. What is especially relevant about Rice's case is that he did not seem to espouse any particular heresy: it was his general nonconformity and nuisance value in the local society and with prospective donors that was condemned. He and his friends formed, really, the first Beat school—and his graduates have been leaders in this kind of art and culture. The school certainly had a zeal of medieval poverty, its teachers often went unpaid; but they continued because the school was theirs, it had no trustees and no administration. (Rice himself was ostracized as a "leader.") I myself taught a summer at Black Mountain.[1] I found it very feeble in the universal culture, but on the other hand nobody hindered me from teaching more scholastically and trying to influence the others. There was a frantic effort for community, resulting in affectionate loyalty and fatal dissensions. It was a justified and significant boast that students who had dropped out of the Ivy League could still get some kind of education at Black Mountain College. The school lasted nearly twenty-five years and then, like a little magazine, folded. Its spirit survives.

IV

Now, in the sixties, a small secession from about twenty colleges and universities would be immensely profitable for American education. I propose that a core faculty of about five professors secede from a school, taking some of their students with them; attach to themselves an equal number of like-minded professionals in the region; collect a few more students; and set up a small unchartered university that would be nothing but an association for teaching-and-learning. Ten teachers would constitute a sufficient faculty for such a *studium generale*. (For comparison, Jefferson's University of Virginia had eight

---

[1] I was discontinued, against my wishes, because of my wicked ways. Not, however, because of my behavior as such but, oddly, because of my public claim of the right to it, which was apparently legally and otherwise dangerous.

teachers; Joseph Priestley's Warrington had a maximum of thirteen.) Instead of five professionals, there could be a few more, some teaching part-time. With a class size of twelve to fifteen for ten teachers, there would be 120 to 150 students.

I choose the class size of twelve to fifteen as a mean in my own not untypical experience. It gives a sufficient weight of thoughts, objections, and questions to oppose and activate the teacher. When the number falls below this, to seven or eight, I begin to feel that I am leading a group therapy; I am overly conscious of the individual personalities coping with the subject, rather than teaching the objective subject. When the number rises to between twenty and thirty, I begin to feel I am lecturing the subject, with a question-and-answer period, and perhaps leading a "discussion." But of course the mean number varies with the subject, the character of the persons, and how the subject is handled. E.g., in teaching a course in writing, I combine several approaches: Structural analyses of classical texts, and these are largely lectures, with questions, that could be given to a group of thirty-five; psychological unblocking exercises, and exercises on points of style and technique, for both of which I like the class of twelve to fifteen; reading and criticism of the students' own writing, which I prefer in groups of five or six and *not* in a classroom. There are similar variations in anything else I would teach; and I presume it is the same for other teachers.

Throughout this book I have explained the advantages of a strong weight of professionals on a faculty. It is especially important in a small school composed entirely of teachers and students in close relation and without administrative rules, for otherwise it can become clubby, like excellent progressive schools or like Black Mountain College. These are lovely intentional communities, but they are not small universities; they do not sharply turn to the world. Furthermore, if a small school purports to be a *studium generale* it must have resources available outside itself. Suppose that a teacher teaches an elementary and a more advanced course, taking two years; then he will want to take his students nearer to real practice in the city, and the professionals have access to such practice.

It is evident, I hope, that I am not thinking of any particular educational experiment or ideology, like Goddard, Antioch, Sarah Lawrence, etc., aiming at democracy, communal living, community service, individual development, creativity, and so forth. These are fine things. But I am proposing simply to take teaching-and-learning in its own terms, for the students and teachers to associate in the traditional way and according to their existing interest, but *entirely dispensing with the external control, administration, bureaucratic machinery, and other excrescences that have swamped our communities of scholars.* I have no doubt that many such faculties, of dissatisfied academics and professionals who would like to teach, are ready in existence. At present there is no dearth of students; but of course such academic and professional faculties would choose the students very strictly, perhaps unduly so.

v

Three problems immediately arise: (1) the economics of the community; (2) its plant, library, and equipment; and (3) its relation to the chartered academic world and the rest of society, that is, the need for accredited degrees.

(1) We are not thinking of a social experiment, so let us pitch our prices according to the current inflated national scale of living. This is psychologically quite unrealistic (and perhaps any merely economic discussion would be), for teachers who would engage in such an experiment would also be less interested in the current standards; and of course, psychologically committed to it, they would have to make the experiment succeed, even if it cost them heavily financially. The professionals would be the doctors, lawyers, reform politicians, etc., who work too hard for too little reward anyway. And such a faculty would find it hard to exclude serious youngsters who could not foot the inflated bill.

Nevertheless, since we are thinking precisely of acting in society and of preparing professionals, we have to take the world as it is. This is the irony of actuality: those who want to transform a system of society, rather than to withdraw from it or destroy it, must operate practically within it. Our economy is administrative and venal through and through, and *therefore* inflated; but it is only the academic administration that we propose withdrawing from!

The relevant comparative figures are:

Median College Salaries, 1961

Professor	$10,250
Associate Professor	8,200
Assistant Professor	6,900
Instructor	5,600
(Assistant Instructor, Preceptor, etc.)	2,000–3,000

Typical College Tuition (plus fees), 1961

Cornell	$1,600 plus 260
Dartmouth	1,550
Harvard	1,520
Columbia	1,450 plus 10
New York University	1,280 plus 100
Swarthmore	1,250 plus 150
Oberlin	1,150 plus 80
University of Chicago	1,140
Amherst	1,150 plus 110

State Colleges for Out-of-State Students, 1961

Michigan	$ 750
Rutgers	500
California	500
North Carolina	500

Let us fix the salaries for teachers in two opposite ways: as a guild of teachers, and as a guild of students. For the first, we can adopt the national median for full professor, $10,000. (This is, of course, lower than the top at the great Eastern schools.) Then, the expenses are:

Salaries	$100,000
Rent (10 rooms, urban middle-class)	4,000
	$104,000

Divided among 150 students, this comes to tuition of $685. Among 120 students, $850. This is $300–500 less than the good liberal arts colleges, and half of the Ivy League. It includes, of course, no extras whatever, importantly no Medical; and there are no endowed library, laboratories, gymnasium, stadium, which are usually, however, paid for by the special "fees," not as "tuition." No school provides books.

Conversely, we might assume that the students as a guild would be satisfied to pay the tuition of an average State university, $500 plus fees. Then,

Income from 150 students	$75,000
Rent	—4,000
	$71,000
Income from 120 students	$60,000
Rent	—4,000
	$56,000

This would pay each teacher $7,100, a little more than the median for Assistant Professor, or $5,600, the median for an Instructor.

Perhaps the teachers and students might compromise on the median for Associate Professor, $8,200! This is for forty weeks. And we must remember that especially the professionals would have subsidiary income.

(2) With regard to plant and equipment, let us envisage several possibilities. But we must keep in mind that this is a *community* of scholars. It would immediately have available for its use 10,000 to 20,000 carefully selected books and some apparatus. Its professional associations would give it some access to the laboratories and equipment that the teaching professionals would happen to be interested in.

It is simplest to think of such a little community as located in a large city, with a municipal library, a Y, and many available part-time professionals. On the other hand, there are obvious charms and advantages to locate in a town and its region; nor need such places be lacking in excellent professionals with a lively local practice. (I do not much picture a school of this kind as isolated in the country.)

But another possibility for providing books and plant is to consider the small university as next to, and unofficially adjunct to, some great university which extends to it friendly services because it is a necessary experiment and a source of good graduate students. The economic independence of the community dissociates it from the great school; the administration of the great school has no responsibility for it whatever; yet the secession of a small faculty need *not* mean a rupture of friendly relations. That is, we can conceive of a free academy set up in the neighborhood of a great university to their mutual advantage.

Historically, this is *almost* familiar. In Germany, our teachers paid directly by the students would be recognized as Private-Docents of the University, officially associated with it and teaching in its classrooms. What we propose is simply the secession and association of these Independents, so that they become again, what they were in the beginning, regent masters of their own guild.

(3) Finally, a major difficulty of any unchartered *ad hoc* association of scholars is that it cannot grant degrees leading to licenses. It is not to be expected, and *it is not desirable,* that young people spend their years and money in study that does not lead to careers in society.

An obvious possible solution is the European plan: to have the graduates matriculate for a term in an accredited school and pass the comprehensives. (E.g., the University of Chicago used to accept candidates for comprehensives after one Quarter, three months, of residence.) To my mind this solution has a theoretical drawback. The comprehensives of an accredited school must necessarily follow the curriculum of that school; and this cannot, of course, be a determining "goal" for the community of scholars which has been teaching-and-learning according to its implicit goals, without extrinsic "motivation." But it is likely—and perhaps I am sanguine—that for many of the students it would not be difficult, after several years of good education, to make up the usual requirements with a semester's cramming.

Far more attractive, however, would be a friendly arrangement whereby graduate and professional schools, that compete for good students, would accept these students on their merits. In this case their first accredited degree would be a master's or doctor's.

VI

How complicated this simple proposal is! We must bring together 150 persons, subject the young to considerable expense, and think of future arrangements that have no real relevance to the living present. Is there no easier way to grow up?

The *studium generale* is, finally, what we mean by the Western World. It *is* complicated, let's face it—but it is not necessarily absurd, it can be viable. Anyway, it is the way we have chosen, and we are committed to it! Our fundamental idea is that the growing social animals become free citizens. They grow into civilization in a way rational to themselves, they understand it, and therefore they continue to have initiative. They have also taken *on* the civilization; they are responsible for it. They are no longer simple social animals confronting God and the other people.[2]

We can think of two different (fictitious) extremes, and see that the *studium generale* is in the middle and is neither of them. Education can be regarded as socialization, to make the young conform harmoniously to society—and this can be a base or noble purpose, depending on the quality of society. Or it may be regarded as the effort to perfect people as such, perhaps giving them defenses against the existing, or any, society, in the interest of liberty. But the Western university rather regards society itself as a drama of persons, in which the educated understand the play and so can invent a new play. *Liberty is, essentially, the exercise of initiative in a mixed city.*

The tendency of contemporary society, collectivized, technocratic, managerial, is to impose a culture on its members, to train them to carry it and perform. Such a society is different from ancient despotism

---

[2] Let me repeat an anecdote of Buber's: An Eastern sage and a Western sage are climbing a mountain. But the Western sage is carrying a heavy box, drops it, falls backward, shoulders it again, struggles on. The Easterner easily races ahead to the top and is soon on his way down. "Why don't you throw away that box?" he says to the other, "then you could easily get up." "But what," says the Westerner, "if I have to get to the top just with my box? Otherwise it is nothing to me."

in that, ideally, it has no elite, though it may have top managers, for decisions are also made by a technological process to maximize the common good. The schools of society are, ideally, partly trade schools and partly finishing schools in conformity. Of course there is not, and probably cannot be, such an ideal social machine. In America, the need for personal co-ordination, democracy-by-consent, is a limit of management as well as a managerial triumph. Other more tyrannical technocracies have other limitations.

But there have been high cultures with a contrary tendency, psychical and cosmological, to by-pass as much as possible the objective tools and institutions of society and civilization, in order to attain holiness, beatitude, or wisdom as directly as possible. Since these are the goals that men seek in the end, other things are illusion, and it is the task of learning to see through them. Schools are then retreats, whose guru, monk, or therapist has the right soul to liberate the right disciples. But of course, every such religious culture is embedded in its civilization, believes its myths, conforms to its social structure, and partly has to be defined as an escape from its troubles.

By and large, we have to say that the city culture of the West is both moral and technical, personal and collective. Yet it is not, as some writers think, a dialectical process of the other two tendencies, for it has a different principle. The principle of the *studium generale* is that civilization has been a continual gift of the Creator Spirit; it consists of inventions, discoveries, insights, art works, highly theorized institutions, methods of workmanship. All of this has vastly accumulated over the ages and become very unwieldly, yet, in the spirit, it is always appropriable. As Socrates would have said, its meaning can be recalled. The advantage of recalling it is that we are then not enslaved to it, we are citizens, and we again have it available as our own. Consider. It is by losing himself in the objective, in inquiry, creation, and craft, that a man becomes something. It is as if a man "makes himself," but of course it is the spirit that makes him. On the other hand, he need not be submerged in the civilization that he inherits, that others made, for if he studies it he will surely find himself there; it is his.

The university, the *studium generale*, is the appropriable city. "Its proper end," said Coleridge, "is civilization with freedom." A city culture is a mixture of clashing influences, foreigners from all parts. The objective culture that we have inherited is by now total confusion; and certainly there is too much of it for anybody to cope with. As if this were not bad enough, the young are kept from learning, by rules, task-work, and extraneous distractions. They have no conversation and they meet no veterans. Nevertheless, there is no other way for them to grow up to be free citizens, to commence, except by discovering, in an earnest moment, that some portion of the objective culture is after all natively their own; it is usable by *them*; it is humane, comprehensible and practicable, and it communicates with everything else. The discovery flashes with spirit.

College
and the
Alternatives

JOHN W. GARDNER

As president of the Carnegie Corporation, a philanthropic foundation, and later Secretary of Health, Education and Welfare in the cabinet of President Johnson, John W. Gardner (1912–) has been one of the most influential figures in contemporary American education. A graduate of Stanford University and holder of a doctorate in psychology from the University of California, Gardner has taught at Connecticut College and Mt. Holyoke College. In 1968 Gardner left his government post to become chairman of The Urban Coalition.

WHO SHOULD GO
TO COLLEGE

All of the conflicting and confusing notions which Americans have concerning equality, excellence and the encouragement of talent may be observed with crystal clarity in the current discussions of "who should go to college." In the years ahead these discussions will become more heated. Pressure of enrollments will make it far harder to get into the better colleges, and there will be lively debate over who has a "right" to a college education.

A good deal of this debate will center around issues of quality versus quantity in education. Douglas Bush eloquently enunciated one extreme position in the phrase, "Education for all is education for none." [1]

Arguments about quality in higher education tend to be heated and rather pointless. There are many reasons why such conversations become muddled, the foremost being that they so often degenerate into arguments over "elite" versus "mass" education. People who engage in these arguments are like the two washerwomen Sydney Smith observed leaning out of their back windows and quarreling with each other across the alley: "They could never agree," Smith said, "because they were arguing from different premises." [2] In the case of arguments over "elite" versus "mass" education, I am convinced that both premises should be vacated, because behind the arguments is the assumption that a society must decide whether it wishes to educate a few people exceedingly well *or* to educate a great number of people rather badly.

This is an imaginary dilemma. It is possible to have excellence in education and at the same time to seek to educate everyone to the limit of his ability. A society such as ours has no choice but to seek the development of human potentialities at all levels. It takes more than an educated elite to run a complex, technological society. Every modern, industrialized society is learning that hard lesson.

The notion that so-called quality education and so-called mass education are mutually exclusive is woefully out of date. It would not have survived at all were there not a few remarkably archaic characters in our midst. We all know that some of the people calling most noisily for quality in education are those who were *never* reconciled to the widespread extension of educational opportunity. To such individuals there is something inherently vulgar about large numbers of people. At the other extreme are the fanatics who believe that the

---

[1] Douglas Bush, "Education for All is Education for None," *New York Times Magazine*, January 9, 1955, p. 13.

[2] W. H. Auden (ed.), *Selected Writings of Sydney Smith*. New York: Farrar, Straus & Cudahy, Inc., 1956, p. xiv.

chief goal for higher education should be to get as many youngsters as possible—regardless of ability—into college classrooms. Such individuals regard quality as a concept smacking faintly of Louis XIV.

But neither extreme speaks for the American people, and neither expresses the true issues that pose themselves today. It would be fatal to allow ourselves to be tempted into an anachronistic debate. *We must seek excellence in a context of concern for all.* A democracy, no less than any other form of society, must foster excellence if it is to survive; and it should not allow the emotional scars of old battles to confuse it on this point.

Educating everyone up to the limit of his ability does not mean sending everyone to college. Part of any final answer to the college problem must be some revision of an altogether false emphasis which the American people are coming to place on college education. This false emphasis is the source of great difficulties for us. In Virginia they tell the story of the kindly Episcopal minister who was asked whether the Episcopal Church was the only path to salvation. The minister shook his head—a bit sadly, perhaps. "No, there are other paths," he said, and then added, "but no gentleman would choose them." Some of our attitudes toward college education verge dangerously on the same position.

There are some people who seem to favor almost limitless expansion of college attendance. One hears the phrase "everyone has a right to go to college." It is easy to dispose of this position in its extreme form. There are some youngsters whose mental deficiency is so severe that they cannot enter the first grade. There are a number of youngsters out of every hundred whose mental limitations make it impossible for them to get as far as junior high school. There are many more who can progress through high school only if they are placed in special programs which take into account their academic limitations. These "slow learners" could not complete high school if they were required to enroll in a college-preparatory curriculum.

It is true that some who fall in this group would not be there if it were not for social and economic handicaps. But for most of them, there is no convincing evidence that social handicaps are a major factor in their academic limitations. Children with severe or moderate intellectual limitations appear not infrequently in families which are able to give them every advantage, and in which the possibilities of treatment have been exhaustively explored. Such children can be helped by intelligent attention, but the hope that any major change can be accomplished in their academic limitations is usually doomed to disappointment.

With each higher grade an increasing number of youngsters find it difficult or impossible to keep up with the work. Some drop out. Some transfer to vocational or industrial arts programs. A great many never complete high school.

Presumably, college students should only be drawn from the group which is able to get through high school. So the question becomes: "Should all high school graduates go to college?" The answer most frequently heard is that "all should go to college who are qualified for it"—but what do we mean by *qualified*? Probably less than 1 per cent of the college-age population is qualified to attend the California Institute of Technology. There are other colleges where 10, 20, 40 or 60 per cent of the college-age population is qualified to attend.

It would be possible to create institutions with standards so low that 90 per cent of the college-age population could qualify. In order to do so it would be necessary only to water down the curriculum and provide simpler subjects. Pushed to its extreme, the logic of this position would lead us to the establishment of institutions at about the intellectual level of summer camps. We could then include almost all of the population in these make-believe colleges.

Let us pursue this depressing thought. If it were certain that almost all of the eighteen- to twenty-two-year-old population could benefit greatly by full-time attendance at "colleges" of this sort, no one could reasonably object. But one must look with extreme skepticism upon the notion that all high school graduates can profit by continued formal schooling. There is no question that they can profit by continued *education*. But the character of this education will vary from one youngster to the next. Some will profit by continued book learning; others by some kind of vocational training; still others by learning on the job. Others may require other kinds of growth experiences.

Because college has gained extraordinary prestige, we are tempted to assume that the only useful learning and growth comes from attending such an institution, listening to professors talk from platforms, and reproducing required information on occasions called examinations. This is an extremely constricting notion. Even in the case of intellectually gifted individuals, it is a mistake to assume that the only kind of learning they can accomplish is in school. Many gifted individuals might be better off if they could be exposed to alternative growth experiences.

In the case of the youngster who is not very talented academically, forced continuance of education may simply prolong a situation in which he is doomed to failure. Many a youngster of low ability has been kept on pointlessly in a school which taught him no vocation, exposed him to continuous failure and then sent him out into the world with a record which convinced employers that he must forever afterward be limited to unskilled or semi-skilled work. This is not a sensible way to conserve human resources.

Properly understood, the college or university is the instrument of *one kind of further education of those whose capacities fit them for that kind of education.* It should not be regarded as the sole means of establishing one's human worth. It should not be seen as the unique key to happiness, self-respect and inner confidence.

We have all done our bit to foster these misconceptions. And the root of the difficulty is our bad habit of assuming that the only meaningful life is the "successful" life, defining success in terms of high personal attainment in the world's eyes. Today attendance at college has become virtually a prerequisite of high attainment in the world's eyes, so that it becomes, in the false value framework we have created, the only passport to a meaningful life. No wonder our colleges are crowded.

The crowding in our colleges is less regrettable than the confusion in our values. *Human dignity and worth should be assessed only in terms of those qualities of mind and spirit that are within the reach of every human being.*

This is not to say that we should not value achievement. We should value it exceedingly. It is simply to say that achievement should not be confused with human worth. Our recognition of the dignity and worth of the individual is based upon moral imperatives and should be of universal application. In other words, everyone has a "right" to that recognition. Being a college graduate involves qualities of mind which can never be universally possessed. Everyone does not have a right to be a college graduate, any more than everyone has a right to run a four-minute mile.

What we are really seeking is what James Conant had in mind when he said that the American people are concerned not only for equality of opportunity but for equality of respect. Every human being wishes to be respected regardless of his ability, and in moral terms we are bound to grant him that right. The more we allow the impression to get abroad that only the college man or woman is worthy of respect in our society, the more we contribute to a fatal confusion which works to the injury of all concerned. If we make the confusing assumption that college is the sole cradle of human dignity, need we be surprised that every citizen demands to be rocked in that cradle?

THE NEED FOR INSTITUTIONAL DIVERSITY

But a scaling down of our emphasis on college education is only part of the answer. Another important part of the answer must be a greatly increased emphasis upon individual differences, upon many kinds of talent, upon the immensely varied ways in which individual potentialities may be realized.

If we develop such an indomitable concern for individual differences, we will learn to laugh at the assumption that a college education is the only avenue to human dignity and social worth. We would educate some youngsters by sending them on to college. We would educate others in other ways. We would develop an enormous variety of patterns to fit the enormous variety of individuals. And no pattern would be regarded as socially superior or involving greater human dignity than any other pattern.

But the plain fact is that college education is firmly associated in the public mind with personal advancement, upward social mobility, market value and self-esteem. And if enough of the American people believe that one must attend college in order to be accorded respect and confidence, then the very unanimity of opinion makes the generalization true.

It is particularly true, unfortunately, in the crude categories of the employment file. A cynical friend of mine said recently, "Everyone has two personalities these days—the one under his hat and the one in his employment file. The latter is the most important—and it is made up of primitive categories. Have you held too many jobs? (Never mind why.) Did you go to a good college? (Never mind if you were the campus beachcomber.) Does your job record show a steady rise in responsibilities? (Never mind if you played politics every inch of the way.)"

If we are to do justice to individual differences, if we are to provide suitable education for each of the young men and women who crowd into our colleges and universities, then we must cultivate diversity in our higher educational system to correspond to the diversity of the clientele. There is no other way to handle within one system the enormously disparate human capacities, levels of preparedness and motivations which flow into our colleges and universities.

But we cannot hope to create or to maintain such diversity unless we honor the various aspects of that diversity. Each of the different kinds of institutions has a significant part to play in creating the total pattern, and each should be allowed to play its role with honor and recognition.

We do not want all institutions to be alike. We want institutions to develop their individualities and to keep those individualities. None must be ashamed of its distinctive features so long as it is doing something that contributes importantly to the total pattern, and so long as it is striving for excellence in performance. The highly selective, small liberal arts college should not be afraid to remain small. The large urban institution should not be ashamed that it is large. The technical institute should not be apologetic about being a technical institute. Each institution should pride itself on the role that it has chosen to play and on the special contribution which it brings to the total pattern of American higher education.

Such diversity is the only possible answer to the fact of individual differences in ability and aspirations. And furthermore, it is the only means of achieving *quality* within a framework of quantity. For we must not forget the primacy of our concern for excellence. We must have diversity, but we must also expect that every institution which makes up that diversity will be striving, in its own way, for excellence. This may require a new way of thinking about excellence in higher education—a conception that would be applicable in terms of the objectives of the institution. As things now stand, the word *excellence* is all too often reserved for the dozen or two dozen institutions which stand at the very zenith of our higher education in terms of faculty distinction, selectivity of students and difficulty of curriculum. In these terms it is simply impossible to speak of a junior college, for example, as excellent. Yet sensible men can easily conceive of excellence in a junior college.

The traditionalist might say, "Of course! Let Princeton create a junior college and one would have an institution of unquestionable excellence!" That may be correct, but it may also lead us down precisely the wrong path. If Princeton Junior College were excellent, it might not be excellent in the most important way that a community college can be excellent. It might simply be a truncated version of Princeton. A comparably meaningless result would be achieved if General Motors tried to add to its line of low-priced cars by marketing the front half of a Cadillac.

We shall have to be more flexible than that in our conception of excellence. We must develop a point of view that permits each kind of institution to achieve excellence *in terms of its own objectives.*

In higher education as in everything else there is no excellent performance without high morale. No morale, no excellence! And in a great many of our colleges and universities the most stubborn enemy of high morale has been a kind of hopelessness on the part of both administration and faculty—hopelessness about ever achieving distinction as an institution. Not only are such attitudes a corrosive influence on morale, they make it virtually certain that the institution will never achieve even that kind of excellence which is within its reach. For there *is* a kind of excellence within the reach of every institution.

In short, we reject the notion that excellence is something that can only be experienced in the most rarified strata of higher education. It may be experienced at every level and in every serious kind of higher education. And not only may it be experienced everywhere, but we must *demand* it everywhere. We must ask for excellence in every form which higher education takes. We should not ask it lightly or amiably or good naturedly; we should demand it vigorously and insistently. We should assert that a stubborn striving for excellence is the price of admission to reputable educational circles, and that those institutions not characterized by this striving are the slatterns of higher education.

We must make the same challenging demands of students. We must never make the insolent and degrading assumption that young people unfitted for the most demanding fields of intellectual endeavor are incapable of rigorous attention to *some sort of standards*. It is an appalling error to assume—as some of our institutions seem to have assumed—that young men and women incapable of the highest standards of intellectual excellence are incapable of any standards whatsoever, and can properly be subjected to shoddy, slovenly and trashy educational fare. College should be a demanding as well as an enriching experience—demanding for the brilliant youngster at a high level of expectation and for the less brilliant at a more modest level.

It is no sin to let average as well as brilliant youngsters into college. It *is* a sin to let any substantial portion of them—average or brilliant —drift through college without effort, without growth and without a goal. That is the real scandal in many of our institutions.

Though we must make enormous concessions to individual differences in aptitude, we may properly expect that every form of education be such as to stretch the individual to the utmost of his potentialities. And we must expect each student to strive for excellence in terms of the kind of excellence that is within his reach. Here again we must recognize that there may be excellence or shoddiness in every line of human endeavor. We must learn to honor excellence (indeed to *demand* it) in every socially accepted human activity, however humble the activity, and to scorn shoddiness, however exalted the activity. As I said in another connection: "An excellent plumber is infinitely more admirable than an incompetent philosopher. The society which scorns excellence in plumbing because plumbing is a humble activity and tolerates shoddiness in philosophy because it is an exalted activity will have neither good plumbing nor good philosophy. Neither its pipes nor its theories will hold water."

OPPORTUNITIES OTHER THAN COLLEGE

Not long ago the mother of two teen-age boys came to me for advice. "Roger made a fine record in high school," she explained, "and when he was a senior we had exciting discussions of all the colleges he was interested in. Now Bobby comes along with terrible grades, and when the question of his future arises a silence descends on the dinner table. It breaks my heart!"

I knew something about Bobby's scholastic limitations, which were notable, and I asked warily what I might do to help.

"The high school principal says that with his record no college will take him," she said, "and that if one did take him he wouldn't last. I can't reconcile myself to that!"

"Have you discussed any possibilities other than college?" I asked.

She shook her head. "His father says he can get him a job driving a delivery truck. But I think he just says that to jar Bobby."

It took some time for me to explain all that I thought was deplorable in her attitude and that of her husband. Parents of academically limited children should not act as though any outcome other than college is a fate worse than death. By doing so they rule out of discussion a world of significant possibilities; and the failure to think constructively about those possibilities is a disfavor to the young person.

The great prestige which college education has achieved in our society leads us to assume—quite incorrectly—that it is the only form of continued learning after high school. The assumption is that the young person either goes to college and continues to learn, or goes to work and stops learning. Most parents, deans, counselors—indeed the young people themselves—have given little or no thought to the many ways of learning and growing which do not involve college. The result is that the path to college appears to be the only exciting possibility, the only path to self-development. No wonder many who lack the qualifications for college insist on having a try at it.

The young person who does not go on to college should look forward to just as active a period of growth and learning in the post-high school years as does the college youngster.

The nature of this continued learning will depend on the young person's interests and capacities. The bright youngster who has stayed out of college for financial reasons will require a different kind of program from that of the youngster who stayed out for lack of ability.

The majority of young people—at least, of boys—who terminate their education short of college do so because they lack academic ability. Most have had unrewarding experiences in the classroom and have a negative attitude toward anything labeled "learning" or "education." Even if they are not bitter about their school experiences, they are likely to feel that, having tried that path and failed, their salvation lies elsewhere. *What they must recognize is that there are many kinds of further learning outside formal high school and college programs. The fact that they have not succeeded in high school simply means that they must continue their learning in other kinds of situations.*

The opportunities for further education of boys and girls who leave the formal educational system are numerous and varied.

Training programs within industrial corporations have expanded enormously and constitute a respectable proportion of all education today. Apprenticeship systems are not as universal as they used to be in the skilled crafts or trades, but they are still in operation in every major industry, and offer wide opportunities for the ambitious youngster. (He must be warned, however, that in some of the older crafts and trades entry is jealously guarded; indeed in some it is held within family lines as a hereditary right.)

A few labor unions have impressive educational programs. The International Ladies Garment Workers Union, for example, conducts European tours, sponsors lecture series and offers a wide variety of courses.

Various branches of government offer jobs to high school graduates which involve an opportunity to learn while working. The Armed Services offer training in a great many occupational specialties.

Night classes in the public schools are breaking all attendance records; and more than one quarter of present attendance is in trade courses for semi-skilled or unskilled workers. These courses offer a surprising range of interesting opportunities for the young person who wishes to test his aptitudes and to develop various skills.

There also exist, in the amazingly variegated pattern of American education, many special schools—art schools, music schools, nursing schools and the like—which should be considered by the young person not going on to college. The boy who wishes to become an X-ray technician and the girl who wishes to be a practical nurse, for example, will find a great many schools throughout the country at which they may receive training.

Correspondence study offers the most flexible opportunities for study beyond high school, but the young people who do not go on to college usually have little enthusiasm for paper-and-pencil work, and that is what correspondence study amounts to. For those who can overcome this handicap, there is an open door to almost any conceivable subject. One can study accountancy or blueprint reading, creative writing or diesel mechanics, watch repairing or dressmaking, fingerprinting or foreign languages, music or petroleum technology. Almost the only limits are one's own interest and ability.

Educational opportunities on radio and television continue to expand. In certain parts of the country the high school graduate can study a considerable range of subjects through this medium—e.g., salesmanship, typing, composition, reading improvement and foreign languages.

Finally, jobs themselves are a form of education. Today most young people have a wide choice of jobs. They should look at the array of jobs available not simply from the standpoint of money and convenience but from the standpoint of their own further growth. If the young man is willing to think hard about his own abilities and interests, and then to look at available jobs as opportunities for self-development, he can look forward to years of learning and growth at least as rewarding as anything a college student might experience.

The possibilities reviewed here are by no means exhaustive, but they suggest the diverse paths open to the noncollege student. Some youngsters will want to get as far away as possible from "book learning" and some will not. Some will want vocational education and others may wish to continue their general education. Some will shun anything labeled a "school" or "course." But all should somehow continue learning.

In order to help young people in this direction, the following steps are essential:

1. We must make available to young people far more information than they now have on post-high school opportunities other than college.

2. Parents, teachers and high school counselors must recognize that if the youngster who is not going to college is to continue his growth and learning he must receive as much sagacious help and counsel as a college-bound student.

3. We must do what we can to alter the negative attitude toward education held by many youngsters who fail to go on to college. They must understand that they have been exposed to only one kind of learning experience and that the failures and frustrations encountered in school are not necessarily predictive of failure in every other kind of learning.

4. We must enable the young person to understand that his stature as an individual and his value as a member of society depend upon continued learning—not just for four years or a decade, but throughout life.

Some Reasonable Alternatives

JOHN KEATS

In 1963, John Keats
(1920–   ) published an
article in Life magazine on
college dropouts but felt more
remained to be written: "It
seemed time to say that
the idea of going to college
has been wildly oversold to the
public. I cannot believe that
a college education would
be a good thing for everybody."
Hence the focus of his book
The Sheepskin Psychosis,
from which this essay is taken.
A newspaperman turned
free-lance writer, Keats also
wrote the two provocative
social commentaries:
The Crack in the Picture
Window (about the construction
industry) and The Insolent
Chariots (about the auto
industry).

With a crust in his pocket,
a merry smile on his frank,
open face, and with his
father's blessings in his heart,
John Youth strode briskly
down the highroad to seek his
fortune in the wide world.

Three hundred pages later,
John would marry the princess
and live in the castle, thoughtfully providing his aging parents with a comfortable
cottage nearby, where he
could visit his mother every
day.

Today, the story is a little different. It goes like this:

Because his mother made him do it, John Youth raced out of the house, through high school and straight into a good college and out the other side, into a good safe job. Without pausing for breath, he dashed off to suburbia with a nice, safe wife who promptly produced three quick children, who began running, too.

Something has happened between Then and Now, which is a pity, for the nature of Youth has not essentially changed. Youngsters still want to see the world. They want to explore on their own; to sniff at the bones of experience like apprehensive but fascinated puppies. They like to fiddle around to no apparent purpose, doing little that seems to make much sense. They have no idea of time, but a great trust in the distant future. Meanwhile, they want the right to make their own mistakes.

The significant change seems to be that we, Youth's elders, have come charging into the scene, urging speed. We want our children to stop wasting time. We hurry them toward adult life, towing them every step of the way, indulging them to the point where they have no opportunity to develop their personalities or sense of responsibility, pressing adult concepts and adult toys upon them as gifts, and demanding that they immediately use them. But young people are not in all this hurry. A good many of them are properly suspicious of it and are by no means sure that we are taking them in a direction they want to go. More than a few want to grow up in their own way, on their own time.

Of course there are exceptions to this pattern, but the over-all impression is that we do not seem to care enough for our children to have the simple decency to let them be themselves. Consider the different views of Steve and his father:

"If Steve doesn't go to college, he will never be able to join the club, and if he doesn't join the club, he will never make any money," the boy's father said. "It's as simple as that, and if he can't see it, he is a damned fool."

"Man," Steve said, "if my Pop wants me to go to college just so I can make a crock of dough and wind up in that goofy club with those other yuks, he is One, Two, Three, O-U-T."

Steve is not thinking of a distant future. It so happens that he intends to go to college, not because he envisions a career, but because all his friends are going, and he wants to live a life of his own, now, with his contemporaries. This is a perfectly legitimate reason for wanting to attend college, and it makes much more sense than his father's reason. It speaks directly to the central, unique value of the collegiate experience.

"The people you meet in college offer you far more of an education than the professors you meet or the courses you take," a Reed senior said.

"You know why the Ivy schools are better than this place?" a Temple sophomore said. "It's because the kids who go there are brighter than we are."

All three youngsters are echoing the thoughts of observers as different as Cardinal Newman and Stephen Leacock: College is the people who attend it.

The Cardinal said that if he had to choose between living in a dormitory or attending classes as a means of acquiring an education, he would choose the dormitory. Mr. Leacock said if he were to found a university, he would first found a smoking room. As funds became available, he said, he would add a library, a dining hall, a dormitory. Were any funds remaining, he might consider hiring a professor.

The view here is that a college is valuable insofar as it resembles a conversation among bright people. Perhaps a father of three sons might believe that $36,000 is a relatively large amount of money to pay for their enjoying four years of chitter-chatter in Princeton's comfortable suites, but he should know that the informal education that begins when classes end is the heart and soul of a college education.

"I know this brilliant atheist," a Catholic student at a city university said. "If you want to know, he's actually my best friend. He's my roommate. It's not that I'm losing my faith, or anything like that. It's just that I never really thought about it before I had to defend it."

"I'd never read anything past *Ivanhoe* in high school," said a boy at a Midwestern university. "But when I came here, I found all these kids from New York talking about guys you never heard of, like Camus and Dostoevsky. It was amazing. I didn't know what they were talking about, but I found out in a hurry. It was either that, or I'd have been out of it."

The Midwestern boy's reasons for wanting to read Camus might seem callow, but the net result could not be called harmful. Many a professor would say that the particular virtue of college lies in the fact that it is the only social institution we have wherein a man may dwell for a time surrounded by a disproportionate number of bright people, against whose wits he hones his; wherein every intellectual facility is provided him; where he is under no obligation other than to speculate as widely and as deeply as he wishes over libraries of information set before him.

The most poignant lessons would seem to be those one learns in youth from one's contemporaries, and at college these are learned in the dining halls, in intellectual argument in a dormitory room, in all the places young men and women meet on and around the campus; in the simple stuff of living in enforced intimacy with a few hundred total strangers. The special quality of these encounters is that they all—even the girl's date in the boy's room—are somehow connected with some degree of concern for affairs of the mind. In no other social institution save primary and secondary school is the ordinary life of the institution concerned with anything of the sort.

How much any student profits from free-form discourse is, of course, up to him. Some will find it boring and pointless. Everything would seem to depend upon the individual student's personality and fund of information. (One Harvard boy took the lofty view that it would waste his time to talk with his freshmen roommates because they did not know enough to be able to speak with him. Their view of him was that his personality was not impressively engaging.) There is no way to measure how much a student will learn from his friends during his college years, and much less can we evaluate the quality of whatever he might have learned. Nor can anyone say how long a student must stay on any particular campus in order to glean all he can from his contemporaries. There is no particular reason to believe the process must take four years. Generally speaking, those who derive most from their collegiate experience are bright youngsters of gregarious nature who were never challenged in mediocre high schools and who come from minimal cultural backgrounds. Those who profit least are well-traveled youngsters who come from intellectual homes and who have attended superior public or private schools. Briefly, the first group learns more things worth learning from the second group than the second group learns from the first. In any event, it is difficult to say that, apart from bringing people together for the purposes of intellectual discourse, a college does anything else that is uniquely valuable.

To be sure, a college provides courses of instruction. But so does a night school. It has a library. But so does any major city. It provides an opportunity for people to learn to live together. So does a rooming-house. It gives youngsters an opportunity to look after themselves. But so does a hobo jungle. College may indeed be a place offering the most convenient and maximum opportunities in all these regards, but it is not the only place in which life's basic lessons may be learned or information acquired. It is unique only in its aspect as a contentious forum.

Not all adolescents are going to profit uniformly from either the formal or the informal education a college can provide. In fact, not all adolescents should attend, and not all of them do. For that matter, there is not the slightest reason, except social convenience, why our colleges concern themselves exclusively with adolescents in the first place. Indeed, there is reason to believe they should not, for as one professor put it (paraphrasing Shaw), "It is a pity that education is wasted on the young."

He was not being flippant, for he went on to say that a man needs some experience in the outside world in order to bring value to the campus; in order to appreciate the insights that the academic world can provide. Proof, he said, lies in the splendid college records made by returned veterans of the Second World War, and in the academic records of industrial executives who attend special humanities programs sponsored at certain colleges by business corporations.

The professor therefore suggested that college should not necessarily be what happens immediately after high school, but that it should be something a growing man can enter, leave, and return to at need at any time of his life. His view embraced the fact that learning—formal and informal—proceeds in fits and starts throughout life, and that all institutions of learning should accommodate themselves to this fact.

Drastic changes would take place in the collegiate world if this line of thinking were pursued, and it is easy to predict that it will be pursued, because the circumstances of national life favor it. As society becomes increasingly affluent and increasingly freed by machines from humdrum chores, there is more time and money to spend on the pleasures of life, which of course include education. We are now seeing a steady increase in the number of housewives who enroll in college once their children are in school. Shorter work hours have increased enrollments in night schools and extension courses. Earlier retirement has made it possible for men in their fifties to embark on college studies preparatory to second careers. There is growing demand for colleges to keep their doors open night and day, all year round. Also part of current thinking is the notion that admission to college might be based on factors other than—and not necessarily including— academic performance in high school. Changes in admission policies would open the doors not only to those who bloomed late, but also to those who for one reason and another did not finish high school, but who during the course of their lives developed aptitude, ability, and need for formal education.

Another suggestion recently heard is that colleges grant credentials other than diplomas and degrees, such as certificates of achievement in subject matter. One professor said this "would shunt out of general education all those whose interests are specific, so that they could go directly to what they wanted at no waste of their time, or of ours." Another professor said he thought the college "should make it possible for an incoming student to first gorge himself on the subject matter he wants, instead of demanding that he first take a lot of subjects he doesn't want, and which often serve to drive him out of education instead of into it."

Their suggestions imply that a college should offer three separate programs. It could reserve its diploma for those students who satisfy the college's scholarly requirements. It could grant a special student a certificate of competence to show a prospective employer. It could offer a different document (since the world seems to cherish documents) to the adolescents who come to college with no well-formed objectives, and who at this moment in their lives might profit more from general survey courses than from deep courses designed as prerequisites to graduate studies.

If a college were to offer these three programs, it would seem wise to keep the lines open among them, so that a student could move without prejudice from one to another as his objectives crystallized in his mind. In any event, current thought tends to regard a student as someone who wishes to study something, and it urges the colleges to accept a candidate at whatever age the student happens to be when he realizes that serious work in the field, at college, will best serve his need.

Rising resentment against the doctrine of publish or perish suggests that the future college will place a premium on good teaching; that teachers will be hired because of their competence in their fields and their ability to communicate what they know, without respect to their formal education. An increasing number of universities now go into the world to find men who have demonstrated their competence. They are hiring unlettered artists, writers, musicians, and dramatists of considerable celebrity. Some of these people are no better able to teach what they know than are some professors, but at least their honors have been won in a more general competition than the academic, and this very fact evokes a certain excitement among the students.

The total shape of current thought and practice suggests that the campus of tomorrow will no longer be almost exclusively populated by late adolescents, but by a student body that contains a more normal balance of young and old, which has a greater concern for realistic study, and which, out of the experience of its members, will provide a far more valuable informal discussion group than any student body of adolescents could. One can only say, Speed the day! for to keep the college doors open at all times to all ages would not only be a service to the general cause of education, but it would almost certainly put an end to the current hysterical insistence that a high school student forfeits all chance of success if he does not win college admission immediately upon high school graduation.

In predicting the shape of future colleges, I am not making original suggestions, but am merely reporting what is now going on. Education, always in flux, is peculiarly sensitive to public mood, despite its apparent remoteness in an ivory tower. It is after all a process of society, and because a good many of the most alert minds in a society will be found in its colleges, changes in the order of things are normally first suggested by the academic community. But changes are almost never effected until the public welcomes them. Moreover, like any other establishment, the academic establishment has a vested interest in remaining exactly as it is. So changes will most probably be made with glacial speed. Yet, ten years from now, the American college will most probably more resemble a community of freely met scholars than it does today. The question is, How much more?

In good part, the answer will depend upon public acceptance of these facts:

Valuable as the collegiate experience can be, it is not always valuable to everyone; no particular magic is worked within an arbitrary four-year period; possession of a diploma is not always a guarantee of anything much; the time for a man to go to college does not necessarily occur during his adolescence; lack of a diploma does not always condemn a lad to limbo; reasonable alternatives to the collegiate experience exist.

By and large, the public mood is such as to allow it to accept these statements as being true, but whether the general public is willing to act on the basis of facts is quite another matter.

Meanwhile, there is much we can do to reduce the crushing weight of anxiety that now bears upon our high school students and their parents. We can begin by remembering how very young the eighteen-year-old is; by realizing how much he may need time to loaf, or hack around, as he calls it. During his apparent aimlessness, he is trying to sort things out. Everyone needs a time for reflection at different stages of his life, and the first stage is set at the moment of high school graduation. The eighteen-year-old is eager to somehow prove himself, but is a bit dubious as to how and where to begin. It is a rare child who flies arrow-straight from home and school directly into his adult career. Most of us—particularly most adolescents—proceed through life more like a blind man making his way up a boulder-strewn hillside. The first job is almost never the last one, nor is the second, nor the third. We live and, as someone hopefully said, learn. The years eighteen to twenty-two are only four out of the seventy, and they are not necessarily the most formative. College authorities assure us that too many students come to college too soon; that the students who will get most out of college, and who are most likely to remain to be graduated, are those who know precisely what they expect the college to do for them. Their deans' thought is that a youngster who spends a year or two in the outside world before coming to college will discover for himself whether possession of a college degree is essential to realization of his developing ambitions.

"The boy of eighteen who is not ready to go to college *can* spend two years that he will later view as respectably spent, and positively spent, and start college at twenty," the dean of admissions at one selective college said. "If it were socially acceptable for a boy to go to work after high school, then two years later he would not suffer the kind of community pressure and high school pressure that comes from being rejected from college today, or not being good enough to get in, or not going where his parents went. By the time he was twenty, he would either be established in a job which both he and the community find acceptable, or he would now be ready to apply for college admission if he found reasons why he should, but in any event, he would no longer be as much in the public eye as the graduating high school senior, and the pressure would be off."

It should not greatly concern us whether a high school senior goes to college, or whether he signs on a commercial fishing boat, or becomes a ranch hand, or migrant laborer, or quits college to go to sea (as Dana did), or joins the Air Force, or apprentices himself to a trade, or takes a job as a bread truck driver, or just plain hits the road for a year or so of aimless wandering. By the time he is eighteen, and presuming that we have raised him to be a responsible, self-reliant lad, we might as well give him a chance to shift for himself a bit. Indeed, by the time he is eighteen we have otherwise done all we can for him except wave good-bye to him and wish him well, advising him that we will always be glad to see him if he wants to drop by from time to time, and that we will always be glad to be of what help we can if he thinks he needs any help. It is well to remember that what he does at this moment is not necessarily what he will do for the rest of his life; that if he has the good qualities we hope he has, he will eventually find his place in this world. Many alternatives to going to college exist, and not all of them are bad. One of the more worth while is travel abroad.

"I know just big bunches of kids who would get a whole lot more out of a trip to Europe," one college senior said. "And their fathers could send them to Europe for four years for about half as much money·as they're paying to send them here."

What would they do in Europe?

"Look at it! Live in it!" the boy said. "Sure, they ought to have some reason to want to go, some idea of what they want to look at. It's the same thing as going to college, you get more out of it if you know what you're doing. But you can't stay there without getting *something* out of it, even just sitting at a cafe having a beer, because it's different.

"Unless," he qualified his statement, "you're just a clod anyway, and if you're a clod you're going to be a clod anywhere. But you take a bright kid who doesn't like college and wants to do something, he's going to flip when he sees Europe. The scales will fall from his eyes. What are we after, anyway? A degree? No. What we're all after is *education*, which is really growing older and having experiences, and meeting other people and getting perspective. Europe is a great place for it—and a lot cheaper than college."

Some parents might object that "going to Europe" sounds like a fairly complicated way of wasting time and money unless there was some specific end in view, but before they speed to that conclusion, they might wish to ask themselves just how *they* spent the past year.

Another perfectly reasonable alternative to college-after-high school is Army enlistment. A rational stranger from another planet might presume that a nation as warlike as ours would hold the soldier in good repute, and expect us to at least understand that bearing arms is one responsibility of male citizenship. No doubt he would be astonished to learn that we look down on the soldier; think the service a waste of time; and that many of our employers view the Army as a place where a man is taught to shirk and loaf.

Actually, the Army is just another social institution that—like college, a business firm, or any other large organization of people—offers loafers and shirkers an opportunity to demonstrate their poor qualities in public. It offers other people infinite opportunities to become what they wish to become. It provides all sorts of vocational training, including work that challenges gifted minds. Army instruction is much more indoctrination than it is education, but many able youngsters are happier with it than they were, or would be, in the free-form college seminar, and they are just as liable to be happier within military discipline than within an unstructured campus or civil life. As one student in an Army school said:

"The Army doesn't horse around. They tell you the deal, you learn it, and that's that."

It is simply not true that Army vocational skills cannot be applied to civilian tasks, as some employers believe. That belief is just as far from reality as the popular belief that all a man does in the service is peel potatoes. If, in fact, all a particular man does in the Army is peel potatoes, the reason for this will be that he is a potato peeler. He would be a potato peeler in civil life, too. The Army is a nation within a nation, self-sufficient and viable. It operates a college, offers college extension courses of all kinds, speaks foreign languages, maintains complicated electronic equipment and power plants, builds every sort of structure, makes roads, drives machines, dredges harbors, fights enemies and—peels potatoes. It works at every kind of profession and trade that one may find in civil life, and perhaps as the civilian world does not, the Army understands that all jobs are necessary and, in that sense, important.

The military service also does something that we might not presume it does. Like college, like any other social institution of some size, it offers an uncertain young man ample opportunity to discover who he is, with respect to a wide cross section of his contemporaries. Its very rigidity encourages self-reliance and inculcates a sense of personal responsibility in those who are most oppressed by paternalistic discipline, because it forces them to seek ways of establishing their personal identity and difference from the ordered ranks.

So the Army serves as haven for those who need to be told what to do, and it serves as a forcing ground of personal decision for those who do not want to be told what to do but who have some difficulty deciding just what it is that they *do* want to do. Meantime, military service offers unparalleled vocational and educational opportunity to any person ready to take advantage of it. It can be a worthy and reasonable alternative to a college education for many a man; perhaps one that imparts certain lessons he would never learn on campus. The most valuable military training programs are not open to short-term draftees, however, but are reserved for high school graduates who volunteer for three- and four-year tours of duty. To youth, four years seems an eternity, but the fact is that nowhere else in our society can a young man receive the dollar equivalent in food, clothing, housing, medical and dental care, recreation facilities, job training, foreign travel, paid vacations, and monthly pay, in the four years immediately following high school.

Another reasonable alternative to college attendance, insofar as the narrow acquisition of a vocational skill is concerned, is apprentice training. There are many apprenticeship programs in our industries; many companies send their employees to training schools and colleges, claiming these programs to be legitimate tax deductions. All such activities should be widely extended, but there are two difficulties. One is that it is difficult to convince parents that, since their child is not college caliber, they should abandon their wistful dream that he is, and so save him a wasted trip to the state university that will predictably toss him back. Second, it is not easy to get it through the status-conscious head of the businessman that he should hire people instead of pieces of paper. He must be brought to see that it is more sensible to hire on the basis of job aptitude and personality than on the basis of possession of a diploma and be made to understand that the companies most successful in the retention of employees are those that provide the hired hands with the greatest possibilities of advancement through company-sponsored educational programs. The businessman probably knows that most jobs are best learned on the job, but it is surely difficult to get him to practice whatever he preaches. Perhaps Mr. Iffert might be able to convince him: [1]

"There are many students who have the job skills of a high school level who go to college now, but who do not, while there, increase in their employable skills," Mr. Iffert said. "Now, because they have gone to college, they think they cannot have jobs demanding only high school job skills, and they are therefore unhappy and unsuccessful if they try a job demanding higher job skills, or they are miserable in taking a job they have been led to believe lies at lower-than-college levels. We must get away from the idea that just because you have a degree, you are automatically qualified for a job that demands skills which you may not have acquired during your college years, and from the idea that just because you do not have a degree, you therefore lack college skills you may have acquired somewhere else."

In short, if an employer demands specific skills or knowledge, and certain traits of character and personality, he should not care where the applicant acquired them.

The important question posed by a high school graduate is really not where, or whether, he is going to college. It is: What is he going to do now? A wise parent would point out sundry possibilities, including college only if the student had academic abilities, aptitudes, and a desire to use them on college work—but leaving the answer much more up to the student than is now the case. Our only entirely legitimate demand is that he do something. We can hope that what

[1] Robert E. Iffert, an official of the Federal Office of Education.

he does will prove wise, but we would be foolish to imagine that such proof will be forthcoming by return mail.

One thing is quite certain: We have been leading our children's lives for them to such an extent that their idea of the importance of winning college admission has become as psychotic as our own. Heretical as it may now seem, candor demands that we should acquaint ourselves and our children with the fact that going to college is not the only path to a useful, happy life. Using the youngsters' own language, we might tell them this:

"College isn't all *that* great. It's great, yes, but not too great. It is mainly just teachers who think college is red, white and blue, *five* trading stamps, and a partridge in a pear tree. Actually, there are about fifty other ways to make the scene, if you want to think about them. But you know something? It takes talent and guts to make the scene in a really great way. If you don't have them, you'll never make it big no matter *how* many colleges you go to. If you do have them, then you'll make it whether you go to college or not."

A Case for Humane Intelligence

MICHAEL O'NEIL

*In 1966 Otto Butz, a
professor of political science
at San Francisco State College,
collected the essays of ten
students under the title:*
To Make a Difference—A
Student Look at America:
Its Values, Its Society,
and Its Systems of Education,
*in which this essay, by
Michael O'Neil (1941–   )
first appeared. Son of a police
officer in southern California
and a veteran of three years
in the U. S. Marine Corps,
O'Neil graduated* magna
cum laude *from
San Francisco State in 1968.
Currently, he is a credit officer
in a bank and working for
his master's degree in
business administration.*

One of the purposes of this collection of essays is to help persuade the American community to re-examine some of its conventional ideas about higher education. In addressing ourselves to this task we are thus making at least two assumptions. We believe that as presently conceived and constituted American higher education is not adequately meeting the challenges of today's evolving world. And we are assuming that if we convincingly demonstrate why and how American higher education ought to be altered, we will, in fact, make a difference. I personally share this faith—both in our ability to make a cogent case in this regard, and in our fellow citizens' willingness to give us a sympathetic hearing. In the course of my own essay, indeed, I will present a plea for the revitalization of faith in general.

Education cannot be considered apart from the society it expresses and serves—local, national, and today increasingly global. To talk meaningfully about American higher education one must therefore also concern oneself with the nature of the contemporary world. And since this world is undergoing a major transition, one must examine the dominant trends that seem to be at work. These trends can be analyzed in many ways, but as I see it, they are most fundamentally twofold. The world is moving toward increasing centralization. And there is a universal striving for mankind's material betterment.

On the surface of it, global integration seems a remote prospect indeed. Intensely nationalistic forces appear to be pulling mankind further and further apart. Yet these forces, no matter how disruptive, are in fact responses to the very kinds of long-range cultural, economic and technological developments that in the end cannot but eliminate them. The centralizing process in our world is taking place almost completely below the level of our awareness. It is largely ignored by our newspapers, our public opinion, and even in the statements and actions of our political leaders. But its roots run deeply and someday it will sprout a tree hitherto seen only in the dreams—or nightmares —of men. For someday some kind of centralizing order and authority are going to have to cope effectively with irreversible changes in human aspirations and techniques that even now greatly affect the lives of people all over the globe. International order and mutual responsibility are clearly called for when a fluctuation on the New York Stock Exchange has world-wide economic repercussions, when a railway jam on Switzerland's St. Gotthard line backs up freight in Scandinavia, when mass communications take the story of Selma, Alabama, to Monrovia, West Africa, and when the industrially advanced nations have the know-how and resources to produce increasingly worrisome surpluses while much of the rest of the world remains on the edge of starvation.

Some interpreters of today's world claim that the trend of centralization is leading toward either a bipolar mobilization of whites versus coloreds, of haves versus have-nots, or of one ideological bloc against another. But these are not realistic alternatives. The logic of contemporary socioeconomic ideas, industrial techniques and military weapons requires nothing less than global world order. Either sovereign nation states are dead or mankind is dead.

I suggested that the second main trend in today's world is the universal drive for material betterment. I realize that there is currently more talk of raising physical standards than there are tangible results in that direction. The gap between rich and poor nations has, in fact, been increasing. Yet even though it suffers temporary setbacks, the battle for a decent standard of living for all peoples cannot be halted. The hearts and minds of human beings everywhere are set on it. In the short run, the frustrations that this quest engenders are bound to be highly explosive. But eventually it is certain to be accomplished. For where there is all this will, it is unthinkable that there is not going to be found a way.

Given these trends, the key questions facing contemporary man concern what *kind* of world order he is going to build, and what he is going to do with himself as *more* than a mere physical organism. On the answers he works out for these questions hangs the future not necessarily of life, but certainly of what we call civilization. And for these answers, we are ourselves responsible.

There are many who claim that science is incompatible with the idea of free will. Perhaps such a view seemed plausible in the past. But it certainly is not today. For today science and technology not only are satisfied to coexist with the notion of free will; their high degree of development and the powers they have unleashed make it absolutely essential that we subscribe to the precepts of free will and personal responsibility. The frontiers of science are theoretically unlimited. Whereas natural catastrophes, disease and starvation were once fatalistically accepted, science and technology now strongly indicate that there will be a day when nothing in the physical life of man, not even death, will be inevitable. We are truly becoming the masters of our physical fate. If we do not soon solve our physical problems, it will be because of our own stupidity and wickedness, not because we do not have the opportunity. Can we intelligently apply the unprecedented knowledge at our command? Can we place it in the service of the ideals of human worth, brotherhood and dignity? Or will we misuse it merely to exploit and manipulate one another?

The trends and circumstances which are reshaping today's world are so vast and complex that in their presence man often stands confused and troubled. He asks questions which his traditional concepts and institutions can no longer answer. In such a transitional world of troubled man, there is great danger that the forces of our age will become the tools of those who want to use their fellows for their own cause or profit. For taken together, our widespread uncertainties along with the nature of today's technology and psychological skills constitute a greater potential for human enslavement than has ever before existed.

At the root of the contemporary threat to our freedom is a very old and much-used conception of man. It is the misanthropic idea that human beings are innately too selfish, stupid, belligerent and divided to willingly join together in mutual advantage and harmony. Applied to today, this Hobbesian argument maintains that the world has become so crowded and complex that men can no longer be effectively coordinated save through some kind of systematic coercion.

Opposed to the pessimistic view of man and its accompanying threat to his freedom is a dynamic conception of the practicability of libertarian and democratic ideals. It is a conception which strives to put in man's service the powers of our age. It is the belief that with these powers man can pull upward his society as he himself ascends. It is a conception which claims that man can remake his institutions and concepts in such a way that they will shape a humane world order.

Above all, the conception of libertarian and democratic ideals is an expression of faith in man, a faith based not on the dictates of an authority or majority but in the creative potentialities of man himself.

It is the belief that if you put faith in man, man will be deserving of this faith and will justify it in practice. It is analogous to the faith that underlies scientific research.

To paraphrase and grossly oversimplify the philosopher of science Charles Sanders Peirce,[1] scientific inquiry, because of man's human limitations, cannot properly start with a priori notions of Truth. That is, because man is not one and the same with the Real, he cannot know Reality. However, to start scientific research, man, whether he realizes and admits it or not, must believe that there *is* a Reality and that it is regular. Otherwise, inquiry is futile; and, indeed, as Jean Paul Sartre tells us, life itself is then absurd. Our best scientists, while not knowing the Real, have nevertheless believed in its existence. And for this reason they have found much of that small part of Reality which we *can* know—namely, the shared opinion of what are conceivable practical consequences in our experiential realm of living. On the basis of their faith, and because of a willingness to constantly test their beliefs or hypotheses about Reality, scientists have, for example, launched Mariner IV.

The conclusion to be drawn here concerns the logical imperative of faith. In science we have believed, and hence we have achieved. What now remains is to extend logical faith beyond science. We need to humbly recognize that man has not yet been seen in the fullness of his being, that there is a Reality about him which has so far escaped us. In order to develop the potentialities of man, we must put faith in man. To launch mankind's beauty and creativity, we must believe in him and be willing to work by trial and error toward his ever greater improvement. We can best do this by constantly improving the implementation of democratic and libertarian ideals. And to effectively implement these ideals, we must develop a practical dedication to them which is as deep as is our dedication to the scientific method.

I do not define libertarian and democratic ideals in accordance with any ideology. I define them experientially. That is, I mean by them

---

[1] Charles Sanders Peirce, *Essays in the Philosophy of Science.* New York: Bobbs-Merrill, 1957.

those concepts and practices which further the development and realization of the faith in man which underlies them. Thus, for example, the proposal to institute world peace by subjugating man to a coercively ordered world society is anathema to libertarian and democratic ideals; for, to name only a few of its gross faults, it admits lack of faith in the potential for ever higher good in mankind; it repels the logic of man's opportunity to participate in the building of an ever greater society; and it refutes the plainly indicated potential of truly free men.

If the forces of our age are put in the service of man, and, directly related to this, if libertarian and democratic ideals are made the guiding principles of the future one world, mankind will enter an unprecedented age of humaneness, abundance, and peace. However, such a world society is a questionable aspect of our future. Its development is dependent upon that more-than-material betterment of man which I earlier mentioned.

Both prerequisite and supplementary to continuous progress toward a humane world order is what I shall call the development of metatelic values and aspirations. I refer to man's need for a conception of human perfectness that is so open-ended, self-transcending and dynamically formative that it can never be claimed to have been fully realized. I mean an abstract, limitless ideal of human potentialities which can serve man as his ultimate inspiration and which he will feel impelled always to redefine and more fully to actualize as he moves from one successful experience to another. I believe such an ideal inspiration and reference for human strivings is essential for two reasons. It implies that no existing set of objectives and arrangements is ever finally sufficient. And it thereby provides a thrust to human unfolding that transcends the cultural expectations of any particular situation. By virtue of this fact, it also provides justification for the libertarian and democratic ideals of which I have spoken. And it at the same time requires that man operate in terms of these ideals if the never-consummated search for his full being is to be possible.

Unfortunately, we live in an age when faith both in the instrumental ideals of liberty and democracy and in the more abstract notion of infinite human perfectibility is neither strong nor widespread. Faith of any kind—in the abstract, in ideals, in man himself—is badly languishing. Nor is our current anti-faith the rational, faith-inspired and creative reaction against dogmatism that earlier in Western history produced many of mankind's greatest moments. Instead, it is an expression of normlessness, confusion, despair, and extreme fear—fear of self, fear of the future, fear of all life. It is a rationalization for inactivity, for failure to sacrifice and plan, for failure to dream. It is rooted in more than the death of *a* God; it stems from the belief that "God is dead" and that no metaphysical orientation is possible or permissible. It is the reason contemporary man finds it so difficult to make moral choices and formulate clear purposes. Contemporary anti-faith is the reason modern man, when not standing inert, is reaching committee-type decisions with his psychiatrist, or finding direction in a bottle of liquor, tranquilizers or pep pills.

We cannot long endure the highly demoralized state which results from anti-faith. This is the major threat to our future in one world. If man too long lives in mental, moral, and social chaos, he inevitably turns to irrational faith. He turns to faith in extremist leaders, material success, scientism, or some other "ism" which, because it eliminates faith in man, leads to tyranny. This is to say that mankind is entirely capable of enslaving himself, of voluntarily committing himself to the collective security, order, and purpose of a tyrannical world state. And given the forces of our age, I am saying that we are entirely capable of developing ourselves into a race of human automatons, eugenically shaped, bureaucratically organized, technologically brainwashed, scientifically coerced, and completely subservient to a pseudo divine collective.

If the foregoing view is correct, it is clear that our most urgent task is the rebuilding of man's faith in man. Yet this is bound to be a most difficult undertaking. We cannot hope to create the kind of faith in man I am talking about overnight. At least for the time being we must work toward this objective indirectly—by demonstrating to all men everywhere the practical and personal benefits of liberalism and democracy. It must be shown what liberal and democratic institutions can do—that they provide the best possible answer to man's need for a coordinating social principle and that they therefore best facilitate his quest freely to participate in the shaping of his own destiny.

Despite all her shortcomings, I believe that the role of demonstrator in the task of restoring faith in man through the effective practice of liberalism and democracy falls to the United States. America commands the greatest force, power and influence in the world today. Also, at least in principle if not always in practice, the United States remains the world's most libertarian and democratic country. It is therefore America's opportunity and duty to exemplify to the world dynamic actualizations of libertarian and democratic ideals. Unless the United States assumes this duty, all that is humane and promising about this country will be lost. America, the idea, will perish.

To call on America for world involvement is not to call on her for world crusade. One does not spread ideals and institutions by exporting economic exploitation and armies. We must give up our obsession with force and power. We must be self-confident enough to enter into relationships on all levels with all peoples, currently friends or foes; and, even more important, after exemplifying the self-evident advantages of our ideals, and while yet engaged in the continuing development of these ideals at home, we Americans must be intelligent enough to realize that all peoples must be free to interpret and institute faith in mankind in accordance with their own indigenous circumstances and values. We must, then, be dedicated not to universally instituting our specific way of life, but to sharing with all the ideals which underlie our way of life.

To be an international exemplar, America must undergo reform at home. Our country has too long held on to outworn and even erroneous ideas which no longer, if ever they did, serve libertarian and democratic ideals. We have too long believed that irresponsible self-interests would automatically produce a progressive, harmonious society. We have relied on a mechanistically conceived market which, even if it ever did promote goods, always ignored men. We have practiced an amoral, anti-leadership politics which has too often responded to conflicting special interests and too seldom to community needs. By moral and intellectual default, we have allowed injustice and poverty to survive in our very midst.

Because many of the concepts by which we are guided have become outdated (if they ever were humanly appropriate), we face an unprecedented challenge to our highest faculty, our creative reason. Whereas in the past we have needed mainly our backs, hands, and practical good sense, today, more than anything else, we must call upon our powers to think penetratingly and imaginatively. To understand and guide the vast forces transforming today's world, to map out our new possibilities and goals, to implement a dynamic conception of libertarian and democratic ideals—to respond to these tremendous challenges we must bring to bear every bit of constructive intelligence we can muster. All our ideas and institutions must be honestly and critically evaluated and all of them must pass the test of appropriateness and, where necessary, be updated or replaced.

The task of providing this infusion of critical and creative reason cannot but fall mainly to our intellectual centers, our American colleges and universities. Of all our institutions, the one that holds the greatest promise and faces the greatest challenges is higher education. It is hardly too much to say that the future of the world depends in important measure on the kind of influences upon American society that can emanate from our colleges and universities.

America is today experiencing an educational revolution. One of the two main aspects of this revolution is the increasingly pivotal role being played by our institutions of higher learning in furnishing the scientific and organizational know-how to operate our industrially based, mass society. America is today turning its higher education into a knowledge industry that is becoming the fulcrum of its national growth. The chief reason for this is that the technical and organizational problems we face are too large and complex to be dealt with by uncoordinated conferences, isolated surveys, governmental studies, and individual research projects. What is needed instead are cooperative, planned syntheses of knowledge and expertise from a wide range of disciplines, which must then be focused on specific problems. And it is mainly by our colleges and universities that this service is being provided. It today constitutes the principal source of their status with the general public and accounts for the biggest portion of their financing.

The other major aspect of America's current educational revolution lies in the fact that more and more of our people are going to college. As one of the consequences of this, almost all of our future leaders—as well as the people who elect them—will have experienced higher education. This means that the quality of their response to our society's problems will depend in large measure on the quality of the education that our colleges and universities have been able to provide them.

It goes without saying that we must make higher education as effective in preparing us for this philosophical and political function as we can. *America's higher learning must concern itself with the continuous redevelopment of ideas, values and institutions which are applicable to our ever changing conditions and inspired by the faith in mankind that underlies liberalism and democracy.* I would call this a third major aspect of our educational revolution. To date, however, this further function of higher education is on the whole little recognized. And it is seriously endangered by the other two developments I have cited—by the development of our colleges and universities into centers of operational know-how, and by their absorption in the job of educating ever greater numbers.

In itself, the application of knowledge for the more efficient operation of our society through our colleges and universities is undoubtedly a good thing. Yet it must be recognized that to provide expertise is not the same thing as significantly to evaluate and alter. That is, it is not adequately to meet the total challenge that education today faces. Moreover, these two distinct functions require different kinds of people and organizations. One cannot expect a force whose business is to help run a system, at the same time also to question its basic assumptions. Indeed, as has become increasingly evident, the more energies our colleges and universities have devoted to solving our society's technical problems, the less they have been concerned with evaluating and recreating its foundations.

The ever larger numbers being handled by our institutions of higher learning also retard the development of the creative function of education. While mass education is certainly a worthy ideal, it is not a sufficient educational achievement by itself. Since many students continue to attend college for economically and socially "practical" reasons, the function of mass education in effect converges with that of servicing the society with expertise. It is then these simultaneous and mutually reinforcing activities that tend to make American institutions of higher learning into the businesslike treadmills whose biggest net contribution is to perpetuate the status quo.

It seems to me a first precondition for the fundamental re-evaluation of our society's current directions that what I am calling the purely educational function of colleges and universities and their role as institutions for specialized training be organizationally separated. Our graduate and professional schools could then be oriented to turning out experts, not claiming at the same time also to be concerned with education in the traditional humanistic sense. And our undergraduate schools could devote themselves to pure education, without feeling it necessary to seek status and financing by pretending to be doing more than that—as is all too often the case at present.

If we utilize our undergraduate schools for general education and creative thinking, and if we gear our graduate and professional schools for training people in the mastery of our physical environment, we would only be taking a further step in a trend already in progress. We would be admitting and coping with the fact that our graduate and professional schools have more and more become training grounds for business and government; that they have contributed very little by way of understanding of our civilization's total situation; and that with their emphasis on highly specialized academic research, they have in fact discouraged the many gifted people on their payrolls from concerning themselves with the new horizons and problems of our age as a whole.

Far too many of our educated people have no idea of the larger assumptions and implications of the expertises they practice. Having been trained in what in effect are vocational studies, they take the existence and morality of the status quo entirely for granted. To remedy this we must make certain that everyone is first exposed to a general education in the complexities of life in their full dimensions, and that during this educational experience they hear not only from expert scholars but also from teachers who will encourage them to think for themselves. Only after they have passed through this truly liberal phase of their education ought they to be admitted to graduate and professional schools. While the purpose of the undergraduate schools should thus be to help people educate themselves as human beings, the chief work of graduate and professional institutions should be to provide the intellectual tools for the society's day-to-day functioning. And contrary to what is now generally the case, the job of teaching and creative thinking should not be rated as any less important and prestigious than that of producing academic or scientific experts. For if anything, the concern with man's needs and life as a whole is a humanly more actualizing and dignifying activity than is the task of training him for specialized roles.

The actual establishment of the kind of division of labor between undergraduate and graduate learning that I am proposing would require a number of basic changes in both types of institutions. To list specific reforms for our graduate schools must fall to someone more qualified than I. At my present level of experience I feel I should confine myself to some of the alterations badly needed in our undergraduate education.

The ideal undergraduate college would not have a program of required courses. It would recognize that a highly structured curriculum is a sign of educational weakness. Its aim would be to help each student develop his individual potential rather than memorize information and work chiefly for grades. It would not conceive of the student's mind as a receptacle into which must be poured a certain volume of facts and figures. It would trust the student to decide for himself what is educationally relevant and what extracurricular activities are worth-while or not. With a basic faith in man, the ideal college would view the student's mind as something individually alive and would try to stimulate it and judge its performance according to its own unique dispositions.

The ideal undergraduate college would recognize that students come to it with their own innate gifts, needs and interests. It would accept and retain only those students who feel genuinely excited by intellectual activity, a criterion that has nothing at all to do with what is called "I.Q." And it would operate on the premise that if given enough time and if appropriately stimulated by their academic environment, most students can be counted on to find their own intellectual challenges and to pursue their studies with their own, self-imposed discipline.

There would be many more kinds of course offerings in the ideal undergraduate college. Especially emphasized would be courses in social and group processes as well as in the various arts—all areas of relevance for our changing and increasingly affluent society. And even more important than the expansion of the number of courses offered would be a radical alteration in the way they are taught and organized. The introductory course in biology, currently a very unpopular subject required at most colleges, provides a good example. In addition to the standard survey course which teaches a mass of biological definitions, the ideal college would offer another course which considers the personal and social implications of the biological knowledge presented and which traces the relationships of this knowledge to all other realms of human experience. All survey courses that concentrate on a mass of data, and all courses designed to force students to "appreciate" something or other, would be limited to future experts in those fields. Only future biologists, for example, would be required to learn a textbook-full of biological definitions. Other students would take a course designed to open to them the wonders that biology is exploring and to enable them to absorb these discoveries into their lives as a whole.

All survey courses in the ideal undergraduate college would be interdisciplinary. It would be realized that the ultimate subject of study is the whole human being in his total context and that every aspect of this subject is inseparably involved in every other. In place of to-day's one-year, specialized course in United States history, for example, the ideal college would offer a three- or four-year course in American civilization, a course which would bring together and transcend all conventional academic disciplines to present a unified, organic conception of America in its full dynamism and complexity.

As I mentioned earlier, today's teaching methods would be radically altered by the ideal undergraduate college. The teaching process would rely heavily upon dialogue between students and professors. Professors will have realized that straight lecturing quickly reaches a point of diminishing returns, that students can be talked at for only a limited span of time, and that they respond best when part of a barely organized, two-way conversation. Being a breeding ground for democratic methods, and posited on the libertarian faith in mankind, the ideal undergraduate college would provide continuous opportunity for teachers and students to cooperatively work out solutions both to academic questions and to the wider range of contemporary and perennial problems of human existence. This, far more than student government, will make students feel part of their education; this, far more than freshman orientation programs, will awaken their intellectual abilities; and this—a simple change in classroom procedure—will do more than any number of speeches by college deans and presidents to overcome the common view among today's students that college means impersonality, futility, intellectual suffocation, and bureaucratic regimentation.

To help make students free to learn, the ideal undergraduate college will have abolished the grading system. It will have realized that the highly competitive grading system of today is detrimental to learning; that it focuses students' attention on grades and not on knowledge; that it too often rewards those regimented students who perfectly distribute their time and effort over a wide, shallow area to produce a good grade point average, and not often enough those creative few who get thoroughly wrapped up in one or two courses. It will have realized that the grading system too often rewards those students who unquestioningly accept the material presented to them as fact and who are intellectually cautious or indeed dead; and not often enough those students who think freely and independently, who deal with problems for which the answers are ambiguous or unknown, and who discover not answers, but new and greater questions. The ideal undergraduate college, then, would determine who stays and who leaves, and who goes to graduate school and who doesn't, and who graduates with honors and who doesn't, and who gets what kind of job recommendation, by means and measurements other than the traditional grading system. Once during each school year, and twice during the freshman year, all students would appear individually before a panel of faculty members. By submitting a written paper, research project or work of art, or by presenting himself orally, or by agreeing to take written examinations, or by any other reasonable means chosen by himself, the student would seek to convince the faculty panel that he has been using well the college's opportunities. Any means of testing that the student chooses would examine his understanding and insight, not his ability to regurgitate "factual" material.

Students would be encouraged to engage in independent research projects and studies. Indeed, entire semesters could be devoted to one wide-ranging and preferably interdisciplinary project or study.

Almost all classes would meet only once a week. This would enable students not only to read, but also to think about assignments before discussing them in class. Some formal class sessions would be canceled and the saved time would be used for scheduled, but informal, meetings between individual students and their professors. Teachers and students would be free not only to discuss the student's academic work, but also to let a spontaneous conversation wander freely.

Courses would be concerned much more with the caliber of the material covered and the quality of student work than with the quantity of either. Busy-work would be eliminated. Compared to today's undergraduate, tomorrow's student would read less, write less, and take fewer exams; but he would converse more, think more, understand more, create more, write better, and deal with far more sophisticated materials.

The ideal undergraduate college would be concerned with expanding man's knowledge of man, not with expanding man's mastery over other men. Existing in an age of intellectual crisis, it would realize that to develop man's mind, it must restore those powers of contemplation which have too long been greatly weakened by Western man's devotion to political, economic, and technological conquest. It would realize that in a quest for rather blind and pure power, we have lost sight of the ends of man, of what man is, of how he should live, and of how our various power achievements could and should serve him.

A major concern of the ideal undergraduate college would be that its graduates enter the world with guiding principles, with a general orientation to life. But despite this fact, the college would not try to force any specific principles upon its students. Instead, it would leave students free to develop their own values. Indeed, the ideal college would strongly encourage students to do so. It would point out to students that they do inevitably have values and that, therefore, they should always admit their presence, and always stand ready both to defend and change them. It would point out to students that failing to admit and practice values leads to a normlessness which inhibits full intellectual and moral development, and that unless one eventually proceeds with clear purposes and goals, he proceeds too long by a wasteful, frustrating, and self-destroying system of trial and error.

The ideal college would teach students that while learning how to think is very important, realizing for what they should think and why, is even more important. It would point out to students that too often pure, unguided reason is used to vanquish, dehumanize, and devour man. It would point out that a humane orientation to life must be more than one of pure reason, that true intelligence is a synthesis of purposes, values, emotions, and reason; and that, therefore, true intelligence is a system of deep and guiding intellectual beliefs. In helping students to develop their own intellectual beliefs, the ideal college would be preparing them to seek constant improvement of society, of mankind, and of themselves.

The ideal undergraduate college would strive to develop in its students a capacity for creativity. Rather than fearing those inner forces which are today very little understood and are called irrational and nonrational, the ideal college would see them as composing a realm of preconsciousness which can lead man to an intuitive knowledge very often more rational than the knowledge which is produced by a simple retracing of intellectual steps already taken. Furthermore, the ideal college would realize that to create is to expand one's mind and release one's inner energies in a constructive direction; and that, therefore, to create is to give one faith in mankind.

Although delightful to attend, the ideal undergraduate college would make exacting demands on its students. It would force them to see social reality not as something affording them justification for self-pity, but as a realm for great opportunity, challenge, and excitement. Even more important, students would be expected to push themselves to the limits of their own powers. The college would know that as society grows more complicated, increasingly stronger men are required to hold it together; and thus the college would practice not equality of education, but equality of educational opportunity for each individual to achieve as far as possible that personal intellectual excellence which this democracy must have from many men in order to survive. Students, then, would be forced to test themselves within themselves. But compared to the labor of today's student, tomorrow's would be far more pleasant; it would be exciting and indeed heroic. For instead of competing against his classmates, the system, and the grading scale, tomorrow's student would reach for the utmost development of his own potentialities. Occasionally, in the pursuit, he might even wreck himself upon something deserving of his effort.

I have established very high ideals for the undergraduate college of tomorrow. I have done this because one must set his ideals high in order to reach the level of bare necessity. I have done this because America must set her educational ideals high in order to stand a chance of surviving her present intellectual crisis. The American college must ask itself what kind of world can be, what kind of world it wants to help build, and how it can best do so. The American college must clearly formulate our world's problems and then it must find, test, develop, and apply solutions. It must send to the world's leadership posts truly educated, not just trained, men. And, of course, to adequately do all this, it must constantly strive to perfect the internal actualizations of its own democratic and libertarian ideals.

Past generations of Westerners and Americans have given the Americans of our generation the blind powers we need in order to fulfill our opportunity to help build that humane world order which is now required. To respond successfully to that opportunity is the tremendous challenge of our generation. If the colleges fail, we all will fail. And if all fail, a humane one world will not materialize, and civilization, both as we've known and envisioned it, will fall.

Challenges are not new in human history. All generations have been required to meet the crisis of their age, and, of course, some generations have met their requirements more effectively than others. Thus it is not true that our age is faced with the crisis of mankind. It is faced with *a* crisis. However, it is true that our age is challenged to an extent never exceeded and rarely equaled, in mankind's life on this planet. And it is also true that in order to successfully meet our challenge, man's mind, more than ever before, must reign supreme.

To the American colleges and universities has fallen the task of playing the world's most significant part in making man's mind supreme. Western civilization has already deeply touched the lives of nearly all the peoples of the earth. America is already a world leader in possession of great powers. Therefore, as civilizations before us, we can, if we complement our power with an overriding intellectual development, become the foremost cultural influence of the emerging world. Out of the ferment of Hellenic Greece came some of Western civilization's most important roots. Out of the ferment of twentieth-century America can come some of the ethical and cosmological visions so essential for the shaping of our evolving global civilization. We need but make humane intelligence supreme in our own country to help make it supreme in the coming world order. The opportunity and responsibility are ours; for our own sake and for the sake of mankind—past, present and future.

I should conclude these thoughts about education in the context of America and the world at large with at least a few words about my own personal relationship to what I have said. I have served three years and nine months in this country's Marine Corps. I believe I served well. I was awarded military commendations. And I was proud to be a member of a force that has played such an important part in meeting some of the *external* threats to this nation and the promise that it has historically represented. From 1959 until 1963 I saw no contradiction between my ideals and military service. But it is now 1966. My country is part of a nightmare as old as man, and thus so am I. I see it as my duty to help abolish that nightmare. And as I now more fully understand it, this cannot be accomplished through the use of military force. Not only does the intrusion of force into today's infinitely complex and deeply felt human developments fail to reach the springs of people's actions. It also cannot but damage the quest for a common, universal human purpose that is the unique opportunity and imperative of our age. More than that, the preoccupation with force leads to an aggravation and mobilization of our anxieties, causes us to regress to a myopic nationalism, and so diverts us both from the great promise of today's world and from the inescapable problems that must be faced if that promise is to be made a reality. It is to that promise that I will look in future for my inspiration. And it is to the analysis and solution of the problems involved in its actualization—problems requiring above all what I have called the application of humane intelligence—that I hope to devote my energies.

Epilogue

In the seventeenth and eighteenth centuries, increasing numbers of people began to believe that men could determine their own fate, shape their own institutions, and gain command of the social forces that buffeted them. Before then, from the beginning, men had believed that all the major features of their lives were determined by immemorial custom or fate or the will of God. It was one of the Copernician turns of history that brought man gradually over two or three centuries to the firm conviction that he could have a hand in shaping his institutions.

No one really knows all the ingredients that went into the change, but we can identify some major elements. One was the emergence with the scientific revolution of a way of thinking that sought objectively identifiable cause-and-effect relationships. People trained in that way of thinking about the physical world were bound to note that the social world, too, had its causes and effects. And with that discovery came, inevitably, the idea that one might manipulate the cause to alter the effect.

America
in the
Twenty-third
Century

JOHN W. GARDNER

At the same time people became less and less inclined to explain their daily lives and institutions in terms of God's will. And that trend has continued to this day. Less and less do men suppose, even those who believe devoutly in a Supreme Being, that God busies himself with the day-to-day microadministration of the world.

While all of this was happening, new modes of transportation and communication were breaking down parochial attitudes all over the world. As men discovered that human institutions and customs varied enormously from one society to the next, it became increasingly difficult to think of one's own institutions as unalterable and increasingly easy to conceive of a society in which men consciously shaped their institutions and customs.

The result is that today any bright high school student can discourse on social forces and institutional change. A few centuries ago, even for learned men, such matters were "given," ordained, not subject to analysis, fixed in the great design of things.

Up to a point the new views were immensely exhilarating. In the writings of our founding fathers, for example, one encounters a mood approaching exaltation as they proceeded to shape a new nation. But more recently another consequence has become apparent: the new views place an enormous—in some instances, an unbearable—burden on the social structures that man has evolved over the centuries. Those structures have become the sole target and receptacle for all man's hope and hostility. He has replaced his fervent prayer to God with a shrill cry of anger against his own institutions. I claim no special insight into the unknowable Deity, but He must be chuckling.

Men can tolerate extraordinary hardship if they think it is an unalterable part of life's travail. But an administered frustration—unsanctioned by religion or custom or deeply rooted values—is more than the spirit can bear. So increasingly men rage at their institutions. All kinds of men rage at all kinds of institutions, here and around the world. Most of them have no clear vision of the kind of world they want to build; they only know they don't want the kind of world they have.

So much for the past and present.

To gain perspective on our own time, I decided not long ago that

I would look three centuries into the future. I am able to do this thanks to a Cornell scientist who recently discovered how man may step off the time dimension and visit the past or future at will. You may be surprised you haven't heard about this, but he's finding his capacity to know the future profitable. He doesn't want to publicize his findings until he has won a few more horse races.

The first thing I learned is that in the last third of the twentieth century, the urge to demolish long-established social institutions succeeded beyond the fondest dreams of the dismantlers. They brought everything tumbling down. Since the hostility to institutions was a product of modern minds, the demolition was most thorough in the most advanced nations.

Unlike the fall of Rome, this decline was not followed by hundreds of years of darkness. In fact, there followed less than a century of chaos and disorder.

In the latter part of the twenty-first century the rebuilding began. Since chaos is always followed by authoritarianism, this was a period of iron rule, world-wide—a world society rigidly organized and controlled. I don't think I shall tell you what language was spoken.

But tyrannies tend to grow lax, even under futuristic methods of thought control. By the end of the twenty-second century, the sternly disciplined institutions of the world society had grown relatively tolerant.

In the new, more permissive atmosphere, men were again allowed to study history—which had been under a ban for two centuries. The effect was electric. Twenty-third century scholars were entranced by the variety of human experience, shocked by the violence and barbarism, saddened by the stupidities and exalted by the achievements of their forebears.

As they studied the history of the twentieth century, they discovered that human expectations had risen sharply in the middle years of the century.

Men came to demand more and more of their institutions—and with greater intransigence. But while aspirations leapt ahead, human institutions remained sluggish—less sluggish to be sure than at any previous time in history, but still inadequately responsive to human need.

Considering the disastrous outcome, twenty-third century scholars concluded that if society is going to release aspirations for institutional change—which is precisely what many twentieth century societies deliberately did—then it had better be sure its institutions are capable of such change. In this respect they found the twentieth century sadly deficient.

Because of failure to design institutions capable of continuous renewal, twentieth century societies showed astonishing sclerotic streaks. Even in the United States, which was then the most adaptable of all societies, the departments of the Federal Government were in grave need of renewal; State government was in most places an old attic full of outworn relics; in most cities, municipal government was a waxwork of stiffly preserved anachronisms; the system of taxation was a tangle of dysfunctional measures; the courts were crippled by archaic organizational arrangements; the unions, the professions, the universities, the corporations, each had spun its own impenetrable web of vested interests.

Such a society could not respond to challenge. And it did not.

But as one twenty-third century scholar put it, "The reformers couldn't have been less interested in the basic adaptability of the society. That posed tough and complex tasks of institutional redesign that bored them to death. They preferred the joys of combat, of villain hunting. As for the rest of society, it was dozing off in front of the television set."

Twentieth century institutions were caught in a savage cross-fire between uncritical lovers and unloving critics. On the one side, those who loved their institutions tended to smother them in the embrace of death, loving their rigidities more than their promise, shielding them from life-giving criticism. On the other side, there arose a breed of critics without love, skilled in demolition but untutored in the arts by which human institutions are nurtured and strengthened and made to flourish.

As twenty-third century leaders proceeded to redesign their own society for continuous renewal, one of them commented on the debt they owed to the twentieth century: "It is not just that we have learned from twentieth century mistakes. We have learned from twentieth century insights. For in that troubled time there were men who were saying just what we are saying now. And had they been heeded, the solutions we have reached would have come 300 years earlier. But no one was listening."